Poland

WORLD BIBLIOGRAPHICAL SERIES

General Editors:
Robert L. Collison (Editor-in-chief)
Sheila R. Herstein
Louis J. Reith
Hans H. Wellisch

VOLUMES IN THE SERIES

VOLUME 32

— Poland —

Richard C. Lewański
Compiler

CLIO PRESS

OXFORD, ENGLAND · SANTA BARBARA, CALIFORNIA

016.9438
L669

© Copyright 1984 by Clio Press Ltd.

British Library Cataloguing in Publication Data

Lewański, Richard C.
Poland. – (World bibliographical series; 32)
1. Poland – Bibliography
I. Title   II. Series
016.9438   Z2521

ISBN 0-903450-58-5

Clio Press Ltd.,
55 St. Thomas' Street,
Oxford OX1 1JG, England.

ABC-Clio Information Services,
Riviera Campus, 2040 Alameda Padre Serra,
Santa Barbara, Ca. 93103, U.S.A.

Designed by Bernard Crossland
Computer typeset by Peter Peregrinus Ltd.
Printed in Great Britain by
Billing and Sons Ltd., Worcester

THE WORLD BIBLIOGRAPHICAL SERIES

This series will eventually cover every country in the world, each in a separate volume comprising annotated entries on works dealing with its history, geography, economy and politics; and with its people, their culture, customs, religion and social organization. Attention will also be paid to current living conditions — housing, education, newspapers, clothing, etc. — that are all too often ignored in standard bibliographies; and to those particular aspects relevant to individual countries. Each volume seeks to achieve, by use of careful selectivity and critical assessment of the literature, an expression of the country and an appreciation of its nature and national aspirations, to guide the reader towards an understanding of its importance. The keynote of the series is to provide, in a uniform format, an interpretation of each country that will express its culture, its place in the world, and the qualities and background that make it unique.

SERIES EDITORS

Robert L. Collison (Editor-in-chief) is Professor Emeritus, Library and Information Studies, University of California, Los Angeles, and is currently the President of the Society of Indexers. Following the war, he served as Reference Librarian for the City of Westminster and later became Librarian to the BBC. During his fifty years as a professional librarian in England and the USA, he has written more than twenty works on bibliography, librarianship, indexing and related subjects.

Sheila R. Herstein is Reference Librarian and Library Instruction Coordinator at the City College of the City University of New York. She has extensive bibliographic experience and recently described her innovations in the field of bibliographic instruction in 'Team teaching and bibliographic instruction', *The Bookmark*, Autumn 1979. In addition, Doctor Herstein co-authored a basic annotated bibliography in history for Funk & Wagnalls *New encyclopedia*, and for several years reviewed books for *Library Journal*.

Louis J. Reith is librarian with the Franciscan Institute, St. Bonaventure University, New York. He received his PhD from Stanford University, California, and later studied at Eberhard-Karls-Universität, Tübingen. In addition to his activities as a librarian, Dr. Reith is a specialist on 16th century German history and the Reformation and has published many articles and papers in both German and English. He was also editor of the *American Society for Reformation Research Newsletter*.

Hans H. Wellisch is Associate Professor at the College of Library and Information Services, University of Maryland, and a member of the American Society of Indexers and the International Federation for Documentation. He is the author of numerous articles and several books on indexing and abstracting, and has most recently published *Indexing and abstracting: an international bibliography*. He also contributes frequently to *Journal of the American Society for Information Science, Library Quarterly,* and *The Indexer*.

v

Contents

Contents

Contents

Contents

Introduction

It is not surprising that every nation fosters an oversimplified and generalized image of its own characteristics and qualities. Many Americans, for example, are deeply convinced of the superiority of their way of life; the British sometimes claim that the English Channel separates the European Continent from the British Isles rather than Britain from Europe; and the Italians often prefer to evaluate themselves by region and have serious doubts about the existence of a single, homogenous Italian nation.

Polish history and literature display messianic characteristics and suggest that, throughout its history, Poland has enjoyed God's special attention, and that even its sufferings represent a sign of grace. They also imply that Poland's role among nations is like Christ's among individuals and that through its adversities Poland will redeem itself and other nations. This Polish mystical approach to history found its best-known spokesmen in Adam Mickiewicz and Andrzej Towiański although it had many more followers in the fields of both Polish philosophy and literature. It is an approach which does have some merits. Indeed, how else could the Polish nation, which for generations was located in the world's worst geopolitical position between two powerful and technically advanced militaristic powers, (Germany and Russia) with populations ten times larger than her own, have survived?

The known history of the Slavic tribes inhabiting the territories in the Odra and Vistula river basins goes back to the 9th Century but oral tradition goes back another two centuries. By the end of the 13th century, a homogenous Polish state had evolved, and this was followed by two centuries of great territorial and cultural expansion that transformed Poland into a multinational commonwealth, a centre of arts and letters, and a refuge for Christian dissidents and Jews. Poland became a propagator and defender of both Christianity and of Western civilization against the Ottoman and Muscovite Empires.

Domestically this was a period when the nobles became increasingly powerful and when the belief that the nobility could take part in con-

Introduction

trolling the royal will was reaffirmed. The 'nobiliary republic' was ruled by 8-12 per cent of the entire population, a very high figure compared with Western countries of the period. The arrogant and arbitrary power of the high nobility became firmly established and the strength of the gentry and the burghers declined while the peasants were reduced to serfdom. However, factions and rivalry persisted and no strong ruling dynasty was able to establish itself. Consequently, the entire country was weakened, thus encouraging foreign interference in Poland's internal affairs.

In spite of efforts to correct Poland's governmental and constitutional problems it eventually became impossible to forestall the aggressive plans of Russia, Prussia and Austria who partitioned the country between them at the end of the 18th century. Notwithstanding this, the seed of reforms enacted during the Stanislavian era formed the basis for cultural resistance and later insurrection. There were frequent outbreaks of revolutionary and military activity during the late 18th century, and during the 19th and early 20th centuries, which kept alive the torch of national independence: Tadeusz Kościuszko's rebellion in 1794; Jan Henryk Dąbrowski's military activities during the period 1797-1803; Józef Poniatowski's fight against the Russians, 1807-15; the establishment of an independent Free City of Cracow 1815-46; the Spring of Nations 1846-48; the November Uprising 1830-31; the January Insurrection 1863-64; and the 1905 revolutionary movements and strikes. During this period writers like Henryk Sienkiewicz, poets like Adam Mickiewicz, composers like Fryderyk Chopin and artists like Jan Matejko contributed substantially towards keeping alive Poland's language, traditions and pride. Others, like Stanisław Wyspiański, Stefan Żeromski, Władysław Reymont, and Maria Konopnicka directed their creative ability towards the peasants and workers, whose participation in the government of pre-partition Poland had been practically nil. These men and women attempted to expand the social basis of the Poland of the future.

When the First World War broke out, the partition powers aligned themselves in opposing camps, eager to barter the future of ethnically Polish territories for Polish political and military support of their cause. However, those promises came too late and commanded little credibility among the Poles, who preferred to rely on their own military effort (led, amongst others by Józef Piłsudski and Józef Haller) and political action (particularly that of Ignacy Paderewski and Roman Dmowski).

An understanding of contemporary Poland must take into account the country's extraordinary history. Although Poland is no longer the vast, multi-ethnic and multidenominational commonwealth of former years, the nation's past relationship with its neighbours continues to play an important role today. In this context it is important to remember that during the Second World War the hostilities affected a much larger portion of Poland's population and had a greater impact on its national economy than was the case in most other countries involved in the conflict. This is why the impact of the Second World War with its destruction and revolutionary changes remain a frequent theme of historical, political and economic studies and of literary and artistic impressions. Polish life has been deeply affected by socioeconomic transformations including: demographic shifts and losses; the processes of urbanization and industrialization; nationalization of the means of production; and integration into the East European Common Market and into a Soviet-run military alliance. Notwithstanding this, the national character has remained largely untouched. Poland's exposed geopolitical position explains why foreign relations and military affairs occupy a paramount place in the life of the country. In spite of all Poland's difficulties a high priority has been repeatedly assigned to the reconstruction and preservation of historical monuments destroyed by war for they serve as a witness of past glories and provide a cohesive influence for present and future generations.

Today, the eyes of the world are again turned towards Poland, a country of contradictions where the rapid advance of heavy and extractive industry has been accompanied by economic depression; where technological progress has failed to erode the country's strong attachment to tradition; and where socioeconomic emancipation has taken place at the same time as a growth in the influence of the Catholic Church. Several recent developments have led some observers to describe the late 1970s and early 1980s as the 'Polish Years'. These developments have included: the ascent of a Polish pontiff to the Holy See (the first non-Italian for several centuries, and the first East European ever); the increasing international appreciation of Polish culture (literature, theatre, music, cinema and posters, for example) evinced by the award of Nobel prizes in literature to a Polish writer and also to a Polish-born Yiddish writer; and the challenge to the Soviet Russian variant of Marxism posed by the *Solidarity* and other protest movements of workers and intellectuals.

In Poland moral and spiritual values still retain, for better or for worse, a higher esteem than purely economic considerations. A cavalry charge against an armoured division or the opposition of lyrical poetry to the truths of economics might seem to many sheer foolishness. However, it is to this kind of spirit and to the indomitable character of her people, that Poland owes its very existence, for without them the

Introduction

nation would not have been able to emerge victorious from a deluge of conflict and warfare. With few exceptions, Poles everywhere in the world, romantics or realists, progressives or conservatives, speak a common language, because they share the same deep feelings of love towards their country and the same faith that eventually their love of liberty will prevail over the forces of constraint.

The bibliography

I hope the present guide, which pays particular attention to Poland's long and crucially important history, will meet the needs of scholars and of the general public. A broad range of subject categories has been included and it is hoped that the works included will provide an interpretation of Poland which will reveal its culture, its place in the world and the qualities and background that make it unique. In the main the arrangement and style follows that of the other volumes in the World Bibliographical Series, although some adaptations have been necessary. The work is a selective and annotated bibliography of English-language material, (books, journals, articles, maps and albums) on all aspects of Polish civilization past and present. Only very exceptionally have non-English titles been included. In such cases the English entries available were judged to be insufficient, or the non-English entries were considered to be of paramount importance, or the nature of the works (bibliographies, art illustrations, road maps, language dictionaries, for example) was such that they remained useful to the English-speaking reader who has no knowledge of Polish.

The compiler has also selected items on the basis of both his judgement of their quality and his knowledge of their general availability. Each entry is located in the section judged to be the most pertinent to its content and cross-references have also been supplied. Items within sections have normally been placed in alphabetical order by author or editor (although some of the history sections, for example, are arranged chronologically and in some of the sections under 'the arts', bibliographic entries on prominent individuals, e.g. Chopin, have been grouped together). The index at the end of the volume provides the reader with ready access to the bibliographic entries listed in the volume.

The annotations are as concise as possible. They normally contain a description of the subject treated and an evaluation of the book in question. In a few cases, when the publication appeared very recently, or was not available in any of the libraries within the reach of the compiler, a reference has been included without an annotation. Books dealing with Slavic or other East European countries in general have sometimes been included usually with a description of the chapters

Introduction

dealing with Poland. On the other hand, books on some general subjects such as the history of Europe or encyclopaedias of music were normally excluded even though they necessarily included information on Poland.

The section on newspapers and journals is not intended to be comprehensive. In addition to the principal titles, which are listed, there is, of course, a large number of other local or specialized dailies and journals that occasionally rise to national prominence (the Silesian *Sobótka* or the Lublin *Kamena*, for example). In addition, the national minorities publish their own periodicals in their respective languages. These include: *Fołks Sztyme* (People's Voice) a Jewish weekly in Yiddish; *Nashe Slovo* (Our Word) a weekly for Ukrainians in Cyrillic; *Auśra* (Dawn) a Lithuanian quarterly; and *Život* (Life) a Czechoslovak review. It should be noted that the general position of periodicals in Poland today is somewhat fluid: some titles have not been reinstated after the emergency and some new titles have been established.

I hope that the present guide, primarily intended as a research tool, will also stimulate scholars to fill the gaps in the English-language material on Poland. It goes without saying, that all suggestions for inclusion and/or replacement of entries in any future edition are most welcome.

Acknowledgements

I am indebted to many libraries, institutes and individuals who assisted me in the compilation of the present work. I would like to mention especially the Biblioteka Norodowa in Warsaw, the Biblioteka Jagiellońska in Cracow, the Biblioteka Uniwersytetu Warszawskiego, The Polish Library in London, the Bibliothèque Polonaise in Paris, the Biblioteca Polacca in Rome, the New York Public Library, Slavonic Division, the Stanford University and Hoover Institution Libraries, the University of California at Berkeley Library, the Johns Hopkins University Center in Bologna, the University and Municipal Archiginnasio Libraries in Bologna, the Biblioteca Nazionale Centrale in Florence, the Institute of Slavonic Studies, University of Pisa, and the Institute of Eastern European Languages and Literatures, University of Udine.

RCL

Polish Libraries Outside Poland

Argentina: Biblioteca Polaca 'Ignacio Domeyko', c. Serrano 2076, Buenos Aires.

Canada: The Polish Library, McGill University, 3479 Peel Street, Montreal. The Canadian-Polish Research Institute, 288 Roncesvalles Avenue, Toronto M6R 2M4.

France: Bibliothèque Polonaise, 6 Quai d'Orleans, Paris 4.

Great Britain: The Polish Library, 238-246 King Street, London W6 0RF; Scottish branch: 42 Cecil Street, Glasgow G12 8RJ.

Italy: Biblioteca Polacca, Palazzo Doria, vicolo Doria, 00187 Roma.

Switzerland: Bibliothèque Polonaise, Castle of Rapperswil.

United States: The Polish Institute of Arts and Sciences Library, 59 East 66th Street, New York 10021. The Polish Roman Catholic Union Library, 984 Milwaukee Avenue, Chicago 22, Illinois.

In addition to the above major Polish libraries, Polish area studies materials are available in most national libraries. Especially rich in Polish materials are: The Library of Congress; the British Library; the Bibliothèque Nationale; the Finnish National and University Library, Helsinki; Oesterreichische Nationalbibliothek; and the Bayerische Staatsbibliothek. University libraries which are especially strong in Polish materials are: Harvard; Columbia; the Hoover Institution; and the University of London. Research institutes whose holdings are particularly valuable for students of Polish studies include the Institut National d'Études Slaves in Paris and the Osteuropa Institut in Munich. Polish émigré associations and Polish foreign societies also hold valuable research sources.

Polish Bookstores and Subscription Services Outside Poland

Austria: Księgarnia Heinz Kolisch, Rathausstrasse 18, A-1010 Wien.
Australia: Polish Book Depot 'Vistula', Daking House, Rawson Place, Sydney, NSW 2000.
Canada: Polish Alliance Press, 1636 Bloor Street West, Toronto, Ontario M6P 1A7.
France: Księgarnia Polska 'Libella', 12 Rue Saint-Louis-en-l'Isle, 75004 Paris 6e; Telephone 326-51-09. Librairie Polonaise, 123 Boulevard Saint Germain, 75006 Paris 6e; Telephone 326-04-42, Telex 250302. La Boutique Polonaise, 25 Rue Drouot, Paris 9e.
Germany (Federal Republic): Księgarnia St. Mikiciuk, Gablonzerstrasse 7/1, 8 München 45.
Great Britain: Cracovia Bookstore, 38 The Avenue, London W13 8LS; Telephone 998 8355. Earlscourt Publications, 129-130 Shepherd's Bush Centre, London W12. Księgarnia Stowarzyszenia Polskich Kombatantów, 238-246 King Street, London W6 0RF; Telephone (01) 748 5522. Orbis Bookstore, 66 Kenway Road, London SW5 0RD; Telephone (01) 370 2210.
Israel: Księgarnia Polska E. Neustein, PO Box 29443, Tel Aviv; Telephone 621 311.
Scandinavia: Svenska Transpol, Box 9014, Solna 9 171-09.
United States: Księgarnia Ludowa, 5347 Chene Street, Detroit, Michigan 482 11. Polish Publications Center, 2917 North Central Park Avenue, Chicago, Illinois 60 618. Polonia Bookstore, 2886 Milwaukee Avenue, Chicago, Illinois 60 618. Szwede Slavic Books, Palo Alto, California 94302, PO Box 1214. Polish Book Store F. Orzechowski, 7970 Summerdale Avenue, Philadelphia, Pennsylvania 19111.

In addition to the above, orders for Polish books and subscriptions for Polish periodicals are handled by all major bookstores and subscription services, and especially by bookstores specializing in importing Slavic books including: Kubon & Sagner in Munich; Nauka in Tokyo; and the

Polish Bookstores and Subscription Services Outside Poland

Four Continent Book Corporation in New York. The official Polish agency in charge of the distribution of books and periodicals abroad is: Ars Polona, ul. Krakowskie przedmieście 7, 00-067 Warsaw. This agency publishes an annual price list of Polish dailies and periodicals and occasional subject checklists, and it also runs an antiquarian department.

List of Pseudonyms

Pseudonym	Real Name
Fay Sibyl Marie Anstruther	Lady Carmichael (Rechnitzer)
General Bór	Tadeusz Komorowski
Ann Su Cardwell	Margaret Low Super
Joseph Conrad	Józef Korzeniowski
T. M. Filip	Tytus Filipowicz
Paweł Jasienica	Leon Lech Beynar
Peter Jordan	Aleksander Tadeusz Lutosławski
Władysław Kania	Zdzisław Stahl
K. S. Karol	Unknown
Jan Karski	Jan Kozielski
Joseph Mark	Andrzej Ciołkosz
S. M. Marvey	Marian Zygmunt Jedlicki
Helen Modjeska	Helena Modrzejewska
Stefan Tadeusz Norwid	Tadeusz Nowacki
Józef Rudnicki	Stefan Mękarski
Rysia	Unknown

The Country and Its People

1 **Poland: its people, its society, its culture.**
Clifford R. Barnett (et al.). New York: Grove Press, 1958.
471p. maps. bibliog. (Survey of World Cultures Series).
A handbook based on the Human Relations Area Files at the Connecticut
Academy of Arts and Sciences, New Haven. Although there are no Poles among
the contributors, this is an encyclopaedic work covering history, geography, demography, politics, religion, government, foreign relations, economics, manpower,
agriculture, education, social organization, health and art.

2 **Poland for beginners.**
Olgierd Budrewicz, translated by Edward Rothert. Warsaw:
Interpress, 1976. 185p. illus.
A witty, entertaining and concise introduction to Poland's beauty and diversified
characteristics. Highly recommended for its readability and clarity. Alfred Bloch's
The real Poland: an anthology of self-perception (Continuum, 1982. 224p.) may be
considered an extension of Budrewicz's book.

3 **Poland in world civilization.**
Roman Dyboski, edited by Ludwik Krzyżanowski. New York:
J. M. Barrett, 1950. xii+285p. map. bibliog.
A profile of Poland's culture and history by a prominent scholar. A classic that
needs to be supplemented by a treatment of the period since the Second World
War.

1

The Country and Its People

4 Portrait of Poland.
Jan Krok-Paszkowski, preface by Czesław Miłosz. London: Thames & Hudson, 1982. illus.

The traditional and modern faces of Poland are revealed by colour illustrations by Bruno Barbey and comments by some of Poland's writers as well as foreign observers.

5 Poland from inside: a symposium.
Survey, special issues, vol. 24 (Autumn 1979), 245p. and vol. 25 (Winter 1980), 213p.

The topics covered are: censorship; the language of propaganda; the flying university (an underground university, constantly changing its location); the security police; the Katyń Woods murders; workers' actions; political opposition; foreign trade; the theatre; criticism of the national economic situation; the traditional image of the past; and personal behaviour.

6 Poland.
Edited by Bernadette Everly Schmitt. Berkeley, California: University of California Press, 1945. xix+500p. bibliog. illus. (United Nations Series).

An encyclopaedic consideration of Poland's political, social and economic life between the two world wars. The contributions by the thirteen Polish and nine American scholars reveal some weaknesses including a certain unevenness of treatment and differences in terminology. This is a well planned and organized, accurate, objective, factual and detached account and the chapter on Polish-US relations is particularly interesting.

7 The tradition of Polish ideals: essays in history and literature.
Edited by Władysław Józef Stankiewicz. London: Orbis, 1981. 288p.

A series of lectures useful as a background study of Poland especially for those, who share the view that a nation's history is best understood in the light of its ideals and traditions. This volume of miscellanea deals with the following topics: poetry; music; great men of Poland; national identity; tolerance; the role of the nobility; and the Warsaw Uprising.

8 Studies in Polish life and history.
A. E. Tennant. New York: Gordon Press, 1977.

9 This is Poland.
Warsaw: Interpress, 1978. 216p. illus.

A kaleidoscope of journalistic impressions of the various faces of Poland both traditional and modern. The articles are taken from major Polish monthlies distributed abroad and offer a colourful and varied panorama of the country.

10 **Poland: the country and its people.**
Translated by Ryszard Wojna. Warsaw: Interpress, 1979.
240p. illus.

A useful popular guide for foreigners. Provides an overview of Poland's history, sociopolitical system and social services and refers to tourism, sport, cultural life, foreign relations, society, youth and education.

Geography

General

11 **Eastern Europe: essays in geographical problems.**
Edited by George Walter Hoffman. New York: Praeger,
1971. xxviii + 502p.

A collection of papers which survey the state of geographical research and
research opportunities. The work also includes essays on: urban development by
Norman J. Pounds; changes in landscape by Dean S. Rugg; agricultural geography by Jack I. Romanowski; industrial geography by F. Ian Hamilton; and
changing regional and local administrative structures by Thomas M. Poulsen.

12 **Poland: landscape and architecture.**
Irena Kostrowicka, Jerzy Kostrowicki. Warsaw: Arkady,
1980. 334p. illus. maps.

In conformity with the traditions of the Arkady Publishing House, this is a
beautiful album showing the architecture and landscape of Poland in the context
of its natural environment, its cultural development and its socioeconomic transformation. After a comprehensive historical introduction six chapters deal with
the major geographical regions of Poland: the Carpathian Mountains and sub-
Carpathian upland; the central plains; the Sudete mountains and Silesia; the
Greater Poland plateau; the Mazovian lowlands; and the seaboard and lakelands.
Includes 497 illustrations, some in colour, and coloured maps.

13 **The geographical bases of contemporary Poland.**
Stanisław Leszczycki. *Journal of Central European Affairs*,
vol. 7, no. 4 (Jan. 1948), p. 357-73.

The author is the former director of the Institute of Geography of the Polish
Academy of Sciences and a professor at Warsaw University.

14 Eastern Europe: a geography of Comecon countries.
Roy E. H. Mellor. New York: Columbia University Press, 1975. x+358p. illus. maps. bibliog.

The book is divided into two parts: the first section deals with the historical, political, economic and physical geography of the region in its entirety, while the ensuing chapters discuss the geography of individual East European countries. The origins of Comecon, Soviet influence, and the economies of developed and developing countries in Eastern Europe are considered separately. Urban and rural populations, migration and the impact of Socialism on the lives of the people are also discussed.

15 National Geographic.
Washington DC: National Geographic Society 1888- .

This journal was previously entitled the *National Geographic Magazine*. The following interesting articles (in chronological order) have been published about Poland: William Joseph Showalter's 'Partitioned Poland' no.1 (1915) p. 88-106; Frederick Walcott's 'Devastated Poland' no.5 (1917) p. 445-52; Maynard Owen Williams' 'Struggling Poland' no.8 (1926) p. 203-44; Melville Bell Grosvenor's 'Poland, land of the white eagle' no.4 (1932) p. 435-36+viii; Maynard Owen Williams' 'The Poland of the Present' no.3 (1933) p. 319-44; 'Bright bits in Poland's mountainous South' no.3 (1935) p. i-viii; Douglas Chandler's 'Flying around the Baltic' no.6 (1938) p. 767-806; 'War clouds over Danzig and Poland's port' no.10 (1939) p. 551-58; William and Alicelia Franklin's 'Historic Danzig: last of the city states' no.11 (1939) p. 677-96; Dorothea D. Everett's and Fred Everett's 'Black acres: a thrilling sketch in the vast volume of who's who among the peoples that make America: a saga of Polish farmers in upstate New York' no.11 (1941) p. 631-52; Delia and Ferdinand Kuhn's 'Poland opens her doors' no.3 (1958) p. 354-98; Peter T. White's 'Springtime of hope in Poland' no.4 (1972) p. 467-501; and Yva Momatiuk's and John Eastcott's 'Poland's mountain people' no.1 (1981) p. 104-29.

16 East-Central Europe: a geographical introduction to seven socialist states.
Richard Hazelet Osborne. London: Chatto & Windus; New York: Praeger, 1967. 384p. maps. bibliog.

A concise account of the physical and economic geography of 'Mid-Europe' ie., the region between Western Europe and the Soviet Union. The author examines territorial developments and the effects of socioeconomic changes on individual countries in the area. Chapter 8 (p. 227-82) deals with Poland.

17 Eastern Europe.
Norman J. G. Pounds. London: Longman; Chicago: Aldine, 1969. 932p. illus. maps. bibliog.

An excellent introduction to the physical, demographic, economic and transport geography of Poland and seven other East European countries. Considerable space is also devoted to historical and environmental geography. The work clearly shows that East European countries present very few characteristics of uniformity or cohesiveness. However, the characteristics which are common to the nations of Eastern Europe include rapid industrialization and various degrees of Soviet interference in their internal affairs.

Geographia Polonica. (Polish Geography.)
See item no. 845.

Historical and political geography, general

18 Kresy: the frontier of Eastern Europe.
Feliks Gross. *Polish Review*, vol. 23, no.2 (1978), p. 3-16.

The 'Kresy' or Polish-Ruthenian 'borderlands' constituted a transitional and shifting divide between Western and Eastern Europe. The region developed into a multi-ethnic area characterized by a diversity of languages and religious faiths, and conflicting attitudes.

19 Poland's Eastern frontiers, 981-1939.
Oskar Halecki. *Journal of Central European Affairs*, vol. 2 (1941), p. 191-207.

The author, a one-time prominent Polish historian who taught at Fordham University, reviews the shifting of the Polish Eastern frontier in relationship to: the Polish ethnic expansion; the federative policy adopted towards the Lithuanian and Ruthenian lands of the Grand Duchy of Lithuania; and to a lesser extent, the federative policy towards smaller neighbours like Livonia or Moldavia.

20 One thousand years of history of the Polish Western frontier.
Zygmunt Kaczmarczyk. *Acta Poloniae Historica*, vol. 5 (1962), p. 72-106.

An historical outline of the principal political, economic and other factors that helped to shape Poland's Western frontier.

21 The Polish-German frontier in the system of international agreements.
Alfons Klafkowski. *Polish Western Affairs*, vol. 1, no.2 (1960), p. 213-45.

Considers legal aspects of the Polish-German frontier along the Odra-Nysa rivers, with reference to: bilateral agreements and multinational treaties; the Polish security system; and the peace treaty with Germany after the Second World War.

22 The stabilization of the Polish Western frontier under Casimir the Great, 1333-1370.
Paul W. Knoll. *Polish Review*, vol. 12, no.4 (Autumn 1967), p. 3-29.

Poland's Western and Eastern boundaries do not coincide with any geographical divides (such as the Baltic Sea in the North and the Carpathian Mountains in the South). Consequently their security depends entirely on the country's political and military strength. Nevertheless, thanks to Casimir's decision to focus Poland's attention on the East, Poland's Western frontier remained practically stationary for four centuries.

Geography. Historical and political geography, general

23 **The logic of the Oder-Neisse frontier.**
Józef Kokot. Poznań, Poland: Wydawnictwo Zachodnie,
1959. xx+289p. tables. bibliog.
The director of the Institute of International Affairs at Opole (central Silesia)
presents juridical, economic and demographic arguments in support of the Polish
claim to a frontier at the Odra-Nysa Line.

24 **The Oder-Neisse boundary and Poland's modernization: the
socio-economic and political impact.**
Z. Anthony Kruszewski. New York: Praeger, 1972.
xviii+245p.
The author argues that the Westward shift of Poland's boundaries after the
Second World War favoured industrialization and other forms of socioeconomic
modernization and was generally advantageous to Poland. He also believes that
the Polish population in territories recovered from Germany, the new settlers from
the over-populated areas of central Poland, and the repatriates from territories
taken over by Russia together form a melting pot of people motivated by a
pioneering spirit and vigorously active in their new place of settlement.

25 **Poland's return to the Baltic and the Odra and Nysa in 1945:
historical and current conditions.**
Gerard Labuda. *Polish Western Affairs*, vol. 16, no.1
(1975), p. 3-36.
From the 13th century onwards, surplus Western European population moved
East, but that trend was reversed in the middle of the 19th century, when growing Western industry not only absorbed an increasing number of the local rural
proletariat, but also attracted people from Eastern Europe. Just before the First
World War, 767,000 Poles were employed in German industry and agriculture, of
which over half a million emigrated to the Rhineland. After the First World War
about one million ethnic Germans found themselves in the refounded Polish
Republic, while an equivalent number of Poles (800,000 in central Silesia,
160,000 in Masuria and Warmia, 50,000 in the Złotów and Bytów districts of
Pomerania) remained under German sovereignty. During the Second World War,
in making its territorial claims towards Germany the Polish government-in-exile
did not foresee the shift in frontiers that the Soviet Union was to impose after the
end of hostilities. The Polish claims were limited to Upper and Opole Silesia,
Cassubia and parts of central Pomerania, and to East Prussia. The Zgorzelec
Treaty with the German Democratic Republic concluded on 6 July 1950 established the Odra-Lusatian Nysa frontier.

26 **Polish conceptions of the Polish-German frontier during World
War II.**
Marian Orzechowski. *Polish Western Affairs*, vol. 11, no.2
(1970), p. 234-70.
The resultant shifts of Polish frontiers after the Second World War were roughly
equivalent to a return to the ethnic Poland of a thousand years ago during the
rule of the House of Piast. The arguments in favour of changing the geographical
axis of the country from the basin of the Vistula to the territories between the
Vistula and the Odra were manifold and revolved around: historical tradition;
military security; the penalization of the aggressor; free and more extensive access
to the sea; geographical compactness; the gaining of economic advantages; free

inland navigation; and religious and ethnic homogeneity. In that last context some Polish writers (see, for example, Józef Kisielewski's *The land gathers ashes*, Melchior Wańkowicz's *In Smetek's footsteps* and Stanisław Wasylewski's *In Opole Silesia*) commented before 1939 on the native Polish and other Slavic population in German-administered territories. The demands in the event of a German defeat were somewhat different than might have been expected: the total elimination of the Eastern Prussian enclave; the incorporation into Poland of Gdańsk (Danzig) and the Vistula estuary; the return to Poland of those German-occupied territories where the ethnically Polish population still represented a majority or a substantial minority (Opole Silesia, Masuria, Western Cassubia); and the establishment of a short, straight Polish-German frontier to facilitate any future defence. In addition the towns of Lwów (Lvov, Lemberg) and Wilno (Vilna, Vilnius) with a preponderantly Polish population were to remain within Poland's borders.

27 Polish political thought and the problem of the Eastern borderlands of Poland, 1918-1939.
Konstanty Symmons-Symonolewicz. *Polish Review*, vol. 4, no.1 (1959), p. 65-81.

Polish rejection of both Nazi and Bolshevik ideology, traditional territorial disputes with Germany and Russia, and the recent memory of tripartite domination made a rapprochement between Poland and neighbouring powers extremely difficult during this period. On the other hand, Poland's reliance on powerful but remote allies proved impractical and disappointing. The only logical alternative seemed a pact between related ethnic minorities (Ukrainians, Belorussians, Lithuanians) even at the cost of granting them autonomous status or promoting their statehood.

28 Germany's Eastern neighbours: problems relating to the Oder-Neisse and the Czech frontier regions.
Elizabeth Wiskemann. London: Oxford University Press, 1964. x + 309p. maps. bibliog.

An outline history of Poland's Northwestern territories, followed by a history and description of the frontier with Germany as it was established in 1919 and then modified after the Second World War. The author analyzes the Polish-German territorial dispute and discusses the resettlement of Germans expelled from Poland, the economic importance of Pomerania, Silesia, Warmia and Masuria to both Poland and Germany, and the problem of the so called 'water-Poles', living under alternating German and Polish rule in the border areas.

Historical and political geography

Northwestern territories

29 German Eastern territories: a manual and book of references dealing with the regions East of the Oder and Neisse.
Edited by Joachim von Braun.   Würzburg: Holzner, 1957. 196p.
Examines the historical, juridical and political background to the German claims to the territories East of the Odra-Nysa line. For several centuries these territories were subject to German administration and nationalization policy.

30 Poland's Western and Northern territories.
F. E. Hamilton.   New York: Oxford University Press, 1975. 48p. illus. (Problem Regions of Europe Series).
A pamphlet which provides a Western view of the controversial Polish-German territorial dispute.

31 Western and Northern Poland: historical outline, nationality problems, legal aspects, new society, economic survey.
Maria Korniłowicz.   Warsaw: Zachodnia Agencja Prasowa, 1962. 534p. illus. maps.
Considers: changes in the Polish-German frontier over the last thousand years; the new border after the Second World War; population transfers and social changes after 1945; Germanization and the extermination of Poles 1939-45; and the economic situation under German and under Polish rule.

National Geographic.
See item no. 15.

Gdańsk, past and present.
See item no. 59.

Pomerania

32 Poland's Baltic coast.
Jerzy Surdykowski (et al.).   Warsaw: Interpress, 1975. 263p. illus.
A panoramic view of the Polish seaboard which examines its history, present conditions, its natural beauty as well as man-made changes, large cities, seaside resorts, and the fisherman's coves of Western and Eastern Pomerania.

Warmia and Masuria

33 **Warmia and Mazury in the 19th and 20th-century history of Poland's territories.**
Tadeusz Cieślak. *Polish Western Affairs*, vol. 6, no.2 (1965), p. 314-28.
Most people in Poland regard Warmia and Masuria as a tourist paradise of lakes and forests, and as a region of timber and fish production. These lands have also witnessed a strenuous resistance on the part of the autochthonous Polish population (surprisingly enough mostly of Lutheran faith) against German efforts to assimilate them. Since the Second World War, frequent social conflicts have taken place between native Masurians and newcomers from central Poland, and some Masurians have chosen to emigrate to West Germany.

National Geographic.
See item no. 15.

Gdańsk, past and present.
See item no. 59.

Szczecin yesterday, today and tomorrow.
See item no. 60.

A guide to Toruń.
See item no. 61.

The role of the Order and the State of the Teutonic Knights in Prussia in the history of Poland.
See item no. 217.

Danzig, and the Polish corridor, threshold of war.
See item no. 218.

The Free City: Danzig and German foreign policy 1919-1934.
See item no. 220.

Hitler's Free City: a history of the Nazi party in Danzig, 1925-1939.
See item no. 221.

The Danzig dilemma: a study of peacemaking by compromise.
See item no. 222.

Silesia

34 **The role of Silesia in Central Europe in the 19th and 20th centuries.**
Henryk Zieliński. *Acta Poloniae Historica*, vol. 22 (1970), p. 108-22.
Discusses the Silesian region as the crossroads of political and dynastic conflicts between Poland, Bohemia, Austro-Hungary, and Germany, and considers Silesia in the context of Central European resources, manufacturing, trade and transport.

Wrocław in the recent history of the Polish state and nation.
See item no. 63.

A guide to Wrocław.
See item no. 64.
Upper Silesia and the Paris Peace Conference.
See item no. 223.

Upper Silesia

35 **Economic-demographic interrelations in developing agricultural regions: a case study of Prussian Upper Silesia, 1840-1914.**
Michael R. Haines. New York: Arno Press, 1977. illus.

36 **The international experiment of Upper Silesia.**
Georges Silvain Kaeckenbeeck. New York: Oxford
University Press, 1942. 867p. maps. bibliog.
The former president of the Arbitral Tribunal of Upper Silesia (1922-37) reports on the settlement of Silesia, including the protection of minorities, labour and property, and the partition of the region.

37 **National self-determination: the example of Upper Silesia.**
Harry Kenneth Rosenthal. *Journal of Contemporary History*, vol. 7, no.3-4 (July-Oct. 1972), p. 231-41.
It is difficult to apply general principles of national self-determination to Upper Silesia, where frequent changes of state allegiance have made dual ethnicity quite common, and where considerations of political and economic convenience often played a more important role than national consciousness.

Chełm territory

38 **The separation of Chełm from Poland.**
Edward Chmielewski. *Polish Review*, vol. 15, no.1 (winter 1970), p. 67-86.
Examines Polish-Ukrainian coexistence in the borderland territory of Chełm which was returned to Poland after the Second World War. Existing ethnic problems had been further complicated by the forced conversion (by both Tsarist and Soviet authorities) of Ukrainians from the Uniate (Eastern Catholic) rite to the Russian Orthodox Church.

Eastern territories

39 **Border of Europe: a study of the Polish Eastern provinces.**
Adam Żółtowski. London: Hollis & Carter, 1950.
xvi+348p. map. bibliog.
Considers those former Polish territories located to the East of the present state
borderline and inhabited by a mixed Polish-Ukrainian-Belorussian-Jewish population. These lands were lost to Poland in 1945 in exchange for extensive territories
in the West, which she regained after several hundred years of German domination.

The seizure of Vilna, October 1920.
See item no. 224.

The establishment of the Soviet regime in Eastern Poland in 1939.
See item no. 225.

Economic geography

40 **The economic regions in Silesia.**
Stanisław Berezowski. *Polish Western Affairs*, vol. 7, no.1-2
(1966), p. 125-63. maps. bibliog.
Provides the background history of the region from the time of the feudal duke-
doms and Polish, Czech and German rule and examines: the economic geography;
the proportion of natives to new settlers in the lower Silesian (Wrocław), central
Silesian (Opole) and upper Silesian (Katowice) regions; employment in each district;
and rail, air, road and water transport.

41 **The Oder river: transport and economic development.**
Edward Bierman. Evanston, Illinois: Northwestern
University Transportation Center, 1973. 247p.
After the territorial changes that followed the Second World War, the river
Vistula ceased to be the S-shaped backbone of Poland. The new redefined Poland
now came to occupy two major river basins: the Vistula and the Odra. The Odra
system represents the major waterway connecting the Upper Silesian mining and
industrial basin with the large port-city conglomeration of Szczecin-Swinoujście.
In the future the Odra will be integrated into an expanded Polish navigation
system, but it already conducts river ships and barges from the Upper Silesian
conurbation to the cities of Opole, Wrocław, Frankfurt-on-the-Odra, Szczecin, and
even Poznań.

42 **Regional structure and economic regions in Poland.**
Kazimierz Dziewoński, Andrzej Wróbel. *Geographia
Polonica*, no.4 (1964), p. 47-58.
A report on the regional structure of the Polish economy as a basis for integra-
tion into economic macroregions. Analyses the regional characteristics of eco-
nomic patterns, and compares economic and administrative divisions.

43 **Opole Silesia: outline of economic geography.**
Ludwik Straszewicz, translated by Karol Jurasz. Warsaw:
Centralny Instytut Informacji Naukowej, Technicznej i
Ekonomicznej, 1965. 251p. illus. maps. bibliog.
Opole is the capital city of central Silesia, midway between Wrocław and Katowice. The book deals with the environmental conditions of the region, its population, metallurgical and light industries, agriculture and forestry, and road, rail and water transport.

44 **Eastern Europe.**
David Turnock. Boston, Massachusetts: Westview Press,
1978. 273p. maps. bibliog.
A study of the industrial geography of Eastern Europe which discusses the resource base and the socioeconomic structure, and supplies essential background information for the eight countries considered. Eastern Europe is examined as a whole in this rather successful attempt at providing a comprehensive survey of the region without obscuring the distinctive characteristics of each area.

Maps and cartography

45 **The history of Polish cartography from the 15th to the 18th century.**
Karol Buczek, translated by Andrzej Potocki. Wrocław,
Poland: Ossolineum, 1966. 135p. 48 maps.
An analytical and systematic outline of Polish cartography by the editor of the impressive series *Monumenta Poloniae Cartographica*, and one of the better-known historians of Polish map making. *Monumenta* published in 1939 by the Polish Academy of Arts and Sciences at Cracow was intended to reproduce all monographs and maps of importance in the history of Polish cartography, beginning with the maps by the father of Polish cartography Bernard Wapowski. (Publication was interrupted by the war).

46 **Atlas historyczny Polski.** (Historical atlas of Poland.)
Władysław Czapliński, Tadeusz Ładogórski. Warsaw:
PPWK, 1979. 4th ed. 54p.+56p. maps. (text in two parts).
Concentrates on political history, including territorial changes and the evolution of the state frontier, with somewhat less emphasis on economic, social and cultural aspects.

47 **Narodowy atlas Polski.** (National atlas of Poland.)
Warsaw: Ossolineum, 1973-78. 186p.+127 maps.
An atlas sponsored and elaborated by the Institute of Geography of the Polish Academy of Sciences illustrating various aspects of life on the basis of post-1970 data. Includes general, analytical, geographical, socioeconomic and sociocultural maps.

13

Geography. Maps and cartography

48 **Road atlas of Poland.**
Warsaw: Państwowe Przedsiębiorstwo Wydawnictw
Kartograficznych, 1980. 6th ed. 216p. maps.

This is the standard road atlas published by the official publishing house for cartographic publications, and new editions are produced periodically. The atlas contains detailed maps geared to the needs of tourists travelling around Poland by car.

Tourism and Travel

Guidebooks

49 Poland: guidebook for tourists.
Adam Bajcar. Warsaw: Interpress, 1977. 320p. illus. maps.
The best popular guide to Poland on the market. It contains a brief description of the country's geography, history and economy supplemented by useful travel information. The guide is arranged by motoring routes and is meant primarily for tourists visiting Poland by car. In addition to this work and the other guides referred to in this section Interpress, Sport i Turystyka, Krajowa Agencja Wydawnicza (KAW) and some local publishers also produce regional, town, mountain and forest guides and albums which provide essential travel and tourist information in English. These include: Paweł Dzianisz's *Bydgoszcz voievodship invites you* (Warsaw: KAW, 1980. 40p.); Kazimierz Kuczman's *Wawel Hill guide book* (Cracow, Poland: KAW, 1980. 112p.); Tadeusz Skutnik's *Stutthof: historical guide* (Warsaw: KAW, 1980. 42p.); E. Kazimierczak's *Łódź yesterday, today and tomorrow* (Łódź, Poland: Wydawnictwo Łódzkie, 1971. 14p. 175 illus.); Romuald Olaczek's *A guide to Łowicz, Arkadia, Nieborów and environs* (Warsaw: Sport i Turystyka, 1975. 104p.); Włodzimierz Wójcikowski's *Lublin: a guide* (Warsaw: KAW, 1977. 32p.); *Majdanek* (Lublin) (Warsaw: KAW, 1980. 132p.); Adam Cichy's *Poznań* (Poznań, Poland: Wydawnictwo Poznańskie, 1978. 20p. 62 illus.); Maciej Jasicki's *Szczecin: landscape and architecture* (Warsaw: Arkady, 1977. xii+28p. 143 illus.); and Krzysztof Jabłoński's *Warsaw: a portrait of the city* (Warsaw: Arkady, 1979. 18p. 107 illus.). Moreover, the Państwowe Przedsiębiorstwo Wydawnictw Kartograficnych (State Enterprise of Cartography) publishes road maps, maps of camping sites, city plans, atlases, and wall maps, often with polyglot explanatory notes.

50 Poland.
Wojciech Giełżyński. Warsaw: Arkady, 1975. 263p. illus.
A lavishly illustrated album (partly in colour) which provides a step-by-step tourist guide from the Baltic coast to the Carpathian mountains. Anecdotes and stories about the past and the present make the text more interesting. The principal aim of the guide is to show Poland's progress in the three decades since the Second World War.

Tourism and Travel. Guidebooks

51 The Poles: how they live and work.
Marc Euclid Heine. New York: Praeger, 1976. 168p. illus. maps. bibliog.

A guidebook and textbook designed for the diligent tourist, who intends to prepare himself in advance for a study visit to Poland. Individual chapters deal with such topics as the national economy, statistics, everyday life, the educational system and the fine arts.

52 Poland.
Marc Euclid Heine. London: Batsford, 1980. 182p. illus. maps.

A brief introduction to contemporary Poland. Some other guides include: the *Nagel guide to Poland* (New York: Hippocrene, 1978. 384p.); and Anne Pawelek's *American in Poland* (New York: Endurance, 1967).

53 Let's visit Poland.
Julian Popescu. London: Burke, 1979. 96p. illus.

A guide suitable for a visitor having a limited amount of time and interested in rapid sightseeing.

54 Travel guide Poland.
Warsaw: Sport i Turystyka, 1970. 401p. illus. maps.

A detailed guidebook containing information on various aspects of Poland's past and present. It offers twenty-eight separate itineraries with descriptions of each locality, city plans, diagrams of historical monuments and an index.

55 Across Poland.
Przemysław Trzeciak. Warsaw: Interpress, 1979. 2nd ed. 125p. illus.

An imaginary journey from the Baltic coast, through the Masurian lakeland, and across the central plains and Southern uplands to the Carpathian mountain range. The informal narrative contributes to the emotional involvement of the reader. Explanations and factual data on the country's history, civilization, economic geography and history of art are also provided.

56 Poland: a guide for young tourists.
Krzysztof Wichrowski, Tadeusz Wojnowski. Warsaw: Interpress, 1980. 256p. illus.

A guide geared to the needs of both young people with limited budgets and youthful interests, and to all those who prefer the outdoor life to luxury accommodation. Contains general information, hints on preparing to travel in Poland, and descriptions of the most interesting cities and regions.

Poland: the country and its people.
See item no. 10.

National Geographic.
See item no. 15.

The European bison (Bison bonasus).
See item no. 68.

Background to Eastern Europe.
See item no. 97.

City guides

Cracow

57 **Cracow from A to Z.**
Jan Adamczewski. Warsaw: Krajowa Agencja Wydawnicza,
1980. 240p. illus. map.
A mini-encyclopaedia of Cracow with a historical introduction.

58 **A guide to Cracow and environs.**
Leszek Ludwikowski. Warsaw: Sport i Turystyka, 1979.
156p. illus. map.
A pocket guide to the ancient capital city of Poland. It includes a chronological
table, visitors' itineraries, general information, and a description of historical
monuments supplemented by information on nearby places of interest such as the
mediaeval salt mines of Wieliczka, Ojców National Park, and the Nazi extermination camp of Auschwitz-Birkenau (Oświęcim-Brzezinka).

Gdańsk

59 **Gdańsk, past and present.**
Bohdan Szermer. Warsaw: Interpress, 1972. 214p. illus.
maps.
Covers the geographical position, thousand-year history, reconstruction and
present role of this ancient Polish town and harbour (Latin: Gedanium, German:
Danzig).

Szczecin

60 **Szczecin yesterday, today and tomorrow.**
Henryk Mąka, translated by Susan
Brice-Wojciechowska. Warsaw: Interpress, 1979. 180p. illus.
A portrait of the great Polish city-port with a retrospective view going back to
the times of early Slavdom, as well as a projection of the developments which are

likely to occur down to the year 2000. Szczecin's maritime role and its economic hinterland are also discussed.

Toruń

61 **A guide to Toruń.**
Eugeniusz Gąsiorowski. Warsaw: Sport i Turystyka, 1972.
130p.
A brief guide to the old town and modern areas of this major city in Cuyavia. The town is famous because it was the birthplace of Nicolaus Copernicus.

Warsaw

62 **A guide to Warsaw and environs.**
Janina Rutkowska. Warsaw: Sport i Turystyka, 1980. 3rd
rev. ed. 350p. illus. map.
The guide begins with a brief history of the city and of its gradual expansion. It also sets out several tourist itineraries to major historical monuments and modern palaces and provides information about transport, streets, hotels and restaurants etc. Excursions are also suggested to nearby points of interest like Chopin's birthplace at Zelazowa Wola, the Kampinos Forest, the ruins of Czersk Castle and Jabłonna Palace.

Wrocław

63 **Wrocław in the recent history of the Polish state and nation.**
Marian Orzechowski. *Polish Western Affairs*, vol. 13, no.2
(1972) p. 305-33.
Wrocław, the capital of Silesia (Latin: Vratislavia, German: Breslau), occupies a particularly important role in Polish history and in contemporary life. It was a seat of a venerable university, a bilingual German and Polish publishing and printing centre, and a seat of the Slavic Literary Society (*Towarzystwo Lite-racko-Słowiańskie*). Even in the period immediately preceding the First World War some 20,000 ethnic Poles lived here, and Polish singing, sport, commercial enterprise, crafts, and youth group activities remained important. By the time the Nazi troops finally capitulated (6 May 1945) three-quarters of the city had been destroyed.

64 **A guide to Wrocław.**
Wanda Roszkowska. Warsaw: Sport i Turystyka, 1970.
200p. map.
A tourist guide to the capital of Silesia which describes the city's geographical position, its climate, history, reconstruction after the Second World War, its post-war expansion and cultural and scientific life. It also suggests tourist itineraries to nearby places of interest.

Flora and Fauna

65 **Where to watch birds in Europe.**
John Gooders. New York: Taplinger, 1978. 2nd ed. 299p.
illus. maps. bibliog.
A well-organized book for nature lovers with maps and species to be expected in
each area. Twenty-seven countries are listed including Poland.

66 **Baltic amber: a palaeobiological study.**
S. Gisle Larsson. Copenhagen: Scandinavian Science Press,
1977. 192p. illus.
A comprehensive study of Baltic amber with an introductory reconstruction of the
amber forest environment of interest to geologists, botanists and entomologists
alike. The author provides a detailed treatment of the ecology of the Baltic forest
and a full consideration of the Baltic amber, in which the Polish and Lithuanian
coasts are particularly rich.

67 **The vegetation of Poland.**
Edited by Władysław Szafer. Warsaw: Państwowe
Wydawnictwo Naukowe; Oxford: Pergamon Press, 1966.
xxxiii+738p. illus. maps.
Foremost Polish experts on the subject describe plant geography, flora, and the
influence of plant cultivation on population migrations and on human progress in
general.

68 **The European bison (Bison bonasus).**
Jan Żabiński. Cracow, Poland: State Council for the
Preservation of Nature, 1960. 26p.
A pamphlet on the European buffalo, whose habitat is now practically limited to
Poland. At the end of the Second World War, the species was almost extinct, but
now, thanks to Polish efforts, there are over 500 animals living under protected
conditions. In addition their habitat in the virgin forest of Białowieża, has been
expanded to the Bieszczady mountains. The author was a famous Polish naturalist
and Warsaw zoo director.

Prehistory and Archaeology

69 The Goths in ancient Poland.
Jan Czarnecki. Coral Gables, Florida: University of Miami
Press, 1975. 184p. bibliog.

A history of the Goths especially in the Odra-Vistula basins, describing Gothic
migrations in Central Europe, between Scandinavia, Poland and Germany. The
history of the Goths in the area is connected with the so-called 'Gothic theory' of
the origin of the Polish nobility. According to this theory (disputed by most
scholars) like the Varengians (Norsemen) in Russia, the Goths were believed to
form the ruling social class after having subdued the local Slavic population.

70 The origins of Poland.
Witold Dzięcioł. London: Veritas, 1966. 311p. maps.

An attempt, published for the millennium of Poland's Christianization, to synthe-
size recent historical findings on the rise of the Polish nation and state. The
volume covers: Poland's role in the formation of mediaeval Europe; the proto-
Polish period; and Poland during the rule of the Piast dynasty when the nation
was conceived as an organic but separate entity of Western Christendom.

71 The beginnings of the Polish state.
Witold Hensel. Warsaw: Państwowe Wydawnictwo
Naukowe, 1960. 178p. illus. maps.

An account which draws together recent findings on Polish prehistory and
proto-Polish civilization. The division between historians using written records and
archaeologists interpreting material remains has now been abandoned, and current
research is based on a combination of all accessible sources. This integrated
method was adopted by the author, who is the director of the Institute of
Material Culture of the Polish Academy of Sciences. The book covers the period
from 4000 BC to 500 AD. The most interesting parts deal with the ethnogenesis
of Poles and of Slavs in general, and provide accounts of the discoveries at
Biskupin, Wiślica and Krotoszyn.

72 **Poland.**
Konrad Jażdżewski. New York: Praeger, 1965. 240p. illus.
maps. bibliog. (Ancient Peoples and Places Series).
This work examines Polish prehistory (Iron and Bronze Ages) and early history.
It considers early hunters, gatherers and farmers, socioeconomic changes in
Poland during the Neolithic times, and cultural exchanges during the migration
period. The author is professor of archaeology and director of the Archaeological
Museum at Łódź.

73 **Unconventional archaeology: new approaches and goals in
Polish archaeology.**
Edited by Romuald Schild. Wrocław, Poland: Ossolineum,
1980. 233p.
A collection of essays dealing with the prehistoric settlements, stone monuments,
and early socioeconomic developments in the Odra and Vistula basins.

74 **The Sarmatians.**
Tadeusz Sulimirski. London: Thames & Hudson, 1970.
267p. illus. maps. bibliog.
Written by a recognized expert on Central-East European archaeology and prehistory, this work succeeds in reconstructing the role of the Sarmatians from scanty
archaeological evidence supplemented by anthropological and linguistic comparative studies, and the testimony of ancient historians. This was an Iranian nation
that once controlled an extensive area from the Ural mountains and Central Asia
to the Ukraine and Poland. Relations between the Sarmatians and other contemporary tribes, like the Scythians, the Goths, the Huns, and the White Croats, as
well as the influence of Sarmatians upon the Slavs during the formative period of
their history are also discussed. The same author has published a more specific
essay entitled 'Sarmatians in the Polish past' (*Polish Review*, vol. 9, 1 (winter
1964), p. 13-72). In addition, *Vanished civilizations*, edited by Edward Bacon,
(London: Thames & Hudson, 1963) contains Sulimirski's 'The forgotten Sarmatians: a once mighty folk scattered among the nations' (p. 279-98. illus. maps.).

Archeologia Polona. (Polish Archaeology.)
See item no. 841.

History

General

75 **Poland.**
Václav L. Beneš, Norman J. G. Pounds.   New York:
Praeger, 1970. 416p. illus. maps.
A sympathetic overview of Polish history including such aspects as economic
history, constitutional development, cultural heritage, and political aspirations.
Less attention is given to recent social changes. Historical, economic, demographic
and political maps are provided.

76 **History of the Polish air force, 1918-1968.**
Jerzy B. Cynk.   Reading, England: Osprey, 1972. 307p.
plates.
In spite of some biased conclusions, this book fills a vacuum in the literature on
the subject, and is full of information on the role of the Polish air force in the
September 1939 campaign, in the Battle of Britain, and during the Warsaw
Uprising of 1944. It also offers an excellent history of the air force of the Polish
People's Republic prior to 1968.

77 **A history of Poland: God's playground.**
Norman Davies.   New York: Columbia University Press,
1981. 560p. 672p. illus.
The work consists of two volumes, volume one is entitled *The origins to 1795* and
volume two *1795 to the present*. This is a comprehensive history of Poland which
is free of national bias and which provides deep historical insights.

78 **A thousand years of Poland.**
Aleksander Gieysztor, Stanisław Herbst, Bogusław
Leśnodorski. Warsaw: Interpress [n.d. but ca.1975]. 260p.
illus. maps.
A beautifully produced short history of Poland by three outstanding historians: A.
Gieysztor 'early Middle Ages', S. Herbst 'late Middle Ages', 'Renaissance', and
B. Leśnodorski 'from the Enlightenment to present day'. A compact presentation
rendered especially attractive by very good graphic layout including many full-
page colour plates.

79 **History of Poland.**
Aleksander Gieysztor, Stefan Kieniewicz, Emanuel
Rostworowski, Janusz Tazbir, Henryk Wereszycki. Warsaw:
Państwowe Wydawnictwo Naukowe, 1980. new ed. 668p.
illus. bibliog. tables.
A book mainly intended for foreign readers. The main emphasis is on political
history, with explanatory sections on the socioeconomic and cultural background.
The work covers events prior to 1939. An excellent volume written by prominent
historians, but with some discrepancies in the treatment of collective undertakings.
Includes chronological tables.

80 **A history of Poland.**
Oskar Halecki, translated by Monica Mary Gardner, Mary
Corbridge Patkaniowska. New York: McKay, 1976.
xiii+366p.
Several other editions of this work have been published: New York (Roy), Chicago (Regnery) and London (Dent), the most recent edition, London: Routledge,
1978, was updated by Antony Polonsky, who wrote the last two chapters. Halecki
attempts to combine his ardent patriotism with objective scholarship and the
result is informative and absorbing, but often biased. The views expressed are
both conservative and deeply Catholic.

81 **The emancipation of the Polish peasants.**
Stefan Kieniewicz, introduction by Arcadius
Kahan. Chicago: Chicago University Press, 1969. xix+285p.
map.
The author explains how countries such as Poland have retained their peasantry
for so long. The book covers the transfer of land to serf-peasants, the abolition of
serfdom, the social emancipation of the rural population, and the new division of
cultivated land brought about by agrarian reform. It also discusses the partial
land reform, which took place on the initiative of the Polish nobility itself, and
Russia's and Austria's attempts to exploit the rural situation by deepening the social
class rift in order to strengthen their political hold on the country.

82 **Poles on the high seas.**
Jerzy Pertek, translated by Alexander T. Jordan. Wrocław:
Ossolineum, 1978. 372p. illus.
A popular but scholarly work on Polish maritime history which covers: the Polish
navy from the 12th to the 18th centuries including the sea battles in which it

took part; Polish sea travellers and discoverers; Poland's seaboard; Poles in foreign navies and merchant marines; and Polish Arctic expeditions.

83 The Cambridge History of Poland.
Edited by William Fiddian Reddaway. Cambridge, England: Cambridge University Press, 1941-1950. 2 vols. xiv+607p. xvi+630p. maps. bibliog. Reprinted, New York: Octagon, 1971.

Sponsored by Harold Temperley, the *Cambridge History of Poland* was planned in the years leading up to the Second World War, and conceived as a team project. In fact, some of the best-known Polish historians (including Władysław Konopczyński, Paweł Skwarczyński, Bronisław Dembowski, Marian Kukiel, Marceli Handelsman, and Stanisław Kutrzeba) contributed articles on the periods of their particular competence and on those aspects of history (military, constitutional, literary, cultural, diplomatic, art) in which they were especially expert. The result of this collaboration would undoubtedly have been a work of the highest quality, had it not been for insufficient coordination (mostly due to war conditions) between the various participants in the undertaking which led to overlapping, gaps, terminological differentiation and unevenness of treatment.

84 Studies in Polish civilization.
Edited by Damian Wandycz. New York: Polish Institute of Arts and Sciences, 1966. 552p.

A collection of contributions delivered at the sessions of the First Congress of Polish Scholars, Scientists and Artists to be held abroad. The volume makes available thirty-eight unabridged papers (out of the 150 read), and abstracts of other papers. The range of topics is very wide with heavy stress on all aspects of Polish history and on Poland's place among Central-Eastern European nations.

85 Chronologia polska. (Polish chronology.)
Bronisław Włodarski. Warsaw: Państwowe Wydawnictwo Naukowe, 1957. 492p.

A valuable reference work containing Polish mediaeval calendars, lists of holidays, comparative tables of various date systems, lists of the saints of the Western and Eastern Churches, lists of diets and of county dietines, lists of Church primates-archbishops, lists of secular dignitaries, a table of Slavonic numbers, and tables of the monarchs and princes of Poland and her neighbours.

Poland from inside: a symposium.
See item no. 5.

The tradition of Polish ideals: essays in history and literature.
See item no. 7.

Studies in Polish life and history.
See item no. 8.

Poland: the country and its people.
See item no. 10.

National Geographic.
See item no. 15.

Atlas historyczny Polski. (Historical atlas of Poland.)
See item no. 46.

Acta Poloniae Historica. (Polish Historical Records.)
See item no. 838.
Kwartalnik Historyczny. (Historical Quarterly.)
See item no. 874.
Przegląd Humanistyczny. (Humanities Review.)
See item no. 884.

Poland within Eastern Europe

86 **East-West relations and the future of Eastern Europe: politics and economics.**
Morris Bornstein (et al.). Winchester, Massachusetts: Allen & Unwin, 1981. 301p.
Expert essays which examine: East-West relations and the history of Soviet-Polish relations within the context of: the changing international situation; the Polish national economy; and the specific problems of the Polish social and political system.

87 **The Soviet bloc: unity and conflict.**
Zbigniew Kazimierz Brzeziński. Cambridge, Massachusetts: Harvard University Press, 1960. 470p. bibliog. Reprinted, New York: Praeger, 1961. 543p.
A general book on Central Eastern Europe by the first Pole to reach the high office of National Security Advisor to the US President. Chapter eleven deals with the Polish challenge to the USSR in October 1956, chapter fourteen with Poland's route to socialism, and chapter fifteen discusses the limits of Polish autonomy.

88 **Slavic civilization through the ages.**
Samuel Hazzard Cross. Cambridge, Massachusetts: Harvard University Press, 1948. 195p.
An excellent synthesis of Slavic cultural history by a prominent scholar. Among the topics discussed in the eight lectures are: the struggle between Poland and Germany; Polish-Russian rivalry; Poland's quest for lands East of the Łaba (Elbe) River; and Russia's drive toward the Baltic Sea.

89 **The making of Central and Eastern Europe.**
Francis Dvornik. London: Polish Research Centre, 1949. iv+350p. maps. bibliog.; New York: Academic International, 1974. 2nd ed. 350p. maps. bibliog.
Written by a well-known expert on Byzantine-Slavic relations, this book contains a wealth of information on the mediaeval history of Bohemia, Poland, Hungary, Croatia, Kievian Rus', and adjacent countries. The main stress is on Poland and Bohemia, Polish-Czech relations and federative efforts.

90 **The Slavs in European history and civilization.**
Francis Dvornik. New Brunswick, New Jersey: Rutgers
University Press, 1962. xxviii + 688p. maps. bibliog.
One of the classics on Slavic countries written by a distinguished Czech scholar
and containing an impressive amount of information. The volume covers Slavic
history and civilization from the 13th to the 17th centuries, and is a continuation
of an earlier book by the same author: *The Slavs, their early history and civilization* (Boston: American Academy, 1956). Almost all chapters deal extensively
with Poland, Polish relations with Bohemia and with other neighbouring countries, Poland's political organization and cultural achievements, the Jagellonian
Commonwealth, social developments, religious reformation, and the growing
threat of Muscovy.

91 **Borderlands of Western civilization: a history of East Central
Europe.**
Oskar Halecki. New York: Ronald Press, 1952. xvi + 503p.
bibliog.
An analysis of East Central European political history based on the following
assumptions: countries between Germany and Russia form a distinct region; this
region is indispensable to the stability of Europe as a whole; the border of
Western civilization coincides roughly with the Eastern border of Poland and of
other Central-Eastern European countries, and is more relevant to historical considerations than the geographical border at the Urals.

92 **Warsaw Pact.**
Andrzej Korboński. *International Conciliation*, no.573 (May
1969), p. 5-73.
A comprehensive article on the Soviet-sponsored military pact for the mutual
security of Eastern European (and some other) countries (The Warsaw Treaty of
Friendship, Co-operation and Mutual Assistance - Warsaw Pact). The historical
background, text of the treaty, institutions, armed forces, relations between participants, relations with the West (NATO), and the consequences of the invasion of
Czechoslovakia are discussed.

93 **Poland and the Slavophil idea.**
Wacław Lednicki. *Slavonic and East European Review*, vol.
7 (1928), p. 128-40, 649-62.
Poles never accepted the Russian version of the Slavophil idea, which they saw as
a device designed to create a Russian hegemony and which represented an
attempt to channel 'smaller Slavic rivers and streams into the great Russian
ocean'. The author was a famous Berkeley professor of Slavic literatures.

94 **Independent Eastern Europe: a history.**
Carlile A. Macartney, Alan Warwick Palmer. New York:
St. Martin's Press; London: Macmillan, 1967. vii + 499p.
A careful and dependable history of countries located between Germany and
Russia ('Inter-Marium') which is crammed with information and sometimes sharp
judgements. The authors believe that Germany and Russia have in the past
influenced the foreign policies and often even the internal structure of smaller
states from Finland to Greece. Hence their decision to treat the area en bloc.

95 **The world of the Slavs.**
Albert Mousset, translated by Margaret Lavenu. London:
Stevens; New York: Praeger, 1950. ix+240p.
A review of Pan-Slavist ideas and of relations between Russia and smaller Slavic states.

96 **Teuton and Slav: the struggle for Central Europe.**
Harmann Schreiber, translated by James Cleugh. New
York: Knopf, 1965. 392p. illus. map. bibliog.
Revises traditional German historiography regarding Eastern Europe, by presenting a new approach to such problems as the German drive to colonize the East; the extermination of Belorussians; and the battle for the domination of the Baltic Sea. German-Slavic relations during the last war are also discussed, as well as their future prospects.

97 **Background to Eastern Europe.**
Frederick Bernard Singleton. Oxford: Pergamon Press, 1965.
226p. maps.
A general treatment of the history of Eastern Europe with some special topics (migrations, nationalism, multi-ethnic empires) discussed separately. A table of industrial resources and suggestions for further reading are also included. Chapter six, section three, p. 153-66 deals with the 'New course in Poland'.

98 **Tensions within the Soviet captive countries.**
Washington, DC: Government Printing Office, 1954.
ix+117p.+147p. (The work is in two separately numbered parts).
One of a series of reports on the internal situation in Eastern Europe prepared at the request of Congress. Part five of the series deals with Poland.

Mediaeval history

99 **The rise of the Polish monarchy: Piast Poland in East Central Europe, 1320-1370.**
Paul W. Knoll. Chicago: Chicago University Press, 1972.
xii+276p. bibliog.
Examines the second period of the Piast monarchy and provides a novel characterization of King Casimir the Great, whom the author considers sentimental and weak rather than astute and unscrupulous. The book is based on a thorough knowledge of the pertinent literature and stresses Casimir's policy of maintaining a balance between the East and the West; a lesson forgotten during the following centuries. Includes genealogical tables and a glossary of place names.

100 Władysław Łokietek and the restoration of the Regnum Poloniae.

Paul W. Knoll. *Medievalia et Humanistica*, vol. 17 (1966), p. 51-78.

After 180 years of feudal fragmentation going back to the last will of Boleslaus (Boleslaw) the Wry-mouthed, who divided his kingdom among his sons, Poland again became a united kingdom in 1320 under Ladislaus (Władysław) I. Thus, regional divisions gave way to a new reunification, and to Eastward expansion. Ladislaus's state had one million inhabitants and stretched over an area of 110,000 square kilometers.

101 German colonization in medieval Poland in the light of the historiography of both nations.

Zdzisław Kaczmarczyk. *Polish Western Affairs*, vol. 11, no.1 (1970), p. 3-40.

Considers the history of German colonization in Poland between the end of the 12th and the 15th centuries, and Polish settlements based on the Magdeburg and Lubeck Law. There exists disagreement on the role and impact of German colonization: German scholars stress the cultural contribution of their gentry, burghers and peasants; the improved technology which was imported; and even suggest that the colonization might have been a simple continuation of the infiltration proposed by 'the conquest theory'. Poles retort, that the policy of the German knights, clergy and bourgeoisie often clashed with Polish national interests; that urban settlements existed in Poland long before German colonization; and that this colonization represented the first step of a political, military and economic expansion towards the East, the eventual aim of which was the elimination of other nations in its path.

102 Tannenberg 1410: 1914.

Geoffrey Evans. London: Hamish Hamilton, 1970. 206p. illus. maps.

The strategic position of the Masurian fields (known in German historiography as Tannenberg, and in Polish as Grunwald) transformed them twice into battlefields that played a decisive role in history. In 1410 the Polish armed forces aided by their Lithuanian and Ruthenian allies crushed the secular power of the Teutonic Knights here. The Order never regained its influence but transformed itself at the first opportunity offered by the Reformation into a secular state allied with Brandenburg.

103 Jagellonian Poland.

Paweł Jasienica (*pseud.*), translated by Alexander T. Jordan. Miami, Florida: American Institute of Polish Culture, 1978. 416p.

Deals with the problems of the Jagellonian Commonwealth between the Middle Ages and the Renaissance (1386-1572) and covers political and military aspects, cultural progress and religious toleration. Although rich in factual information, this book offers a personal rather than scholarly approach, with an emphasis on the international implications of personal unions, family ties, and the intermarriage of Jagellonians.

thth century)

104 **The problem of feudalism in Poland up to the beginning of the 16th century.**
Paweł Skwarczyński. *Slavonic and East European Review*, vol. 24, no. 83 (June 1956), p. 292-310.
Some scholars doubt that the Western European feudal system based on the sovereignty-vassalage relationship can be extended to Poland. The Polish feudal system was in any case considerably less developed than that in Western Europe, while peasant serfdom persisted much longer.

Modern history (16th-18th century)

105 **Sigismund I of Poland: Renaissance king and patron.**
Kenneth F. Lewalski. *Studies in the Renaissance*, vol. 14 (1966-67), p. 49-72.
The era of Zygmunt (Sigismund) I 'the Old' of the Jagellonian dynasty, and of his Italian-born wife, Bona Sforza, was marked by a flourishing of Renaissance civilization in Poland. The king was a generous patron of learning, the arts and literature.

106 **L'Union de Lublin: ses origines et son rôle historique.** (The Lublin Union: its origins and its historical role.)
Juliusz Bardach. *Acta Poloniae Historica*, vol. 21 (1970), p. 69-92.
Written on the occasion of the 400th anniversary of the event (1 July 1569), the article analyses: the causes of the Union; the personal union at Krewo in 1385; the gradual social and institutional transformation of the Grand Duchy of Lithuania under Polish influence; the functioning of the Union after 1569 ('The Commonwealth of Both Nations'); the historical consequences of the union; and other comparable unions in European history (such as the Kalmar Union of Scandinavian countries, and the Habsburg Empire). According to the author, the uniqueness of the Lublin Union lies in its durability. He also examines the differences between the attitude towards Belorussia, Lithuania and the Ukraine later expounded by Polish federalists (who were led by Józef Piłsudski) who advocated a new Polish-Lithuanian-Ukrainian union, and the rightists (led by Roman Dmowski) who wanted to absorb within the boundaries of post-First World War Poland as many Eastern Slavs and Lithuanians as possible.

107 **The siege of Vienna.**
John Stoye. London: Collins, 1963; New York: Holt, 1965. 349p. illus. maps.
An account of the siege (July-September 1683), and the rescue and pursuit campaign led by John III Sobieski, the Polish king, and commander of the allied Polish and Imperial forces who liberated the capital city of the Habsburg Empire. The work is lively and clear and the author has a skilful style. Based mostly on Austrian and Turkish sources.

108 **The king's honor and the king's cardinal: the War of the Polish Succession.**
John L. Sutton. Lexington, Kentucky: University Press of Kentucky, 1980. 250p. maps.
Examines the War for the Polish Succession, that broke out in Europe after the death of Augustus II, the Strong, in 1733. An Austro-Russo-Saxonian coalition supported Frederick Augustus Wettin, while France, Savoy and Sweden sided with Stanisław Leszczyński. The war ended in 1738 with Frederick ascending the Polish throne as Augustus III (1696-1763).

109 **The first partition of Poland.**
Herbert Harold Kaplan. New York: Columbia University Press, 1962. xvi+215p. illus.
A well-researched and well-balanced presentation of one of the crucial periods of Polish history. This account investigates in depth the interaction between internal attempts to renew the country and external schemes to destroy it.

110 **Polish politics and national reform, 1775-1788.**
Daniel Stone. Boulder, Colorado: East European Quarterly, 1976. 122p.
Covers the period from the Bar Confederacy to the Great Diet, that voted the famous 'May Constitution' (3 May 1791) which, to a considerable extent, reflects US constitutional principles. This entire period was characterized by persistent efforts by Polish patriots to save the country from a foreign invasion through a radical socioeconomic reform and a consequent reinforcement of internal institutions.

111 **The government of Poland.**
Jean-Jacques Rousseau. New York: Bobbs, 1972.
This is the most recent edition of Rousseau's comments on Poland's political system in the late 18th century. The work was originally prepared at the request of King Stanisław Poniatowski and to some extent influenced the Polish Third of May (1791) constitution.

112 **The last king of Poland and his contemporaries.**
Robert Nisbet Bain. Reprint, New York: Arno Press, 1971. xviii+296p. First published in London in 1919.
The importance of the 'Stanislavian era' of King Stanisław II Poniatowski (1732-98), for Polish culture and arts is largely the result of the intellectual and progressive milieu that the king created around himself. This began with the famous 'Thursday Dinners' to which he used to invite the most prominent representatives of the enlighted contemporary élite.

113 **The second partition of Poland: a study in diplomatic history.**
Robert Howard Lord. Cambridge, Massachusetts: Harvard
University Press, 1915. 586p. bibliog. Reprinted, New York:
AMS Press, 1969. 596p.

This is not just the only book in English on the subject, but a classic of historiography in its own right which deals with Poland's partitions in general.

114 **Kościuszko and Pułaski.**
Jan Stanisław Kopczewski. Warsaw: Interpress, 1976.
328p. illus.

A beautifully illustrated book which provides comparative biographies of the two
major heroes of the Polish and American struggles for independence. They are
considered brothers-in-arms in spite of the fact that their paths never crossed.

115 **The third partition of Poland.**
Robert Howard Lord. *Slavonic and East European
Review*, vol. 3 (March 1925), p. 481-98.

A companion article to the author's earlier book *The second partition of Poland:
a study in diplomatic history* (q.v.) on partial partitions of Poland. The present
article deals with probably the most tragic event in Polish history marking what
seemed to be at the time *finis Poloniae* (the end of Poland).

Contemporary history (19th-early 20th century)

116 **The lands of partitioned Poland, 1795-1918.**
Piotr Stefan Wandycz. Seattle, Washington: University of
Washington Press, 1975. xvi+431p. maps. bibliog.

Analyses Poland's history under foreign occupation emphasizing the importance of
culture in national survival. This survey is aimed at the scholar, who is not a
specialist in East Central European history. Individual chapters deal with such
topics as the Napoleonic Wars, the Romantic insurrections, organic work and
positivism, 'Young Poland', and the country's rebirth.

117 **Napoleon's campaign in Poland, 1806-1807.**
F. Loraine Petre. New York: Hippocrene, 1975.
xxv+354p. illus. maps.

Although first published in 1901 this book is still relevant. The defeat inflicted by
France upon the two partitioning powers (Austria and Prussia) raised new hopes
among many Poles, who joined the Grand Army. However, Napoleon's exclusive
concern was for French grandeur, and he failed to deliver the promised political
changes which, in the main, had caused Poles to follow his colours.

118 **The lands between: the history of East-Central Europe since the Congress of Vienna.**
Alan Warwick Palmer. London: Weidenfeld & Nicolson; New York: Macmillan, 1970. x+405p. maps.
The land between the Baltic and the Black Seas is inhabited by a mosaic of nations that daily face the political, military and cultural problem of maintaining their distinct ethnic identity in the face of overwhelming political and economic pressures. How to avoid getting squeezed between the two continental giants Germany and Russia has been for over two centuries the main problem of the East-Central European countries.

119 **Czartoryski and the European unity, 1770-1861.**
Marian Kukiel. Princeton, New Jersey: Princeton University Press, 1955. xviii+354p. illus. maps. bibliog.
Reprinted, Westport, Connecticut: Greenwood Press, 1981.
The best study available in English on the ideology and activities of Adam Jerzy Czartoryski the 'uncrowned king of Poland' and leader of the conservative wing of the Great Emigration, who participated in practically every major event from the Grand Diet to the January Insurrection. The book stresses public affairs, showing Czartoryski's efforts to regain independence through a variety of means. After the failure of his plan to form an alliance between an independent Poland and Russia, he dedicated his life to liberating Poland as part of a universal design for a free and united Europe. He considered the maintenance of the national cultural heritage to be the decisive factor in preserving nationality and a pre-condition of Poland's future resurrection.

120 **Antecedents of revolution: Alexander I and the Polish Kingdom, 1815-1825.**
Frank W. Thackeray. New York: Columbia University Press, 1980. 187p. bibliog.
Analyses Tsar Alexander's attitude towards Poland, and derivative Polish hopes and disappointments. Also considers the role played by the tsar's advisors, the most important of which was initially his friend, Adam Czartoryski. Later, however, Czartoryski became Alexander's greatest antagonist.

121 **Romantic nationalism and liberalism: Joachim Lelewel and the Polish national idea.**
Joan S. Skurnowicz. Boulder, Colorado: East European Monographs, 1981. 224p.
A biographical essay concerning Joachim Lelewel (1786-1861) the well-known progressive leader (he headed the democratic wing of the Great Emigration) and outstanding Polish historian, mostly from the point of view of his scholarly contribution and methodology.

122 **National solidarity and organic work in Prussian Poland, 1815-1914.**
William W. Hagen. *Journal of Modern History*, vol. 44, no.1 (1972), p. 38-64.

The author shows that when the Prussian government tried to enforce Germanization on the Poles, their reaction was to set up social and economic institutions which would strengthen their cohesion as a nation and their ability to resist. For the hundred years between the Congress of Vienna and the outbreak of the First World War, Poles formed one tenth of the population of the Kingdom of Prussia. The author teaches at the University of California at Davis.

123 **Politics and economics in Congress Poland, 1815-1865.**
Robert F. Leslie. *Past and Present*, vol. 8 (1955), p. 43-63.

It was the English view that Poland's struggle for independence was actually a popular demand for good government based on liberal institutions. However, it was, in fact, a liberation movement against foreign oppression and a struggle for economic justice. The 'Congress Kingdom' (or in Polish 'Kongresówka') designates the part of Poland occupied by Russia after the Congress of Vienna.

124 **Polish politics and the Revolution of November 1830.**
Robert F. Leslie. London: Athlone Press; New York: De Graff, 1956. xii+306p. maps. Reprinted, Westport, Connecticut: Greenwood Press.

A well-organized, lucid and thorough study based mostly on Polish sources. In the author's view the nationalist insurrection (November Uprising) in Russian Poland represented the last challenge to Russia by pre-partition, nobility-ruled Poland, while the solution of the peasants' problem represented the decisive factor in the country's future.

125 **1848: the romantic and democratic revolutions in Europe.**
Jean Sigmann, translated by Lovett F. Edwards. London: Harper, 1973. 352p.

A readable book which discusses national, political and ethnic forces at work in Europe during the Spring of Nations. As well as the major uprisings that took place in Poland in 1831 and in 1863, there were insurrections in Silesia, Pomerania, and particularly in Greater Poland and Galicia between 1846-48. Polish military and political leaders were also prominent in revolutionary movements in Hungary (Henryk Dembiński), Germany (Ludwik Mierosławski) and Italy (Adam Mickiewicz). In most cases requests for national autonomy were accompanied by demands for socioeconomic emancipation.

126 **The multinational empire: nationalism and national reform in the Habsburg monarchy, 1848-1918.**
Robert A. Kann. New York: Columbia University Press, 1950. 2 vols. 444p.+423p. maps. bibliog.

A comprehensive study of ethnic problems in the Habsburg Danubian Empire which extended towards the Balkans and the Carpathians, and comprised the 'Kingdom of Galicia and Lodomeria', and included the metropolitan cities of Kraków (Cracow) and Lwów (Lvov). The author discusses problems of supranational organization, of cooperation between various national entities, and relations

History. Contemporary history (19th-early 20th century)

between German, Hungarian and Slavic components during the period from the Spring of Nations till the end of the Second World War. The Habsburgs resided in Poland at the town of Żywiec (Cieszyn Silesia) during the interwar period, and a Habsburg archduke was a colonel in the Polish army, while Habsburg breweries are still the source of the well-known Żywiec beer.

127 **The origins and practice of 'organic work' in Poland: 1795-1863.**

Stanislaus A. Blejwas. *Polish Review*, vol. 15, no.4 (autumn 1970), p. 23-54.

Examines the origins of the ideology that developed after the abortive January 1863 Uprising which repudiated Romantic revolutionary tendencies in favour of economic, cultural and educational advancement. This meant a practical reversal of priorities in national goals.

128 **Reform and insurrection in Russian Poland, 1856-1865.**

Robert F. Leslie. London: Athlone Press, 1963. 284p. Reprinted, Westport, Connecticut: Greenwood Press.

The author suggests that the January 1863 Insurrection, the last uprising of the Romantic period, was the first modern revolution, even though its basic aim was the restoration of the pre-partition régime in Poland. The book is important, though somewhat controversial in its conclusions.

129 **Wielopolski's reforms and their failure before the Uprising of 1863.**

Irena M. Roseveare. *Antemurale* vol. 15 (1971), p. 87-214.

The revolutionary ideas springing from the November 1831 Uprising and the Spring of Nations were not implemented. Andrzej Zamoyski and Aleksander Wielopolski led a movement to postpone political aspirations in favour of the country's economic and cultural advancement ('organic work'). Wielopolski made a bid for administrative reforms and cultural and economic self-government, but his efforts failed to produce concessions from Russia. Rather than granting preferential treatment to the Polish nobility, the *Ukaz* of 2 March 1862 handed over ownership of their land to the peasants. The objective was obviously to stir up social hatred among Poles and to penalize the nobility for its patriotism.

130 **The futile compromise considered: Wielopolski and Russian policy, 1861-1863.**

Stanley Żyżniewski. *American Historical Review* vol. 70, no.2 (Jan. 1965), p. 395-412.

Russian attempts to find a *modus vivendi* with the Poles ranged from a recognition of Poland's separate identity to plans for its complete abolition. Marquis Alexander Wielopolski was responsible for the last effort to find a compromise, the failure of which contributed to the outbreak of the January 1863 Uprising. Lack of foresight, *ad hoc* decisions, an autocratic approach and unwillingness to offer concessions on the part of the Russians, as well as Wielopolski's personal unpopularity, appear to have been the decisive reasons for the ultimate failure to reach a compromise.

History. Contemporary history (19th-early 20th century)

131 **The history of Poland since 1863.**
Edited by Robert F. Leslie. London: Cambridge University
Press, 1980. 528p. maps.

The volume spans three major periods of recent Polish history: the period from
1863 to the First World War which was characterised by foreign domination, the
interwar period of complete independance and of 'authoritarian democracy', and
the post-war times of Communist domination and of limited independence as
formulated in the 'Brezhnev doctrine'. The book offers a good balance between
politicoideological, socioeconomic and cultural-intellectual history, and a full discussion of the present institutional structure. The other authors who contribute to
the volume are: Antony Polonsky, Jan Ciechanowski and Zbigniew Pełczyński.

132 **The history of the 'Proletariat': the emergence of Marxism in
the Kingdom of Poland, 1870-1887.**
Norman M. Naimark. Boulder, Colorado: East European
Quarterly, 1979. 329p.

The dynamic development of industry and urbanization in the Congress Kingdom
in the 1870s and 1880s, the tsarist agrarian reform of 1864, and the appearance
of a working class created the necessary conditions for the establishment of the
first Marxist party. The 'Proletariat' considered socialism to be a broader concept
than Poland's independence and did not hesitate to advocate compulsion to
achieve its goals. The author attempts to provide a parallel study of the Polish
and Russian revolutionary movements: the percentage of workers active in the
Marxist movement in Poland was twice as large as in Russia, while in Russia
students were much more numerous than in Poland. Another characteristic
feature of the Marxist movement in Poland was the participation of some
noblemen which helped to bridge the gap between the workers and the intelligentsia. Biographies of Polish socialists are included in an appendix.

133 **Prussian Poland in the German Empire, 1871-1900.**
Richard Blanke. Boulder, Colorado: East European
Monographs, 1981. 280p.

134 **Germanizing Prussian Poland: the H.K.T. society and the
struggle for the Eastern marches in the German Empire,
1894-1919.**
Richard Wonser Tims. New York: Columbia University
Press, 1941. 312p. illus. bibliog.

The Bismarck government of Prussia sponsored a semi-official organization, the
aim of which was to assimiliate, or to eliminate, Poles in territories under Prussian administration. The organization was known as the HKT (from its leaders
Hansemann, Kennemann and Tiedemann), or as the 'Hakata'. In Poland it
became a synonym for German chauvinism and persecution.

Inter-war history

135 Rebirth of the Polish Republic: a study in the diplomatic history of Europe, 1914-1920.
Tytus Komarnicki. London: Heinemann, 1957. xiii+776p. maps. bibliog.

An important contribution on Poland's resurgence after the First World War. The author, a former Polish diplomat, international lawyer and university professor, has produced a well-documented book on the reemergence of the Polish state after the Versailles Peace Conference. A large part of the work is devoted to the problem of Poland's Eastern boundaries, while less attention is given to the Silesian plebiscite, the Cieszyn question and the Wilno issue. A substantial section of the book deals with Piłsudski's plan for self-determination and a confederation of the Eastern European countries from the Caucasus to the Baltic Sea. This plan clashed with Lenin's design for a protective belt around Russia consisting of satellite states, and achieved through a social revolution promoted by the Soviet Union.

136 The Polish problem at the Paris Peace Conference: a study of the policies of the great powers and the Poles, 1918-1919.
Kay Lundgreen-Nielsen, translated by Alison Borch-Johansen. Odense, Denmark: Odense University Press, 1979. 606p. maps. bibliog.

A well-written and well-researched study which: discusses the attitudes of Józef Piłsudski and Roman Dmowski; analyses Allied reaction to the aspirations of various Polish groups; considers Polish border problems and the question of ethnic and religious minorities; and contrasts the attitudes of French and British decision-makers.

137 White Eagle, Red Star: the Polish-Soviet war 1919-1920.
Norman Davies. New York: St. Martin's Press, 1972. 318p. illus. maps.; London: Macdonald, 1974. 332p. illus. maps.

A pioneer work in English describing the entire Polish-Soviet War, and giving detailed accounts of both political and military aspects, as well as discussing the role of such leaders as Józef Piłsudski, Mikhail Tukhachevsky, Symon Petlura and Ludjan Żeligowski. The book shows how the conflict affected the development of Soviet foreign policy and throws light on the way the theory of a 'world revolution' gave way to the 'socialism in one country' ideology.

138 Polish federalism 1919-1920 and its historical antecedents.
Piotr Stefan Wandycz. *East European Quarterly*, vol. 4 (1970), p. 25-39.

The roots of the Polish federal idea go back to the multinational Jagellonian monarchy, the predecessor of the Habsburg Empire. Józef Piłsudski, immediately after the First World War, supported the Polish Commonwealth idea of a Polish-Lithuanian-Ukrainian federative state and for that purpose encouraged General Lucjan Żeligowski's annexation of Wilno (the capital of Lithuania which had a predominantly Polish population) and Symon Petlura's liberation of Kiev (the capital of the Ukraine which has an important Polish minority).

139 Memories of a Polish revolutionary and soldier.
Józef Piłsudski. London: Faber & Faber, 1931. 377p. illus. maps. Reprinted, 1971.

A selection of the earlier writings of this prestigious Polish leader who in his youth fought for socialism and social justice as well as for the freedom of his country. After four decades of forced oblivion his portraits have recently reappeared all over Poland.

140 The eighteenth decisive battle of the world: Warsaw, 1920.
Edgar Vincent d' Abernon. London: Hodder & Stoughton, 1931. 178p. map.

The defeat of the Red Army led by Mikhail Tukhachevsky at the line of the Vistula river is also known in Polish history as 'The Miracle of the Vistula'. This 'miraculous' concept was reinforced by the presence on the Polish side of the papal nuncio Achille Ratti, who later became Pope Pius XI. From this victory Józef Piłsudski emerged as the only commanding officer ever to have inflicted a definite defeat on the Soviet armed forces. Politically, if they had won at the Vistula, the Russians would probably have joined forces with the Communist revolutionary movement in Germany.

141 Joseph Piłsudski: a European federalist, 1918-1922.
Marian Kamil Dziewanowski. Stanford, California: Hoover Institution, 1969. xvi + 380p.

Józef Piłsudski, the commander of the Polish Legions during the First World War and the first head of state of the reborn Poland, cherished a federal programme. However, he was handicapped by the weakness of his operational base: Poland's economy was ruined; its armed forces were weak; its civil service was only patched together; and its allies were remote and unreliable. His aim was to reinstate the former federation between the Crown of Poland and the Grand Duchy of Lithuania transforming it into a base for a broader Central European Federation capable of resisting German and/or Russian pressures. His plan did not succeed, not so much because of Russian military power but because of the caution of the Lithuanians and Ukrainians, who feared that the new organic federation might serve as a smoke-screen for Polish hegemony, and that the original autonomy of each component part might be gradually eroded in favour of Polish leadership.

142 The birth of the parliamentary system in Poland after World War I.
Michał Pietrzak. *Acta Poloniae Historica*, vol. 22 (1970), p. 193-206.

In spite of some shortcomings, the inter-war parliamentary democracy allowed the entire community a share in the political life of the country, and enabled all classes to struggle for their socioeconomic advancement.

143 **East and Central Europe between the two world wars.**
Joseph Rothschild. Seattle, Washington: University of
Washington Press, 1974. 420p. maps.
A comprehensive and meticulously written book which includes an exceptionally
good chapter on Poland. This chapter covers: internal politics; parliamentary
debates; ethnic tensions; the impact of the economic crisis; territorial revisionism;
and foreign relations.

144 **Bitter glory: the history of independent Poland, 1918-1939.**
Richard M. Watt. New York: Simon & Schuster, 1979.
511p. bibliog.
A comprehensive and clearly written history of Poland during the interwar period.
The approach is descriptive rather than interpretative, and special attention is
given to the part played by Józef Piłsudski.

145 **Politics in independent Poland 1921-1939: the crisis of
constitutional government.**
Antony Polonsky. Oxford: Clarendon Press, 1972.
xvi+572p. maps. bibliog.
A concise, comprehensive, clear and very-well researched study of the inter-war
period in Polish history. This work was hailed by some reviewers as a milestone
in Polish contemporary historiography. The author is rather critical of the Piłsudski régime, and asserts that it was largely responsible for the difficult period that
followed the Marshal's death: when nationalities problems became more acute;
when because of the breakdown in international relations Poland seemed set on a
collision course; when the economic situation was difficult; and when authori-
tarianism was on the rise in the institutional structure. It is unfortunate that the
author's efforts at objectivity have led him to exclude all emotional factors: there
is no room in the book for personal feelings, literary impressions, or references to
Poland's historical heritage.

146 **Piłsudski's coup d'état.**
Joseph Rothschild. New York: Columbia University Press,
1966. xii+435p. maps. bibliog.
An able study of the background to Piłsudski's coup d'état, the seizure of power
itself and the consolidation of the Piłsudski régime. The study is based on a
detailed examination of archival material some of which has not been examined
before. The author analyzes the crucial events in the inter-war period and provides an account of Piłsudski's political philosophy and action. He stresses the
'Grand Marshal's' opposition to any form of explicit dictatorship. It should be
noted that, surprisingly enough, the Paris branch of the authors' family, the
House of Rothschild, is closely connected with Polish affairs through the marriage
of Diana Rothschild to a high ranking Polish diplomat, Anatol Mühlstein.

147 **Joseph Piłsudski, 1867-1967.**
Marian Kamil Dziewanowski. *Eastern European Quarterly*,
vol. 2 (1969), p. 359-83.
Even one hundred years after his birth, and despite certain anachronistic and
authoritarian aspects of his government, Piłsudski remains for many Poles the
symbol of Polish independence regained after the Partitions period. In addition he

is remembered for his relentless struggle against the Russian threat and for the extension of ethnic and religious toleration toward minority groups. Piłsudski also had enough political foresight to rely more on Poland's own strength than on promises from Western allies, and to propose preventative military action against Nazi Germany at a time when both Britain and France were experimenting with appeasement.

148 **The little dictators.**
Antony Polonsky. London: Routledge, 1975. xii+212p. maps. bibliog.

Examines the history of the Central European countries between the two World Wars and provides a lengthy introduction on the pre-1918 and post-1939 periods.

149 **Poland: key to Europe.**
Raymond Leslie Buell. New York: Knopf, 1939. 3rd. ed. xi+406p+xvp. map.

A sympathetic but scholarly view of Poland's problems during the years preceding the outbreak of the Second World War. Details: German-Polish and Germanic-Slavic relations; Nazi aims in Eastern Europe; the general historical background; the reemergence of Poland as an independent nation after the First World War; the century of partitions; the political system during the inter-war period; the agrarian question; overpopulation and emigration; economic conditions and prospects; ethnic minorities; and foreign policy.

Second World War

German invasion

150 **The war Hitler won: the fall of Poland, September 1939.**
Nicholas Bethell. New York: Holt, 1973. 472p. illus. maps. chronological table. bibliog.

A well-written and researched account of the first six weeks of the Second World War. The author discusses: the German invasion of Poland; French and British reactions to the invasion; the Russian invasion of Eastern Poland; and the fall of Poland. The account, which is more journalistic than scholarly, concentrates on the military aspects and exposes the ineptitude of many of the British and French leaders.

151 **The German campaign in Poland.**
Robert M. Kennedy. Washington, DC: Department of the Army, 1956. xii+141p. illus. maps. bibliog.

A US officer describes the September 1939 campaign from the point of view of military tactics and strategy. Some background information on the origin of the Polish-German conflict, Polish and German army organization and strength at the beginning of operations, and the conduct of the war is included.

152 **The last European war, September 1939-December 1941.**
John Lukacs.   Garden City, New York: Doubleday, 1976.
562p.

The German-Polish war, which quickly escalated into a European and world conflict, is described in detail. Reference is made to: its diplomatic antecedents; France's reluctance to come to the aid of her ally; Britain's policy of appeasement; and German hopes that the Western powers would exert pressure on Poland to surrender to German demands. A description is included of the German strategy of Blitzkrieg, the success of which was partly fostered by immobility in the West.

153 **The cavalry of World War II.**
Jarosław Piekałkiewicz.   London: Orbis, 1979. 256p. illus.
maps.

A detailed chronological account of those military campaigns of the Second World War, in which cavalry units were employed, with particular reference to the use of cavalry in Poland during the 1939 campaign. Every aspect of cavalry life is presented with the help of well-chosen illustrations. In addition individual formations of cavalry units are examined.

German administration

154 **Nazi rule in Poland, 1939-1945.**
Tadeusz Cyprian, Jerzy Sawicki.   Warsaw: Polonia, 1961.
261p. illus.

An account by Poland's representative at the Nuremberg trials.

155 **Hans Frank's diary.**
Edited by Stanisław Piotrowski.   Warsaw: Państwowe
Wydawnictwo Naukowe, 1961. 320p.

A systematic day-by-day register of Nazi crimes committed in Poland during the occupation years, recorded with typical German thoroughness. Hans Frank was the Governor General of those occupied lands of Poland which were not fully incorporated into the Third Reich and which constituted a separate political entity. His declarations, which comprise 11,000 typewritten pages, represent some of the most revealing evidence which came to light during the Nuremberg trials.

156 **Genocide 1939-1945.**
Szymon Datner, Janusz Gumkowski, Kazimierz
Leszczyński.   Warsaw: Zachodnia Agencja Prasowa, 1962.
334p. illus.

Examines: the crimes committed by the German military establishment during the September 1939 campaign in Poland; the extermination of the Polish population in the territories incorporated into the Reich; the mass extermination camps; the execution of civilians; and the 'pacification' of villages. Includes a chronological index of the localities where extermination took place.

157 **Polish society under German occupation: the General gouvernement 1939-1944.**
Jan Tomasz Gross. Princeton, New Jersey: Princeton University Press, 1979. v+343p.
Analyses the pattern of German behaviour and the Polish response during the occupation period. In the author's opinion the absence of any German-sponsored institutions in Poland was largely responsible for the emergence of a Polish underground state. Nazi brutality persuaded the Poles that they had very little to lose from guerrilla-style resistance to the occupation forces. The book offers a fresh perspective to a much discussed and written about subject.

158 **Silesia in German eyes, 1939-1945.**
Kazimierz Popiołek, translated by Andrzej Potocki. Katowice, Poland: Instytut Śląski, 1964. 238p.
A well-known expert on Silesian history discusses German attempts to bring about the total destruction of the Polish language, cultural life, and economic property in occupied Silesian lands during the Second World War. The Polish resistance movement in the area is also discussed. The book is based on German sources.

159 **Fighting Auschwitz.**
Józef Garliński. London: Friedmann; New York: Holmes & Meier, 1975. 327p. illus. maps. bibliog.
A factual and painstakingly researched account of the resistance movement inside Auschwitz (Oświęcim) concentration and extermination camp. The movement was led by a member of the underground Home Army, who voluntarily became the Auschwitz inmate with the responsibility of organizing the resistance. The author, a former camp prisoner, is also the current president of the Association of Polish Writers Abroad which is based in London.

160 **Commandant at Auschwitz.**
Rudolf Hoess, translated by Constantine Fitzgibbon. London: Weidenfeld & Nicolson, 1959. 252p. Reprinted, Cleveland, Ohio: World Publishing Co., 1960. 285p.; New York: Popular Library, 1969. 240p.
Written in prison while the author awaited trial and execution, this cold-blooded and horrifying volume is nevertheless an important historical document. It shows how a mediocre but basically civilised person can become a cog in an extermination machine without taking a moral stance on the mass murder of millions of human beings. A naïve autobiography dwelling in detail on the technicalities of extermination practices.

161 **Anus mundi: 1,500 days at Auschwitz/Birkenau.**
Wiesław Kielar, translated by Suzanne Flatauer. New York: Times Books, 1980. 312p. illus.
Well-written and highly moving memoirs of a Polish survivor of the camp. The work provides a different perspective on the subject compared with other books and is free of any personal bias.

162 **The death camp Treblinka: a documentary.**
Edited by Alexander Donat. New York: Schocken, 1979.
320p. illus. maps. bibliog.

Treblinka, Northeast of Warsaw, was an extermination camp for Jews and gypsies, as distinct from the various slave labour camps, where forced labour preceded extermination. It existed from July 1942 till August 1943, when a desperate revolt broke out. Only 60 inmates survived while almost one million people perished. On the site of Treblinka there is today an impressive monument surrounded by 17,000 symbolic tombstones, which have been erected by the Polish authorities.

163 **Treblinka.**
Jean François Steiner, translated by Helen Weaver, with a preface by Simone de Beauvoir. London: Weidenfeld & Nicolson, 1967. xiii+336p. Reprinted, New York: New American Library, 1979. 304p.

Relates the resistance efforts of the few people who survived the Nazi extermination programme at Treblinka, near Białystok, in Northeastern Poland. At times the author seems to be more shocked by the passivity of the victims than by the cruelty of the executioners.

164 **Axis rule in occupied Europe.**
Rafał Lemkin. Washington, DC: Carnegie Endowment for International Peace, 1944. xxxviii+674p.

This work deals with occupation law and the system of government imposed upon European countries by the Axis powers. The author is a prominent Polish lawyer and the originator of the concept of genocide. Chapter 24 (p. 221-31) deals with Poland.

165 **Inter arma non silent musae: the war and the culture 1939-1945.**
Edited by Czesław Madajczyk. Warsaw: Państwowy Instytut Wydawniczy, 1977. 656p.

A collection of miscellaneous essays on the influence of the Second World War on the intellectual life and culture of the nations involved. The volume includes contributions on: cultural life in German concentration camps; the resistance as expressed in art; the cultural policy of the German occupation authorities; and the ways in which Poles tried to evade the control of their cultural life. The contributions are in English, French, German and Russian.

Jews

166 **Jewish resistance in Nazi-occupied Eastern Europe: with a historical survey of the Jew as fighter and soldier in the Diaspora.**
Reuben Ainsztein. New York: Harper & Row, 1974. 970p. map. bibliog.
A systematic survey of Jewish resistance and partisan guerrilla activities in Poland and the Soviet Union. Contains an excellent account of the Warsaw Ghetto Uprising.

167 **The Black Book of Polish Jewry: an account of the martyrdom of Polish Jewry under the Nazi occupation.**
Edited by Jakub Apenszlak. New York: American Federation of Polish Jews & Roy, 1943. xvi + 343p. illus; Reprinted, New York: Fertig, 1982.
An invaluable source book on the martyrdom of Polish Jews in German-occupied Poland. Although the account is shocking enough as it stands, the full details of many of the Nazi crimes did not come to light until after the book's publication ie., at the end of the war.

168 **Righteous among nations: how Poles helped the Jews 1939-1945.**
Edited by Władysław Bartoszewski, Zofia Lewin. London: Earlscourt Publications, 1969. 834p. Also published under the title: *The Samaritans: heroes of the holocaust.* New York: Twayne, 1970. 442p.
A saga of individual experiences of sacrifice, martyrdom and dedication to the Jewish cause in Nazi occupied Poland.

169 **Roads to extinction: essays on the holocaust.**
Philip Friedman. New York: Jewish Social Studies, 1980. 610p.
A selection of writings by this well-known Polish-Jewish historian which describes life and death in the ghettos of Łódź (renamed Litzmannstadt by the Germans), Lublin (Lüben) and Lwów (Lemberg). Also considers resistance and collaborationism, and the Nazi impact on modern Jewish history.

170 **Poland's ghettos.**
Alfred Katz. New York: Twayne, 1970. 175p.
Considers the living conditions in the ghettos organized by the Nazis in five major Polish cities (Warsaw, Cracow, Łódź, Białystok, Wilno).

171 **The bravest battle: the twenty-eight days of the Warsaw Ghetto Uprising.**
Dan Kurzman. New York: Putnam, 1976. 386p. illus. map.

A step-by-step account of what was termed 'a modern Masada': the last stand of 60,000 poorly armed Jews led by Mordechai Anielewicz, against regular German troops equipped with armour and artillery, and aided by tactical air force support under the high command of SS Major-General Jürgen Stroop.

172 **Uprising in the Warsaw ghetto.**
Ber Mark, translated by Gershon Freidlin. New York: Schocken, 1975. 209p. map. bibliog.

An exhaustive account of the fierce and heroic resistance of the Warsaw Jews based on letters, manifestoes, memoirs, and records from Jewish, Polish and German sources. The author, the founder of the Jewish Historical Institute in Poland, tells how 2,000 SS troops were dispatched on 19 April 1943 to destroy the Jewish district of the capital city.

173 **Polish-Jewish relations during the Second World War.**
Emanuel Ringelblum, introduction by Joseph Kermish. New York: Fertig, 1976. xxxix+330p. First published, Jerusalem: Yad Vashem, 1974.

A well-researched study on the complex relationship between the Jewish and Polish communities during the German occupation of Poland. A brief introduction on pre-war Polish-Jewish relations is followed by chapters on Polish-Jewish economic relations, Polish aid to the ghettos and to Jews in hiding, and the various Polish attitudes towards the Jews from solidarity to anti-Semitism.

Polish underground

174 **A memoir of the Warsaw uprising.**
Miron Białoszewski, translated by Madeleine G. Levine. Ann Arbor, Michigan: Ardis, 1977. 234p.

A highly detailed record of the author's ordeal during the August-October 1944 insurrection in the besieged Polish capital.

175 **The Warsaw Rising in 1944.**
Jan M. Ciechanowski. London: Cambridge University Press, 1974. 332p. map. bibliog.

Describes the background to, and the events of, the Warsaw Uprising which was organized by the Polish Home Army. The insurrection had two aims: to expel the German occupation forces and to aid the Soviet offensive approaching the line of the Vistula River; and to ensure that the liberation of Warsaw by Russians did not lead to the installation of a Soviet-supported and oriented administration in the capital. The military, diplomatic and political implications of the uprising are analyzed.

176 **The unseen and silent: adventures from the underground movement narrated by paratroopers of the Polish Home Army.**
Translated by George Iranek-Osmecki, foreword by General Władysław Anders. London: Sheed & Ward, 1954.
xvii+350p. illus. maps.

Parachutists of the Home Army maintained communications between underground military and civilian authorities in occupied Poland, and the Polish high command and government-in-exile in London.

177 **Story of a secret state.**
Jan Karski (*pseud.*). Boston, Massachusetts: Houghton Mifflin, 1944. vi+391p.

The author presents his reminiscences concerning his participation in the Polish underground during the Second World War. He describes the unique situation in which the Polish authorities, appointed by the government-in-exile in London, exercised political, military and educational functions from secret hideouts in Poland while eluding the surveillance of the German occupation forces.

178 **The secret army.**
Tadeusz Komorowski. London: Gollancz; New York: Macmillan, 1950. xiv+407p. maps.

A historical report on the organization of the Polish underground Home Army (by far the largest and most efficient Polish clandestine military organization during the Second World War) by its commanding officer 'General Bór'. Based on documents available in the West and on the author's personal memoirs, this book provides a vivid account of the tragic events of the period 1939-44.

179 **Fighting Warsaw: the story of the Polish underground state, 1939-1945.**
Stefan Korboński, translated by Franciszek Bauer-Czarnomski. New York: Macmillan; London: Allen & Unwin, 1956. vi+495p. Reprinted, New York: Funk & Wagnall, 1968 and Boulder, Colorado: East European Monographs, 1978.

This book is written with a sense of humour and without rancour and provides an extremely personal account of relations within the Polish government-in-exile, the frustrations the government encountered, and its problems with the homeland underground organization. During the Second World War, Poland not only had a very large and active underground army (totalling approximately 300,000) but is was actually administered by a government in hiding which organized underground courts, secret education and civil resistance. The author, who was the last leader of this government, has also written *The Polish underground state: a guide to the underground, 1939-1945* (Boulder, Colorado: East European Monographs, 1978. 268p.), translated by Marta Erdman, which includes chapters on: the structure of underground institutions; the organization and activities of the Home Army; the impact of the Katyń Woods massacre; the Warsaw Uprising; and the relationship between the Home Army (loyal to the legitimate Polish government-in-exile) and the smaller communist-sponsored resistance group. There are a number of interesting anecdotes which make this a lively book to read.

History. Second World War. Government-in-exile

180 **Seventy days: a diary of the Warsaw Insurrection of 1944.**
Wacław Zagórski, translated by John Welsh, introduction by
Tadeusz Bór-Komorowski. London: F. Muller, 1957. 267p.
illus.; London: Hamilton, 1959. 223p.

The author does not discuss in this diary the political validity of the uprising, but
offers a soldier's account of the facts and feelings experienced by the participants.
General Komorowski, the Commander-in-Chief of the Polish underground Home
Army at the time of the uprising, who on instructions from the Polish government-in-exile issued the order to begin the combat, gives a summary of the
military situation on the German-Russian front at the start of the battle. The
Warsaw Uprising left an indelible impression on a whole generation of Poles.

181 **Nothing but honour: the story of the Warsaw Uprising 1944.**
Janusz Kazimierz Zawodny. London: Macmillan; Stanford,
California: Hoover Institution, 1978. 328p. bibliog.

A meticulously researched and objective analysis of the history of the only major
battle of the Second World War, where an irregular military organization which
was inadequately armed, challenged and held off for 63 days a regular army
equipped with artillery and armour and which was supported by an air force. The
Poles hoped to free their capital city by their own means in advance of the arrival
of Soviet troops, so as to claim the credit for the expulsion of the Germans, and
to establish a non-Communist government. The aims of the Russians were, of
course, quite different: they wanted the Home Army (which owed allegiance to
the Polish government in London) to exhaust its forces in the uneven combat
against the Germans as a prelude to the establishment of a Soviet-backed administration. For this reason, not only did the Soviet army itself fail to aid the
insurgents, but it did its best to prevent Allied assistance.

The tradition of Polish ideals: essays in history and literature.
See item no. 7.

Government-in-exile

182 **The Black Book of Poland.**
New York: Putnam by authorization of the Polish
Government, 1942. xiv+615p. illus. maps.

Documentary material released by the Polish government-in-exile in London.

183 **Defeat in victory.**
Jan M. Ciechanowski. Garden City, New York:
Doubleday, 1947. xvi+397p.; London: Gollancz, 1948. 415p.

A documentary history concerning secret negotiations with the US authorities
conducted by the Polish government-in-exile. The author, who was at the time
Polish ambassador to Washington, presents his personal views and describes the
situation with remarkable insight, immediacy and restraint.

History. Second World War. Government-in-exile

184 **Documents concerning German-Polish relations and the outbreak of hostilities between Great Britain and Germany on 3rd September 1939.**
London: HM Stationery Office, 1939. xxviii+195p.
These documents were issued by the Polish government-in-exile in London.

185 **The German Fifth Column in Poland.**
London: Polish Ministry of Information, 1941. 157p.
Reproduces documents released by the Polish government-in-exile in London.

186 **The German New Order in Poland.**
London: Hutchinson, 1942. xiv+585p. illus. maps.
A collection of documents issued by the Polish government-in-exile in London.

187 **Exile governments: Spanish and Polish.**
Alicja Iwańska. Cambridge, Massachusetts: Schenkman, 1981. 192p. bibliog.

188 **Warsaw in exile.**
Stefan Korboński. New York: Praeger; London: Allen & Unwin, 1966. xiv+329p.
A commentary on Polish exile politics and on the attitude of the Western Allies towards Polish political leaders and parties in London. The author was one of the top figures of the Polish Peasant Party and of the war-time resistance movement.

189 **The pattern of Soviet domination.**
Stanisław Mikołajczyk. London: Sampson Low, 1948. xiv+353p.; New York: McGraw-Hill, 1948. xiii+310p. illus. (The US edition has the title: *The rape of Poland: pattern of Soviet agression*).
The memoirs of the leader of the Polish Peasant Party in exile, and Poland's prime minister in London after the tragic death of General Sikorski in 1943. The Western Allies urged him to try to reach an agreement with the Soviet-supported Polish Committee of National Liberation in Lublin promising their support. His experiences and his disappointments are the theme of his memoirs.

190 **The Polish White Book: official documents concerning Polish-German and Polish-Soviet relations, 1933-1939.**
London: Polish Ministry of Foreign Affairs, 1940. xvii+222p.
This collection of documents was published by the Polish government-in-exile in London.

Polish forces in the West

191 **An army in exile: the story of the Second Polish Corps.**
Władysław Anders, introduction by Sir Harold Macmillan,
foreword by Viscount Alexander of Tunis. London, New
York: Macmillan, 1949. xvi+320p. illus. maps. Reprinted,
London: Battery Press, 1981. xvi+320p.
One of the basic documents of the Second World War, a succinct account by one
of the chief Polish and Allied military leaders. General Anders won several
important battles for the Allied cause, including the famous battle of Monte
Cassino. However, he did not have an opportunity to return to Poland and establish the political system he and his soldiers had fought for. After the war he
remained in exile, playing an important part in the émigré government and refus-
ing till the end to enter into any compromise which involved the Soviet domination of Poland. He is buried at the Monte Cassino Polish war cemetery.

192 **Poles in the battle of Western Europe.**
Witold Biegański. Warsaw: Interpress, 1971. 158p.
A popular history of the organization of the Polish armed forces in Western
Europe after the September 1939 campaign which considers their part in: the
invasion of Normandy; the liberation of France; airborne operations at Arnhem;
the 'Overlord' naval operations; and air force support. The military operations of
the First Armoured Division and of the First Parachute Brigade are described,
and are supplemented by a brief account of Polish participation in the liberation
movements in France and Belgium.

193 **Monte Cassino: the historic battle.**
Charles Connell, foreword by Władysław Anders. London:
Elek, 1963. 206p. illus. maps.
An account of this decisive battle in the Italian campaign which was fought
gallantly and victoriously by the Polish Army 2nd Corps commanded by General
Anders. The conquest of the Monte Cassino mountain peak and fortified German
positions at the monastery broke through the Gustav Line defences and opened
the road to Rome to the Allies. Based largely on eye-witness accounts.

194 **Destiny can wait.**
Foreword by Lord Portal of Hungerford. London:
Heinemann, 1949. xvi+402p.
Recounts the story of the Polish Air Force during the Second World War, its
contribution to the Allied cause in general and its participation in air battles,
including the Battle of Britain.

195 **Poland, S.O.E., and the Allies.**
Józef Garliński, translated by Paul Stevenson. London:
Allen & Unwin, 1969. 248p. illus. maps.
A well-documented account of the Polish underground. The author was a partici-
pant in the actions of the Home Army, and an observer of the assistance given by
the British Special Operations Executive, whose task was to encourage native
resistance to the occupying forces. The book discusses in detail: the reconstitution

of the Polish armed forces on British soil; the development of the Polish Air Force in England; the liaison system between the Poles in Britain and those in the homeland; the use of Home Army intelligence by the Allies; guerrilla fighting against the German armed forces; the Warsaw Uprising; and the Soviet attitude towards the Polish government-in-exile and the Home Army.

196 Accident: the death of General Sikorski.
David John Irving. London: Kimber, 1967. 231p. illus. maps.

This book does not solve the mystery of the death of Poland's émigré government prime minister and Commander-in-Chief of the Polish forces in the West. The reader retains a distinct feeling that the air crash was not due to purely mechanical failures, and gaps do exist in the information unearthed by the enquiry. Parties who might have welcomed Sikorski's disappearance from the stage included: certain Polish circles which were disturbed by Sikorski's allegedly too conciliatory attitude in negotiations with the Russians; top Allied leaders, who made personal commitments regarding peace treaty conditions and guarantees to Poland of which Sikorski was the only trustee; and Soviet leaders who considered Sikorski a hard negotiator because of his strong Allied support and his close personal links with Western summit leaders.

197 They saved London.
Bernard Newman. London: Werner Laurie, 1952. 192p.

The history of the Polish airmen who participated in the Battle of Britain. Military historians credit them with the destruction of about one tenth of all enemy aircraft shot down over England.

198 Poles on the seas in the Second World War.
Jerzy Pertek. *Polish Western Affairs*, vol. 18, no.2 (1977), p. 255-78. bibliog.

In view of the overwhelming superiority of the German navy, Polish ships withdrew to British bases at the beginning of the hostilities in 1939. From here they continued to serve the Allied cause throughout the war. In Poland, the military bases of Westerplatte, Oksywie and Hel, on the Northern seaboard, as well as the partisans in Gdańsk, gained the admiration of the enemy by their heroic resistance. Three Polish submarines sought refuge in Swedish ports, while another submarine *Orzeł* managed to penetrate the sounds. The destroyers *Piorun*, *Burza* and *Błyskawica* took part in many Allied operations. Altogether, the Polish navy in the West numbered two cruisers, seven destroyers, three escorts and five submarines. The Polish merchant marine carried Allied troops from overseas and participated in convoy transport. In addition, many individual Poles served in Allied navies, including Admiral William S. Maxwell-Dzwonkowski, who on 2 September 1945 was in command of the battleship *Missouri*, on board which the Japanese signed an unconditional surrender.

199 The Polish armed forces in exile.
Michael Alfred Peszke. *Polish Review*, vol. 26, no.1 (1981), p. 67-113. bibliog.

An informative article concerning the activities of the Polish armed forces in the West between September 1939 and July 1941. In May 1945 the Polish armed forces abroad consisted of 220,000 men in active service and included: four divisions, three brigades, fourteen air force squadrons.

200 The battle for Cassino.
Janusz Piekałkiewicz.   London: Orbis, 1980. 224p. illus.
maps.
The book is based on communiqués from both sides and throws new light on the
conduct of the battle and on some controversial issues surrounding the Allied
strategy. For example, it considers whether the siege and the bombing of the
monastery were absolutely necessary.

201 In Allied London.
Edward Raczyński, introduction by Sir John
Wheeler-Bennet.   London: Weidenfeld & Nicolson, 1962.
xiv+381p. illus.
The diary of a prominent diplomat and statesman who was one of the most
important figures in both war-time 'Polish' London and Polish émigré politics,
and who became president of the Polish 'exile state'. Includes brief biographies of
Polish military and political émigré leaders.

202 Parachute general.
Stanisław Sosabowski, foreword by General Sir Richard
Gale.   London: Kimber, 1961. 159p. maps.
The author narrates his experiences as the commanding officer of the Polish
Autonomous Parachutist Brigade (*Samodzielna Brygada Spadochronowa*), which
took part in the combined operations of the British air and land forces at Arnhem
in Eastern Holland (17-26 September 1944). Also published under the title *Freely
I served*.

203 The assassination of Winston Churchill.
Carlos Thompson.   London: Colin Smythe, 1969. 472p.
illus.
A journalistic inquiry into one of the unsolved mysteries of the Second World
War: the tragic death at Gibraltar in 1943 of the Polish political and military
leader Władysław Sikorski. The book is a reaction to Rolf Hochhuth's play *The
Soldiers* which charges Winston Churchill with responsibility for the 'accident'.

Soviet intervention

204 The inhuman land.
Józef Czapski, foreword by Daniel Halévy, translated by
Gerard Hopkins.   New York: Sheed & Ward; London:
Chatto & Windus, 1951. xvi+301p.
The autobiography of a Polish artist, who was released following the German
attack on Russia and converted overnight from an object of potential extermina-
tion into a comrade-in-arms. He calls Russia an 'inhuman land' not so much
because of the starvation or the unbearable climate, nor even because of the

secret police atrocities, but above all because of the omnipresence of a dehuman-
ized society. Czapski is one of the very few officers, from the Starobielsk and
Kozielsk internment camps, who escaped the appalling massacre at the Katyń
forest.

205 **Katyn: crime without parallel.**
Louis Fitzgibbon. New York: Scribner, 1971. 285p. illus.
map.
A serious and well-documented book on the murder of 4,200 Polish officers in the
Katyń Woods. The discovery of this mass murder and its subsequent attribution
by both a commission of the International Red Cross and the Polish government-in-exile to the Soviet Army led to a crisis in Russian-Polish relations.

206 **A world apart.**
Gustaw Herling-Grudziński, translated by Joseph Marek
(*pseud.*). New York: Roy; London: Heinemann, 1951.
262p. illus.; New York: New American Library, 1952. 256p.
illus.
The author, now a prominent Polish émigré writer, was an inmate of a Soviet
hard labour 'correctional' camp in Karelia during the Second World War. He
describes the inhuman conditions of life in Stalinist camps.

207 **The origin of the Lublin government.**
George H. Janczewski. *Slavonic and East European
Review*, vol. 50, no.120 (July 1972), p. 410-33.
A clear account of the events that led to the formation of the Polska Partia
Robotnicza (Polish Workers' Party) and the Związek Patriotów Polskich (Association of Polish Patriots), and then to their transformation into the Lublin provisional government after the Red Army entered that town on 23 July 1944. The
name of that Soviet-supported administration, which was established in opposition
to the Polish government-in-exile in London and to the Home Army, was the
Polski Komitet Wyzwolenia Narodowego (Polish Committee of National Liberation).

208 **Poles in the European resistance movement 1939-1945.**
Mieczysław Juchniewicz. Warsaw: Interpress, 1972. 178p.
illus.
This book summarizes Polish participation in underground movements and guerrilla warfare in Belgium, France, Central Europe, the Balkans, Yugoslavia and
the Soviet Union (especially in Belorussia and the Ukraine).

209 **Great Britain, the Soviet Union and the Polish government in
exile (1939-1945).**
George V. Kacewicz. The Hague: Nijhoff, 1979. xv+255p.
This work focuses on the diplomatic controversies surrounding the Polish government-in-exile in London, British foreign policy and Soviet demands. It describes
the attitude of Poles towards British and Soviet aims during the chairmanship of
Sikorski and Mikołajczyk. The Polish armed forces in Britain, the Teheran decision on Poland's frontiers, and the breaking of Polish-Soviet relations after the

Katyń revelation are also discussed. Appendices include the Anglo-Polish Treaty, the Molotov-Ribbentrop Pact, the Treaty of Riga (1921), and the Yalta agreement.

210 **Katyn Forest massacre: final report of the select committee to conduct an investigation and to study the facts, evidence and circumstances... pursuant to H. Res. 390 and H. Res. 539. (82nd Congress, 2nd Session, House of Representatives report no. 2505).**
Washington, DC: Government Printing Office, 1952.
iii+45p.

The conclusions of the International Red Cross commission which inspected Katyń Forest at the invitation of the German authorities and attributed the responsibility for the massacre to the Soviet authorities were never accepted by the government of the USSR. Indeed, it was the attribution of responsibility for the killings to the Soviet authorities by the Polish government-in-exile in London which was given as the reason for the breaking off of Soviet-Polish relations by the Russians.

211 **The Katyn Wood murder.**
Józef Mackiewicz, foreword by Arthur Bliss Lane. London: Hollis & Carter, 1951. vi+252p. illus.

A conclusive exposure of Soviet responsibility for this atrocity which was concealed for a long time in an attempt to appease Stalin. The author visited Katyń when the International Red Cross representatives investigated the murder at the request of the German authorities. The book also explores the impact of the discovery of the Katyń massacre on Polish-Russian relations.

212 **The beginnings of communist rule in Poland, December 1943-June 1945.**
Edited by Antony Polonsky, Bolesław Drukier. London: Routledge & Kegan Paul, 1980. 464p. illus.

A detailed account covering the period from the establishment of the Krajowa Rada Narodowa (Homeland National Council) in Lublin to the enlargement of the provisional government by the inclusion of a certain number of non-communist politicians. Based on documents recently made available. Includes a glossary of organizations, a list of pseudonyms, and biographical data.

213 **The Polish Army in the battle of Berlin 1945.**
Zdzisław Stąpor. *Historia Militaris Polonica*, vol. 1 (1974), p. 211-33.

Polish armed forces remaining under the supreme command of the Soviet Commander-in-Chief participated actively in the conquest of the German capital city. A total of 185,000 men, 3,000 guns, 500 tanks and 320 planes took part in the operation which led victorious Polish and Russian troops to the Brandenburg Gate.

214 **Death in the forest: the story of the Katyń Forest massacre.**
Janusz Kazimierz Zawodny. Notre Dame, Indiana: Notre
Dame University Press, 1962. xvii+235p. bibliog.
A reconstruction of the Katyń massacre followed by an analysis of the moral
responsibility and future implications. The author, Professor of International
Relations at Claremont Graduate School, interviewed seventy key persons.

Regional history

Cracow

215 **The Free City of Cracow, 1815-1846.**
Stefan Kieniewicz. *Slavonic and East European Review*,
vol. 26 (1947), p. 69-86.
The Free City of Cracow (Kraków), known also as the Republic of Cracow,
covered 1,164 sq. km. and during this period had about 100,000 inhabitants. It
was established by the Congress of Vienna and placed under the protection of the
three partitioning powers, but after the abortive insurrection of 1846 it was abolished and incorporated into Austria.

Odra River basin

216 **The Odra: an album.**
Ignacy Rutkiewicz, photographs by Jan
Popławski. Warsaw: Interpress, 1977. 276p. illus.
A historical essay on the regions situated along the course of Odra (Oder) River,
which the Piast dynasty ruled until 1675. Since these lands were returned to
Poland in 1945, they have been resettled by Poles expelled from territories in the
East. In addition partially Germanized Pomeranians and Silesians have been re-
Polonized, 'ghost towns' have been rebuilt and cultural centres created.

Pomerania

217 **The role of the Order and the State of the Teutonic Knights
in Prussia in the history of Poland.**
Marian Biskup. *Polish Western Affairs*, vol. 7, no.2
(1966), p. 337-65.
After a careful analysis, the author reaches conclusions rather unfavourable to the
Teutonic Order: they used the wealth of Pomeranian towns and villages to expand
into Polish and Lithuanian lands; they represented the avant-guard of the German
drive towards the East; they cut off Poles and Lithuanians from access to the sea;

they abused religion for secular goals; and last, but not least, for centuries they poisoned the good will and friendly relations between Germans and Poles.

218 Danzig, and the Polish corridor, threshold of war.
Nendeln, Liechtenstein: Kraus-Thomson, 1979. 5 vols.
The work is divided into three parts; part 1: The German claims; part 2: The Polish reply; and part 3: The League of Nations as arbitrator. Each part presents one view of the Danzig problem which was the immediate cause of the outbreak of the Second World War. Poland and Nazi Germany came into conflict over Danzig because Poland needed free access to the sea and this requirement clashed with the German aspiration of integrating East Prussia with the rest of the Reich.

219 The Teutonic Order in Prussia.
Karol Górski. *Mediaevalia et Humanistica*, vol. 17 (1966), p. 20-37.
The historical role of the Prussian and Livonian branches of the Teutonic Order is hard to evaluate impartially because of the gulf between German scholars, who tend to present Prussia as the backbone of the West in Eastern Europe, and Polish and other East European historians, who hold the Order responsible for the poisoning of relations between peoples living in that part of Europe.

220 The Free City: Danzig and German foreign policy 1919-1934.
Christoph M. Kimmich. New Haven, Connecticut: Yale University Press, 1968. 196p.
The creation of a free city at the mouth of the Vistula was an Allied sanction against Germany intended to contribute to the security of Europe, while at the same time satisfying the ethnic claims of Danzig Germans and the historic and economic arguments of Poland. The experiment was not a success: Germany felt humiliated by foreign supervision, while Poland saw her maritime trade under foreign control at its most sensitive point. German policy in the area consisted of firstly attempting to gain complete economic control through financial and trade measures, and secondly the seizure of political control through a continuous irredentist action designed to transform the free city into a thorn in Poland's side.

221 Hitler's Free City: a history of the Nazi party in Danzig, 1925-1939.
Herbert S. Levine. Chicago: University of Chicago Press, 1973. xii+223p. bibliog.
A clearly written and well-documented presentation of the history of the National Socialist German Workers' Party (NSDAP) in Danzig, and of the free city's relations with the League of Nations, Poland and Germany. The methods of government adopted in the free city by the Nazis were modelled on those used in the Third Reich itself but inspite of electoral malpractices, they obtained only 59 per cent of the popular vote. In 1937 all other political parties were outlawed, and a sharp conflict developed between the President of the Senate, Hermann Rauschning, and the Nazi leader Albert Forster.

222 The Danzig dilemma: a study of peacemaking by compromise.
John Brown Mason.   Stanford, California: Stanford
University Press, 1946. 377p. bibliog.

It is the author's opinion, that the creation of a free city under the protection of
the League of Nations was a useful experiment. He asserts that despite numerous
political, economic and administrative problems, the experiment serves as an
example for similar endeavours in areas of limited territorial extension, where the
interests of various countries are difficult to reconcile.

Silesia

223 Upper Silesia and the Paris Peace Conference.
Joseph F. Harrington, Jr.   *Polish Review*, vol. 19, no.2
(1974), p. 25-45.

Considers the ethnic and economic problems of Upper Silesia (Katowice) and
Central Silesia (Opole) after the First World War. The Versailles Peace Treaty
left the Western part of the coal-rich Upper Silesia and all of Opole Silesia (both
with a predominately Polish population) within Germany's frontiers.

Eastern borderlands

224 The seizure of Vilna, October 1920.
Richard C. Lukas.   *Historian*, vol. 23 (Feb. 1961), p.
234-46.

After the Red Army had been driven back from the Vistula line, Józef Piłsudski
gave General Żeligowski confidential instructions to liberate Wilno. This project
was particularly close to Piłsudski's heart for in common with many other prominent Poles, he was born in Lithuania. Żeligowski's mission was successful, and
with the support of the local predominantly Polish population, he established a
satellite state called *Litwa Środkowa* (Central Lithuania). It soon joined the rest
of Poland, and it's existence is now known mostly to stamp collectors.

225 The establishment of the Soviet regime in Eastern Poland in 1939.
Wiktor Sukiennicki.   *Journal of Central European Affairs* ,
vol. 23, no.2 (July 1963), p. 191-218.

When the Russians entered the Lwów, Wilno and Białystok regions, as a result of
the Molotov-Ribbentrop Pact of 1939, they fraudulently tried to present the military
occupation as a political takeover approved by a popular plebiscite.

Population

226 **Population politics in Poland.**
J. Besemeres. *East Central Europe*, vol. 3, no.2 (1976), p. 127-76. tables.
Poland's population recently passed the thirty-six million mark (it had totalled 23.6 million in 1946). However, although the country once had a rapid rate of population increase, growth came close to zero in 1969. The present demographic policy favours more births through the provision of state aid to offset living costs.

227 **War migrations in the Western territories, 1939-1945.**
Sygmunt Dulczewski. *Polish Western Affairs*, vol. 6, no.2 (1965), p. 290-313.
Examines the migration of Polish workers to the West during the Second World War. Also compares the humiliating, contemptuous and vindictive treatment of Poles in Germany after the German victories to the later more humanitarian and generous treatment of Germans in Pomerania, Silesia, and Masuria when these territories came under Polish administration.

228 **Research into demographic history of Poland: a provisional summing up.**
Irena Gieysztor. *Acta Poloniae Historica*, vol. 18 (1968), p. 5-17.
A comparison of demographic trends in Poland and in the rest of Europe. The author studies the influence of epidemic illnesses and the development of agrarian technology upon the rate of population growth. Includes a historical population chart (1820-1900) and population density chart (1000-1965).

229 **Post-World War II and recent regional and rural-urban migrations in Poland and Czechoslovakia.**
Jiri Thomas Kolaja. *Polish Western Affairs*, vol. 5, no.1 (1964), p. 120-44. maps.

A comparative study of Poland and Czechoslovakia which examines: war population losses; post-war urban-rural migrations; the expansion of large cities; the impact of industrial growth; and regional redistribution.

230 **Populations censuses in East Central Europe in the twentieth century.**
Leszek Antoni Kosiński. *East European Quarterly*, vol. 5, no.3 (Sept. 1971), p. 279-301. map. tables. bibliog.

Provides a guide to the censuses taken in the 20th century in eight East-Central European countries including Poland. Also supplies a chronology and details of territorial extensions.

231 **Demographic developments in the Soviet Union and Eastern Europe.**
Leszek Antoni Kosiński. New York: Praeger, 1977. xx+342p.

A contribution to the 1st International Slavic Conference at Banff, Alberta, in 1974.

232 **Population and migration trends in Eastern Europe.**
Edited by Huey Louis Kostanick. Boston, Massachusetts: Westview Press, 1978. 247p. map.

A collection of papers with introductory remarks and a summary by the editor. The book deals with the mobility of population and demographic trends in Eastern Europe, with special reference to the effects of socioeconomic planning on urbanization and industrial relocation.

233 **Sociological problems of the Western territories.**
Władysław Markiewicz. *Polish Western Affairs*, vol. 6, no.2 (1965), p. 266-89.

Discusses the problems connected with the repopulation of the recovered Western territories. The immigrant population came from the overcrowded central lands and from Eastern regions incorporated into the Soviet Union. It also consisted of Poles who had emigrated returning home after the war. The author considers: the adaptation of native Poles, who had previously lived under German administration; the transformation of the occupational structure; the acceptance of modern social values; and the social integration of heterogeneous demographic groups.

Population

234 The German exodus: a selective study on the post World War II expulsion of the German population and its effects.
Geza Charles Paikert. The Hague, Netherlands: Nijhoff, 1962. x+97p.

Millions of Germans fled from the victorious Soviet and Polish armies towards the end of the Second World War, while others were expelled from lands restored to Poland and Czechoslovakia. These latter territories were partially inhabited by ethnic Poles and to some extent they have now been resettled by Poles expelled from the Soviet Union, re-emigrants returning from the West, and immigrants from overcrowded central Poland. The effects of these changes have extended into such fields as economics, industry, religion, ethnicity and dialectology.

235 The population of Poland.
Warsaw: Państwowe Wydawnictwo Naukowe, 1975. 143p. charts. tables.

A report prepared by the Committee on Demographic Studies of the Polish Academy of Sciences in response to World Population Year, which was declared by the United Nations in 1974. Provides background historical information, census data and projections of future demographic developments.

236 Demography of the new Poland.
Edward Rosset. *Acta Poloniae Historica*, vol. 16 (1967), p. 109-37.

The author, a leading Polish demographer, describes major factors which have influenced recent demographic changes in Poland: the shifting of frontiers during and after the Second World War; war losses and the consequent decline in population growth; and the new socioeconomic system. The war resulted not only in the deaths of many of those serving in the armed forces but also in the genocide of the labour and extermination camps. On the other hand the hostilities produced a considerable amount of repatriation together with the resettlement of former German citizens of Polish extraction. The article examines the structure of Poland's population according to age, sex, nationality, source of income and life expectancy.

237 Postwar population transfers in Europe: 1945-1955.
Joseph B. Schechtman. Philadelphia: University of Philadelphia Press, 1963. 408p.

Discusses population movements in Europe with particular reference to the results of the defeat of Germany and her allies in 1945, and the USSR'S Westward expansion.

238 The expulsion of the German population from the territories east of the Oder-Neisse Line.
Theodor Schieder, translated by Vivian Stranders. Bonn, GFR: Federal Ministry for Expellees, 1959. xii+370p.

A collection of documents on the exodus of German nationals from territories recovered by Poland after the Second World War. It involved both 'Reichsdeutsche' (German citizens) and 'Volksdeutsche' (foreign citizens of German ethnic extraction). Following Germany's defeat these two groups of people found their homes and property in either Poland or Czechoslovakia, and they left either voluntarily, or compulsorily. Many of them had settled in Poland during the War itself, others had lived there for generations. Over one million residents of Polish extraction in such regions as Opole Silesia and Masuria, for example, were allowed to stay.

239 **The sociological aspects of demographic changes in Polish western territories.**
Janusz Ziółkowski. *Polish Western Affairs*, vol. 3, no.1 (1962), p. 3-37.
Considers population density in Pomerania and Silesia before and after the last war. Examines: the birth rate; age brackets; the proportion of men to women; migratory movements (voluntary resettlement, forced expulsion and repatriation); the integration of the local native population and newcomers; the bilingual population and their re-Polonization; and the social integration of new settlers and their adjustment to their new living conditions and environment.

Poland: its people, its society, its culture.
See item no. 1.

Economic-demographic interrelations in developing agricultural regions: a case study of Prussian Upper Silesia, 1840-1914.
See item no. 35.

Nationalities (Ethnic Minorities)

General

240 The national minorities in Poland in 1918-1939.
Marian Marek Drozdowski. *Acta Poloniae Historica*, vol. 22 (1970), p. 226-51.

This article examines: ethnic and religious minorities in inter-war Poland; the repatriation agreements between Poland, Russia and Germany, 1919-24; the legal position of minorities and its international implications; the criterion of national consciousness adopted by Polish statistics; the main currents of Ukrainian, Belorussian, Lithuanian, Jewish and German political movements; the interaction between various minority groups and their parliamentary representation; and the interference in Polish internal affairs by neighbouring countries using the excuse of national minority protection. According to the 1921 census, minorities accounted for 31.4 per cent of Poland's population. Some 8.6 per cent of the minorities were Jews with no compact area of habitation and no foreign state affiliation, and 17 per cent were Ukrainians and Belorussians, equally ethnically attached to Poland and Russia, who wished to establish an independent state of their own.

241 Germans, Poles and Jews: the nationality conflict in the Prussian east, 1772-1914.
William W. Hagen. Chicago: University of Chicago Press, 1980. 406p. maps.

During the partitions period the Jewish population in the Prussian-administered part of Western Poland were faced with a dilemma for they had a feeling of loyalty both towards the native population of the area and to the new masters. This was especially true during the pro-Jewish Bismarck policy, and moreover there was a linguistic affinity between the Aszkenazim Yiddish-speaking Jews and Germans.

242 **Poland and her national minorities, 1919-1939: a case study.**
Stephan Horak. New York: Vantage Press, 1961. 260p.
illus. bibliog.

An opinionated and often superficial view of Poland's inter-war policy towards
ethnic minorities written by an American Ukrainian, who favours national self-
determination and the right of all ethnic groups to secede. In his opinion multinational states must chose between suppressing ethnic minorities or disappearing
altogether from the political map.

243 **The politics of ethnicity in Eastern Europe.**
George Klein, Milan J. Reban. Boulder, Colorado: East
European Quarterly, 1981. 279p.

Surveys the attempts of various East European governments to centralize their
power and to render their countries ethnically homogenous, and considers the
variety or reactions from affected minority groups.

244 **Nationalism in Eastern Europe.**
Edited by Peter Sugar, Ivo Lederer. Seattle, Washington:
University of Washington Press, 1969. vii+465p.

Edited by well-known experts on nationality problems, this book contains a
chapter on Polish nationalism written by Peter Brock (p. 310-72) which offers an
overview of Polish national and social thought with special regard to minority
groups.

245 **Foreigners in Poland in the 10th-15th centuries: their role in
the opinion of the Polish medieval community.**
Benedykt Zientara. *Acta Poloniae Historica*, vol. 29
(1974), p. 5-27.

Up to the middle of the 13th century foreigners were welcome in Poland as the
purveyors of new ideas and trends, but after that time their increasing number
began to evoke xenophobic reactions. The author is professor of history at the
University of Warsaw.

Cassubians

246 **Florjan Cenova and the Kashub question.**
Peter Brock. *East European Quarterly*, vol. 11, no.3 (Sept.
1968), p. 259-94.

The Cassubians with their own language and civilization, are considered by some
to be the last remaining tribe of the Westernmost Slavs, which over a thousand
years ago were overrun, and either exterminated or assimilated by the Germans.
On the other hand there are those who regard the Cassubian language as a Polish
regional dialect and consider the Cassubians to be a Pomeranian tribe. Cenova
(also spelt Ceynowa) was a 19th-century Cassubian leader, writer and ethnographer, who helped organize an armed raid against the town of Stargard during

Nationalities (Ethnic Minorities). Ukrainians

the Spring of Nations period, and favoured an inter-Slavic alliance against Germany's push towards the East.

247 The Cassubian civilization.
Adam Fischer, Friedrich Lorentz, Tadeusz Lehr-Spławiński, preface by Bronisław Malinowski. London: Faber, 1935. xxvi+407p. illus. Reprinted, New York: AMS Press, 1977.
This is the only major book in English on the subject and it is written by prominent scholars. Cassubians, together with the Sorabians of Lusatia, are the only residual Slavic tribes, who succeeded in maintaining their identity within Germany. They occupy a position similar to that of the Friulans in Italy or the Frisians in the Netherlands.

Ukrainians

248 Ukrainians in present-day Poland.
Zenon Karpatiuk. *Ukrainian Quarterly*, vol. 33, no.4 (1977), p. 348-65.
The Ukrainian minority in Poland lives in the Southeastern corner of the country, mostly in and around the cities of Chełm, Hrubieszów, Jarosław, Przemyśl, and Sanok. After the Second World War part of that minority was repatriated into the Soviet Union and some other Ukrainians were resettled in Westernmost Poland. In 1956 the Ukrainian Socio-Cultural Society was allowed to organize, and subsequently periodicals and books in the Ukrainian language appeared. In addition, and unlike the situation in the Soviet Ukraine, the Ukrainian Catholic Uniate Church of Eastern rite was allowed to carry out limited activities. The total number of Ukrainians in Poland today is estimated at between 180,000 and 350,000.

249 Ukrainians in present-day Poland.
Olha Mussakovska. *Ukrainian Review*, vol. 6, no.4 (1959), p. 72-79.
Since the border changes after the Second World War, the Ukrainian minority in Poland has dwindled to a fraction of its pre-war strength. Also, several tens of thousands of Ukrainians from former Galicia and Volynia have resettled in Western Pomerania and in Lower Silesia. After the war the Westernmost Ukrainian tribes (Bojki, Łemki) were partially resettled in the Soviet Ukraine (75,000), and partially (35,000) in the Silesian district of Lubin-Lignica. The Ukrainian association *Ukrayins'ke Suspil'no-Kul'turne Tovarystvo* has, since 1958, produced a weekly publication entitled *Nashe Slovo* (Our Word).

Jews

250 [Jews in Poland].
Moshe Avidian. In: *Encyclopaedia Judaica*. Jerusalem:
Keter, 1971. vol. 13, p. 710-90. maps. bibliog. illus.

Separate chapters deal with early settlements, legal status, economic activities, cultural and social life, and the background history of the Jewish community in Poland; the holocaust period is treated on a regional basis. The chapters on recent history deal with: the Jewish resistance; Polish-Jewish relations during the Second World War; the Jews in Poland in the post-war period; and Poland's relations with Israel. There is also a map of Jewish communities in Poland, a map indicating the demographic distribution of Jews, as well as illustrations of Jewish costumes, architecture, and life in the ghettos.

251 The scapegoats: the exodus of the remnants of Polish Jewry.
Józef Banas, translated by Tadeusz Szafer. London:
Weidenfeld & Nicolson, 1979. 221p. illus.

A non-academic but readable account based on some primary sources and the author's first-hand experiences. Focuses on the 1967-68 struggle for power within the Polish Communist party. During this period the earlier massive Jewish influence was replaced by an anti-Semitic trend led by Mieczysław Moczar, a leader of 'national Communist' orientation. As a result, many Polish Jews, including high party officials, emigrated to Israel. Poland also served as a transit land for pre-war Polish Jews, who after being repatriated from the Soviet Union decided to settle in Israel.

252 The golden tradition: Jewish life and thought in Eastern Europe.
Edited by Lucy S. Dawidowicz. New York: Holt, 1967.
502p.

Sixty brief essays by, and on, representatives of various Jewish ideological currents (Hebrew and Yiddish, Zionist and assimilatory, socialist and orthodox). The book discusses problems arising from emancipation and from participation in the life of gentile society. It is immaginatively documented by primary sources, especially memoirs, and represents a valuable contribution to the literature on Polish, Lithuanian, Belorussian and Ukrainian Jewry, and on the place of Jews in the political, social, economic and cultural life of the respective countries.

253 Images before my eyes: a photographic history of Jewish life in Poland, 1864-1939.
Lucjan Dobroszycki, Barbara Kirshenblatt-Gimblett. New
York: Schocken in association with the YIVO Institute of
Jewish Research, 1977. xviii+269p. bibliog. 300 illus.

A beautifully produced album featuring three hundred photos selected from the YIVO (New York) collection of 10,000 pictures. The book depicts traditional life styles, political struggle, bourgeois customs, the intelligentsia and the Zionist movement of Polish Jewry from the January 1863 Uprising to the Second World War. Ethnic data and population figures are provided and there is also a chapter on the pre-war Yiddish cinema.

254 **History of Jews in Russia and Poland from earliest times until the present day.**
Simon Dubnov. Philadelphia: Jewish Publication Society of America, 1916-20. 3 vols. bibliog. Reprinted, Ann Arbor, Michigan: University of Michigan Press, 1967. 4 vols. with a supplement covering the period from the Congress of Vienna to the emergence of Hitler. Cranbury, New Jersey: A. S. Barnes, 1972. 840p.

The classic work on Eastern European Jewry which contains many chapters on the Jews in Poland and in the Polish multinational commonwealth. Many other references to Polish Jewry in the homeland and in the diaspora are scattered throughout the book.

255 **Studies on Polish Jewry 1919-1939: the interplay of social, economic and political factors in the struggle of a minority for its existence.**
Edited by Joshua A. Fishman. New York: YIVO Institute of Jewish Research, 1974. 294p. + 538p. maps.

256 **Polish Jewish historiography between the two wars 1918-1939.**
Philip Friedman. *Jewish Social Studies*, vol. 11 (1949), p. 373-408.

The author of this essay was a prominent Jewish-Polish historian residing in the United States.

257 **On the age of destruction: Jews of Poland between two world wars.**
Celia Heller (Stopnicka). New York: Columbia University Press, 1977. Reprinted, New York: Schocken, 1980. 369p. illus.

A sociological, sociocultural and sociopsychological study of the status of Polish Jewry. An original contribution to the research on the Jewish political groups of this period: accomodationist, oppositional, revolutionary and assimilationist. Based on Polish and Yiddish sources.

258 **The legacy of Polish Jewry: a history of Polish Jews in the interwar years, 1919-1939.**
Harry M. Rabinowicz. New York: Yoseloff, 1965. 256p.

Ethnic Jews and Poles of Jewish extraction played a vital role in many fields of Polish life including finance, business, literature, the cinema, medicine and the law. This situation sometimes prompted a hostile reaction from ethnic Poles, especially in those cases where Jews occupied more important and better paid positions in a particular field of activity.

259 Jewish culture in Eastern Europe: the classical period.
Moses Avigdor Shulvass. Jerusalem: KTAV, 1975. 180p.
A survey of the intellectual and cultural life of Polish Jewry from the 15th century to the early 17th century, during which period Eastern Europe became the world centre of Jewish learning.

260 The Jews in Medieval Poland.
Adam Vetulani. *Jewish Journal of Sociology*, vol. 4 (1964), p. 274-94.
Various privileges issued in the Middle Ages by Polish kings and regional dukes attracted a large number of Jews from the diaspora, where they were subject to persecution. Together with other ethnic groups (including Germans, Flamands, and Armenians) they were expected to settle in towns depopulated as a result of Tatar expansionism, and to engage in trades, arts and crafts. The author was a prominent scholar of Polish legal history.

261 The Jews of Poland: a social and economic history of the Jewish community in Poland from 1100 to 1800.
Bernard D. Weinryb. Philadelphia: Jewish Publication Society, 1973. 424p. bibliog.
A good history of Polish Jewry based on both Jewish and Christian sources. The author maintains a balance both between political, ideological and socioeconomic history as well as between the periods of suffering and alienation on the one hand, and those of privileged status and full participation in the life of Polish society on the other.

262 A necessary cruelty: the emergence of official anti-Semitism in Poland, 1936-1939.
Edward D. Wynot, Jr. *American Historical Review*, vol. 76, no.4 (Oct. 1971), p. 1035-58.
Piłsudski's successors included an anti-Semitic component in their eclectic internal policy. They did it for practical rather than for ideological reasons, hoping to attract to their programme certain radical nationalistic elements. Their success was very limited and made the situation of the newly created Camp of National Unity (*Obóz Zjednoczenia Narodowego*), which was organized in March 1937 as an all-inclusive union of those supporting the government, even more precarious.

Jewish resistance in Nazi-occupied Eastern Europe: with a historical survey of the Jew as fighter and soldier in the Diaspora.
See item no. 166.

The Black Book of Polish Jewry: an account of the martyrdom of Polish Jewry under the Nazi occupation.
See item no. 167.

Righteous among nations: how Poles helped the Jews 1939-1945.
See item no. 168.

Roads to extinction: essays on the holocaust.
See item no. 169.

Poland's ghettos.
See item no. 170.

Nationalities (Ethnic Minorities). Germans

The bravest battle: the twenty-eight days of the Warsaw Ghetto Uprising.
See item no. 171.

Uprising in the Warsaw ghetto.
See item no. 172.

Polish-Jewish relations during the Second World War.
See item no. 173.

Recent studies related to the history of the Jews in Poland from earliest times to the partitions period.
See item no. 822.

Germans

263 **The number of Germans in Poland in the years 1931-1959 against the background of German losses in the Second World War.**
Stanisław Waszak. *Polish Western Affairs*, vol. 1, no.2 (1960), p. 246-89. charts. tables.

Discusses the structure of the German ethnic group in Poland and German efforts to classify Cassubians and Masurians, and at times also the inhabitants of the Carpathians (*Górale*), as independent ethnic groups with strong Germanic influences. Also considers German nationals in Poland in 1939 on a regional basis with reference to mono and bilingual Germans, Catholics and Protestants. The author contrasts pre-war German claims concerning overpopulation and the need for territorial expansion into more sparsely populated regions with the post-war phenomenon of labour shortages in West Germany and the need to import labour.

264 **The Polish Germans, 1919-1939: national minority in a multinational state.**
Edward D. Wynot, Jr. *Polish Review*, vol. 17, no.1 (Winter 1972), p. 23-64. bibliog.

A discussion of the demographic, economic, social, cultural and political life of Polish Germans during these years. The author concentrates predominantly upon their internal condition and avoids all but a perfunctory mention of the role played by this element in foreign affairs.

Karaites

265 **Karaims in Poland.**
Ananiasz Zajączkowski. Warsaw: Państwowe Wydawnictwo
Naukowe, 1961. 114p.

Karaims (or Karaites) are a minority group of both national and denominational
character. They speak a mediaeval version of a Turkic dialect, and are considered
to be a sect of Judaism. Before the Second World War, several thousand Karaites
lived in Poland near Wilno (now Vilnius), mostly in the little township of Troki.
At present a few hundred Karaites still live in Poland and they have organized a
Karaite Religious Union.

Scots

266 **Papers relating to the Scots in Poland, 1575-1793.**
Edited by Archibald Francis Steuart, translated by Mackay
Thomson. Edinburgh: Constable, 1915. xxxix+362p.

The old relationship between Scots and Poles acquired new vigour during the
Second World War, when some Polish troops were stationed in Scotland. The
warm attitude of the Scots towards Poland is often attributed to substantially
similar traits of character between the two nations. During the period covered by
this book James III Stuart (the 'Old Pretender') married Polish princess Clemen-
tine Sobieska. The book discusses: the activities of Scottish merchants in Poland
and especially in Pomerania; Scottish mercenary troops in the service of Polish
and Lithuanian lords; and Polish-Scottish connections during the Reformation and
Counter-Reformation.

Poles Abroad (Polonia)

General

267 **Employment-seeking emigrations of the Poles world-wide.**
Edited by Celina Bobińska, Andrzej Pilch. Cracow:
Jagellonian University, 1975. 194p. maps.
Eight essays on various categories of Polish emigrants who have settled in different areas of the world. Different periods are considered for each region. Individual studies deal with 'seasonal' or 'indefinite' emigrants (i.e. temporary or permanent), for political as well as economic reasons. Polish emigrants of all categories are known as 'Polonia' and tend to keep up their contacts with the Old Country (*stary kraj*) for generations. Numerically they are equal to approximately a quarter of Poland's native population.

268 **Polish emigrants in Europe.**
Andrzej Kwilecki. *Polish Western Affairs*, vol. 17, no.1-2
(1976), p. 83-92.
A study of Poles living in the West, their conditions of life, and their role as representatives of Polish civilization. Also discusses Polish groups living in Eastern European countries, where in most cases they represent a native population which has been settled for centuries and which was not repatriated after the Second World War.

269 **['Polonia'].**
Polish Western Affairs, vol. 17, no.1-2 (1976).
A special issue dedicated to the problems of Poles abroad. The articles deal with: different forms of cooperation and relations with the home country; trends and changes in the everyday life of émigré Poles; their adaptation to the new environment; Polish ethnic minorities in Western Europe and in the Americas; the participation of Poles in foreign wars for independence and in the underground move-

ments during the Second World War; and research on the history of 'Polonia'. Most of the contributions are provided by scholars and officers of the 'Polonia' Association sponsored by the Polish government to promote cooperation between the homeland and Poles abroad.

270 **The Polish peasant in Europe and America.**
Florian Znaniecki, William Isaac Thomas. Chicago:
University of Chicago Press, 1918-1920. 5 vols. New rev.
ed., New York: Dover, 1958. xv+2,250p.

One of the world's sociological classics that not only made an exceptional contribution to the understanding of Polish émigré society in the United States, but also exercised a profound influence on sociology as a whole, marking the beginning of a truly experimental method of research in that discipline. The authors made a significant attempt to combine a theoretical analysis of social factors with subjective experiences. The pioneering significance of this study (whose value is now, after years of social change, mainly historical) overshadowed the initial goal of the work which was limited to an examination of Polish society in the United States.

271 **Emigration from Poland in the nineteenth and twentieth centuries.**
Jerzy Zubrzycki. *Population Studies*, vol. 6 (1953), p. 248-72.

The author is a well-known Australian sociologist of Polish extraction, and a student of Polish emigration problems, especially in Britain and in the British Commonwealth countries. Polish 19th and 20th-century emigration embraces both political and gainful expatriation, 'for freedom' and 'for bread'.

Panorama Polska: Nasza Ojczyzna. (The Polish panorama: our fatherland.)
See item no. 850.

Africa

272 **The Poles in Africa, 1517-1939.**
Edmund A. Bojarski. *Explorers' Journal*, vol. 35, no.2 (1957), p. 9-10; no.3, p. 27-29; no.4, p. 18-26; vol. 36, no.1 (1958), p. 9-13.

Polish participation in the exploration of Africa goes back to the beginning of the 16th century, when Jan and Stanisław Łaski visited Egypt. Later, Maurycy Beniowski explored Madagascar, Jan Potocki the Maghreb, Józef Sułkowski Egypt, Józef Sękowski Nubia and Ethiopia, Leon Cienkowski Sudan, and Stefan Szolc-Rogoziński the Cameroons. In recent times a prominent anthropologist and ethnologist, Jan Czekanowski, has conducted research in Uganda and in Rwanda-Burundi, while Kazimierz Michałowski became world-famous for his archaeological discoveries in Upper Egypt, Sudan and Nubia.

Canada

273 Sir Casimir Stanislaus Gzowski: a biography.
Ludwik Kos-Rabcewicz-Zubkowski, W. E.
Greening. Toronto: Burns & MacEachern, 1959. 213p.
Gzowski was a most distinguished Polish Canadian. He was responsible for the
construction of several railroads and the International Bridge at the Niagara
Falls, and at one time was Acting Governor of Ontario.

274 The Poles in Canada: Polish contribution to the development of Canada; Outstanding Polish Canadians.
Ludwik Kos-Rabcewicz-Zubkowski. Montreal: Canadian
Centennial Commission, 1968. xvi+202p.
Traces the Polish presence in Canada back to the discovery of Labrador in 1476
by a Jean Scolus (Johannes Scolvus, mentioned in French sources as 'a Polish
lord' and claimed by some to have been a Pole - Jan z Kolna). Also describes the
present Polish minority group of some 350,000 strong.

275 A member of a distinguished family: the Polish group in Canada.
Henry Radecki. Toronto: McClelland & Stewart, 1976.
240p. illus. maps. bibliog. (Generations: a History of
Canada's Peoples Series).
A social history of Poles in Canada. The author deals with several aspects of the
subject including: cultural development; religion; language patterns; ethnic asso-
ciations; the pace of assimilation; and folk art. The book was sponsored by the
Canadian Multiculturalism Program of the Secretary of State.

276 The Polish past in Canada: contributions to the history of the Poles in Canada and of the Polish-Canadian relations.
Edited by Wiktor Turek, introduction by Watson
Kirkconnel. Toronto: Canadian-Polish Congress, 1960.
138p. illus.
An outline of Canadian-Polish connections edited by a pioneer of research on the
subject and a leader of Polish cultural activities in Canada.

277 Polish contribution to arts and sciences in Canada.
Andrzej Wołodkiewicz. Montreal: White Eagle Press,
1969. 363p.
An introductory outline of the history of Polish Canadians is followed by biographical information on some 1,000 Canadian Poles including scholars, artists
and technicians, who came to Canada in three distinct periods: 1776-1890;
1890-1938; and the period after 1939.

**Polonica Canadiana: a bibliographical list of the Canadian Polish
imprints for the years 1848-1957.**
See item no. 834.

United States

278 **Poles in the history and culture of the United States of America.**
Edited by Grzegorz Babiński. Wrocław, Poland: Ossolineum, 1979. 223p.

A collection of lectures delivered at a symposium held in Warsaw in 1976. The papers discuss: the contributions of Poles to the development of the United States; the history of Polish settlements in America; the fields in which Poles have been active in the United States; and the changes in Polish life in America since immigration began. The work was sponsored by the Polish Academy of Sciences' Committee for Poles Abroad.

279 **Who's who in Polish America: a biographical directory of Polish-American leaders and distinguished Poles resident in the Americas.**
Edited by Franciszek Bolek. New York: Harbinger, 1943. 3rd ed. 572p. Reprinted, New York: Arno Press, 1970. 582p.

Five thousand biographical sketches of living and deceased Poles from North and South America.

280 **For God and country: the rise of Polish and Lithuanian ethnic consciousness in America, 1860-1910.**
Victor Greene. Wisconsin: State Historical Society, 1975. 202p. illus.

Considers the development of national consciousness among the Polish community in the United States. The author recounts the struggle for control over the Polish-American community which took place between the lay Polish National Alliance and the church-connected Polish Roman Catholic Union. The book also provides background information about the rise of an 'immigrant capital' in Chicago.

281 **Poles in the United States of America, 1776-1865.**
Bohdan Grzeloński, translated by Robert Strybel. Warsaw: Interpress, 1977. 240p. illus. bibliog.

A collection of essays which consider: the part played by the Poles in two crucial events in US history, the American Revolution and the Civil War; the first Polish immigrants to the US who arrived in 1608; the career of Jan Ursyn Niemcewicz, the first biographer of George Washington; and the history of the Polish refugees who went to the United States after the two abortive insurrections in Poland in 1830 and 1863.

Poles Abroad (Polonia). United States

282 **Polish past in America, 1608-1865.**
Mieczysław Haiman.   Chicago: Polish Roman Catholic
Union, 1939. xiv+178p. illus. maps. Reprinted, Chicago:
Polish Museum of America, 1974. 178p.
Although they lack the rigorous scholarly approach of more recent works, Hai-
man's examinations of Polish-American relations laid the foundations for all
future research on the subject.

283 **Polish pioneers in California.**
Mieczysław Haiman.   Chicago: Polish Roman Catholic
Union, 1940. 83p.
Haiman was the pioneer of 'Polonia' regional and local history in America and
this book was followed by his *Polish pioneers of Pennsylvania* (1941. 72p.). More
recently his research has been supplemented by that of historians and sociologists
of a younger generation including: Richard Bernard's *The Poles in Oklahoma*
(1980. 96p. illus.); Angela Pienkos' (editor) *Ethnic politics in urban America: the
Polish experience in four cities* (1978. illus.); T. L. Baker's *The first Polish
Americans: Silesian settlements in Texas* (1970. 268p. illus.); Edward R. Kan-
towicz's *Polish-American politics in Chicago, 1888-1940* (1975. xi+260p. maps.);
Arthur Evans Wood's *Hamtramck: a sociological study of a Polish-American
community* (1955. 253p. illus.); Milton Kosberg's *The Polish colony of California, 1876-1914* (1952); Ewa Morawska's *The maintenance of ethnicity: case
study of a Polish community in Greater Boston* (1977); Eugene Obidinski's *Ethnic to status group: a study of Polish Americans in Buffalo* (1981); and Joseph
Parot's *Polish Catholics in Chicago, 1850-1920: Religious history* (1981. 410p.).

284 **Jamestown pioneers from Poland... in commemoration of the
arrival of the first Poles in America, 1608-1958.**
Jamestown, Virginia: Polish American Congress, 1958. 89p.
illus.
The first Polish immigrants to arrive in Jamestown were not unskilled labourers
or poverty-ridden peasants but glass blowers and tar makers, recruited by Captain
John Smith (1580-1631) on his second voyage to Virginia.

285 **My name is million: an illustrated history of the Poles in
America.**
Wiesław S. Kuniczak.   Garden City, New York:
Doubleday, 1978. 182p.
An attractively produced popular history of Polish Americans written by a well-
known author, who unfortunately paid too little attention to historical accuracy
and is responsible for a large number of embellishments. The reader should be
mindful of these inaccuracies.

286 **Polish place names in the U.S.**
Elżbieta Lyra, Franciszek Lyra.   *Geographia Polonica*, vol.
11 (1967), p. 29-38. map.
A geographical nomenclature of places bearing names of Polish etymological origin correlated with the distribution pattern of Americans of Polish descent.

287 **Poles in America: bicentennial essays.**
Edited by Frank Mocha. Stevens Point, Wisconsin:
Worzalla, 1978. 781p. map.

Miscellaneous essays on Polish learning and civilization, combined with an encyclopaedia of facts on US 'Polonia'. This is a useful source book and guide to
Polish American institutions and organizations. The work deals specifically with
the following subjects: Polish history; education; religion (Polish Brethren); learning; and literature. It also provides a who's who in 'Polonia' America and
information about great Polish Americans.

288 **The transplanted family: a study of social adjustment of the**
Polish immigrant family to the United States after the
Second World War.
Danuta Mostwin. New York: Arno Press, 1981. (American
Ethnic Groups Series).

289 **The Polish Americans: whence and whither.**
Theresita Polzin. Pulaski, Wisconsin: Franciscan
Publishers, 1973. 282p.

In spite of some doubtful affirmations and conclusions, this book contains useful
information on the history and demography of Polish immigration to the United
States during the colonial era (1608-1776) and during the period from independence to the end of the Second World War. It also supplies statistical data and
descriptions of Polish organizations, as well as discussing the process and the
problems associated with the assimilation and integration of Poles into American
society.

290 **The Poles in America, 1608-1972: a chronology and fact**
book.
Frank Renkiewicz. Dobbes Ferry, New York: Oceana,
1973. viii+128p. bibliog.

A history of Poles in the United States since the Jamestown landing. The author
also reproduces documents concerning the Polish-American past and provides an
appendix consisting of excerpts from the US censuses of 1910 and 1960 relating
to Poles in America and to Americans of Polish extraction.

291 **Polish-American community life: a survey and research.**
Irwin T. Sanders, Ewa Morawska. New York: Community
Sociology Monograph Series, 1975. 300p. bibliog.

A very useful survey of the Polish American minority which analyzes the cultural
transformation process of local Polish-American communities. Includes a valuable
comprehensive bibliography on the evolution of the Polish-American community
and the problems it faces. The book was sponsored jointly by Boston University
and the Polish Institute of Arts and Sciences in the United States.

Poles Abroad (Polonia). Australia

292 **Poles in American history and tradition.**
Joseph Anthony Wytrwal. Detroit: Endurance Press, 1969.
498p. bibliog.
A history of Polish immigrants in the United States since 1608. The subjects
dealt with include: the difficulties of assimilation; the contributions made by Poles
to the development of American society; the conflict between the Polish and Irish
Catholic hierarchies; and political refugee immigrants. Unfortunately, the author
fails to adequately distinguish important facts from details of little consequence.

293 **Polish Americans: status competition in an ethnic community.**
Helena Znaniecki (née Lopata). Englewood Cliffs, New
Jersey: Prentice Hall, 1976. xvii+174p. bibliog.
A well-written sociological analysis of the US 'Polonia' which amplifies and
revises *Polish peasant in Europe and America* (q.v.). A compact and readable
survey of the Polish ethnic group in the United States which stresses the two
salient features of the American Polish community ie., life style and status competition.

The history of the education of Polish immigrants in the U.S.
See item no. 647.

Bloods of their blood: an anthology of Polish American poetry.
See item no. 722.

Polish-American Studies.
See item no. 852.

Polish-American Studies.
See item no. 853.

Dziennik Związkowy. (Alliance Daily.)
See item no. 872.

Nowy Dziennik. (The New Daily.)
See item no. 878.

Australia

294 **The count: life of Sir Paul Edmund Strzelecki, explorer and
scientist.**
Geoffrey Rawson. London: Heinemann, 1954. xix+214p.
illus. maps. bibliog.
Paweł Strzelecki (1797-1873) was a famous Polish explorer and geologist, who
travelled widely in Oceania, Australia and Tasmania and, among other things,
bestowed the name 'Mount Kościuszko' on the highest peak of the Australian
Alps.

Austria

295 The Poles in the Austrian Empire.
Piotr Stefan Wandycz. *Austrian History Yearbook*, vol. 3, part 2 (1967), p. 261-86.
After the partitions of Poland and the assignment of the southern portion of the country to Austria, many Poles became prominent in the internal affairs of the Habsburg monarchy: Karol Badeni became the Prime Minister; Agenor Gołuchowski, Lieutenant-General of Galicia; his son Minister of Foreign Affairs; Leon Biliński and Julian Dunajewski Ministers of Finance; and Franciszek Smolka, President of the Chamber of Deputies. Among the patrons of the arts and sciences Karol Lanckoroński was the most prominent. The majority of Polish nationals, however, lived in a precarious economic situation for there was overpopulation in rural areas and the German-speaking lands experienced a greater degree of industrial development. However, thanks to the federal system of government, political control was much more liberal than in the regions occupied by Prussia and Russia.

Great Britain

296 The Poles in Great Britain, 1914-1919.
Norman Davies. *Slavonic and East European Review*, vol. 50, no.118 (Jan. 1972), p. 63-89.
Considers the role played by Poles (numbering some 40-50,000 people) who emigrated to Great Britain during the First World War. Polish emigrants in Britain in this period were in the main a working-class group of socialist orientation. It was in London that the socialist party journal *Robotnik* had first been printed in 1893. The Polish National Committee (*Komitet Narodowy Polski*) headed by W. Sobański was officially recognized in October 1917.

297 Polish guide to London. (Polski Londyn: Informator przewodnik.)
Bohdan Olgierd Jeżewski. London: Centre for Poles Abroad, 10th ed., 1976. 128p. maps.
A directory which provides information concerning: Polish organizations; publishers; business; churches; cultural institutions; clubs; military veterans; hotels; bookstores; émigré authorities; and monuments.

298 Between two cultures: migrants and minorities in Britain.
Edited by James L. Watson. Oxford, England: Blackwell, 1977. 338p.
Includes a chapter entitled 'The Poles: an exile community in Britain' by Sheila Petterson-Horko. The author is a social anthropologist sympathetic to Poland, with a thorough personal knowledge of the Polish community in Britain (her husband, Tadeusz Horko, was for many years editor-in-chief of the Polish daily *Dziennik Polski* in London). In the author's opinion, although two thirds of the

Poles Abroad (Polonia). Soviet Union

Poles residing in Britain are by now British subjects, at heart they still represent an émigré society dreaming of an eventual return to the homeland. This chapter also emphasizes the mutual influence which the British and the Poles have had on each other.

299 **Polish immigrants in Britain: a study of adjustment.**
Jerzy Zubrzycki, preface by René Clemens, Florian Znaniecki. The Hague: Nijhoff, 1956. xix+219p. bibliog.
A sociological and historical investigation of the present Polish community in Britain, which mainly consists of post-1940 émigrés. The author is a well-known Polish-Australian sociologist.

Soviet Union

300 **The Polish minority in Lithuania, 1918-1926.**
Vladas Krivickas. *Slavonic and East European Review*, vol. 53, no.130 (Jan. 1975) p. 78-91.
Discusses the position of the Polish minority in Lithuania and the Lithuanian nationality policy. Lithuanian statistics for 1923 show a Polish ethnic minority of 3.3 per cent, while corresponding Polish figures present a percentage figure three times as high. The Polish minority, however, wielded considerable economic power (Poles owned three quarters of the large farms, for example) and Polish cultural influence extended above and beyond the numerical strength of the Polish-speaking minority. Furthermore, between the wars, the Lithuanian republic included only the former Samogitia (*Žmudź*) region of the historical grand duchy. The social conflict between Polish landlords and Lithuanian smallholders, the forced establishment by Poland of a Central Lithuanian state federated with Poland, and the political and ethnic loss of the capital city of Wilno (Vilnius) were all factors that created resentment towards Poland and prevented any Polish-Lithuanian accommodation during the inter-war years. Today many Poles feel an attachment to Lithuania and would favour some sort of affiliation between the two historically and culturally related nations.

301 **The Poles in the Soviet Union.**
Witold S. Sworakowski. *Polish Review*, vol. 19, no.3-4 (1974), p. 143-50.
A study of the present composition and distribution of the Polish ethnic group in the Soviet Union based on Soviet census data. The author was director of the Hoover Institution library at Stanford, California.

Language

Texts

302 Let's learn Polish.
Zofia Batsgen. Warsaw: Wiedza Powszechna, 1978. 4th ed.
276p. illus.
A popular manual with many illustrations. A useful book but graphically poor and with occasional mistakes.

303 An outline of the history of Polish language.
Jan Niecisław Baudouin de Courtenay. In: *Baudouin de Courtenay anthology.* Edited by Edward Stankiewicz.
Bloomington, Indiana: Indiana University Press, 1972. p. 323-55.
This book deals with the Polish linguistic system, phonetic changes and alterations, and dialectical differentiation in pronunciation. The author is a famous authority on Slavic linguistics.

304 Introduction to the Polish language.
Sigmund S. Birkenmayer, Zbigniew Folejewski. New York: Kościuszko Foundation, 1978. 3rd ed. xx + 146p. + 36p.
A concise and accessible textbook which was published on the occasion of Poland's millennium and is intended for students of Polish as a second language. The volume is supplemented by *A modern Polish reader* by Sigmund S. Birkenmayer and Jerzy R. Krzyżanowski (University Park, Pennsylvania State University, 1970. iv + 188p.).

Language. Texts

305 **Polish reference grammar.**
Maria Brooks (Zagórska). The Hague: Mouton, 1975.
580p.
An advanced reference grammar with review exercises. The book follows the
terminology and methodology of Schenker's *Beginning Polish* (q.v.). Special
features of the work include: a table of genders; a table of consonantal alterations; a table concerning the formation of the present tense; and a dictionary of
verbs.

306 **Essentials of Polish grammar for English-speaking students.**
Mary Corbridge-Patkaniowska, Arthur
Prudden-Coleman. Glasgow: Książnica Polska, 1944. 618p.
Reissued in 1974 in the 'Teach yourself' series.
A textbook compiled during the war to meet the needs of English-speaking people
who came into contact with the Polish armed forces and Polish civilians. Its
vocabulary and usage are now somewhat out of date.

307 **Guide to Slavonic languages.**
Reginald G. A. DeBray. London: Dent, 1969. 2nd ed.
824p. bibliog.
A popular survey of the history and main features of the Slavic languages and
dialects by a professor at the School of Slavonic and East European Studies of
the University of London. This work provides useful comparative studies of
inter-Slavic linguistic relationships and is valuable for people who possess a sound
knowledge of one Slavic language but wish to learn another. Section eleven (p.
589-672) deals with the history of the Polish language, the alphabet, pronunciation, dialects, characteristic features, grammar, and word order and includes
selected texts.

308 **An introductory English-Polish contrastive grammar.**
Jacek Fisiak (et al.). Warsaw: Państwowe Wydawnictwo
Naukowe, 1978. 257p.
A comparative grammar of Polish and English stressing the differences between
the two languages. This type of grammar is particularly useful for students, who
wish to assimilate the diversities between their mother tongue and the language
studied. The author is one of the better known scholars of English philology in
Poland.

309 **The problem of Polish phonemes.**
Zbigniew Folejewski. *Scando-Slavica*, vol. 2 (1956), p.
87-92.
Considers: the sounds (vowels and consonants) of Polish; phonetical permutations;
intonation and accent; palatalization of consonants; and the general characteristics
of the Polish phonemic system.

310 **Contrastive Polish-English consonantal phonology.**
Edmund Gussman. Warsaw: Państwowe Wydawnictwo
Naukowe, 1978. 176p.

Attempts to approach problems of contrastive phonology within the general
framework of generative grammar. Individual chapters deal with the theory and
practice of Polish phonology as well as with phonological processes underlying
consonantal alterations in Polish.

311 **Jan Baudouin de Courtenay: his place in the history of
linguistic science.**
E. F. K. Koerner. *Canadian Slavonic Papers*, vol. 14, no.4
(1972), p. 663-83.

A bio-bibliographical essay stressing Baudouin de Courtenay's contribution to
modern linguistic thought and to phonology.

312 **Mówimy po polsku: a beginner's course of Polish.**
Warsaw: Wiedza Powszechna, 1977. 4th ed. 328p.

Includes conversations, exercises, a grammar, and a small glossary. Recordings
are also available.

313 **Communicating in Polish.**
Bernard Penny, Krystyna Malinowska. Washington, DC:
US State Department Foreign Service Institute, 1974. 260p.
illus.

This textbook was written with the aim of preparing students for life and work in
Poland. It is supposed to be not only a manual but also a guide which will help
to ensure that the foreigner is well received in the country.

314 **Polish conjugation.**
Alexander M. Schenker. *Word*, vol. 10, (1954), p. 469-81.

A description of verbal inflection in modern, colloquial Polish which is only
suitable for experts. The author is a professor at Yale University.

315 **Polish declension: a descriptive analysis of the declension of
nouns, adjectives, pronouns and numerals.**
Alexander M. Schenker. The Hague: Mouton, 1964. 105p.
bibliog.

This book deals with nouns, adjectives, pronouns and numerals while a more
recent publication by Roland Sussex entitled *Attributive adjectives in Polish*
(Humanities Press, 1975) is limited to a consideration of adjectives.

Language. Texts

316 Beginning Polish.
Alexander M. Schenker. New Haven, Connecticut: Yale University Press, 1973. 2 vols. 2nd rev. ed. viii+491p.+xi+452p.

The most modern and comprehensive textbook of the Polish language at present available in English. It is suitable for classroom instruction, as well as for private students and provides: consecutive lessons and drills; a glossary; a phonetic survey; and a consideration of morphology and syntax. Tapes are also available.

317 The Slavic literary languages: formation and development.
Edited by Alexander M. Schenker, Edward Stankiewicz. New Haven, Connecticut: Yale University Press, 1980. 287p. bibliog.

A collection of thirteen essays each on an individual Slavic language. An emphasis is placed on the cultural and ideological background to the development of each literary language. The editors are prominent Polish Slavists.

318 The phonological development of Polish.
Zdzisław Stieber, translated by Elias Schwarz, foreword by Edward Stankiewicz. Ann Arbor, Michigan: University of Michigan Press, 1968. 100p. bibliog.

'Presents phonology as a successive series of systems each valid during a given limited period'. This volume provides a structuralist approach to the history of the Polish language and contains a great deal of useful factual information even though it concentrates primarily on the phonology of modern Polish dialects, rather than on the phonology of contemporary standard Polish.

319 An introduction to Polish.
Gerald Stone. Oxford, England: Oxford University Press, 1980. xi+110p.

This book provides a good start for the beginner and explains the essentials of Polish grammar, although the more complex features are omitted. It includes a glossary of 800 words. A similar work is Oscar Swan's *A concise grammar of Polish* (University of America Press, 1978).

320 The Polish language.
Stanisław Westfal. *Antemurale*, vol. 10 (1966), p. 3-108.

A posthumous paper prepared for publication by Józef Trypućko. The article discusses: mediaeval Polish; Polish dialects and their influence on literary language; relics of Old Polish vocabulary and grammar in the contemporary Polish language; the influence of other languages on Polish; some Polish-English kinships; some etymologies; modern Polish phonetics and structure; and the Cassubian language. The author lectured in Polish at the University of Glasgow.

A selected bibliography of Slavic linguistics.
See item no. 832.

Dictionaries

321 Polish-English and English-Polish dictionary: Słownik polsko-angielski i angielsko-polski.
Kazimierz Bulas, Francis J. Whitfield. The Hague: Mouton, 1961. xii+1,037p.+xi+783p. Reprinted, New York: Kościuszko Foundation, 1973.

Several editions of this dictionary were published both in Poland by Państwowe Wydawnictwo Naukowe, and abroad. The 1973 edition was sponsored by the Kościuszko Foundation in New York, and hence often referred to as the 'Kościuszko dictionary', and was compiled by both a team of Polish-born scholars and an American lexicographer, an ideal situation for a balanced bilingual dictionary. It is considered the best, most complete and most modern Polish-English dictionary. This was especially the case before the 'Stanisławski dictionary' (q.v.) had been thoroughly revised and greatly enlarged.

322 English-Polish and Polish-English dictionary of science and technology.
Sergiusz Czerni, Maria Skrzyńska. Warsaw: Wydawnictwo Naukowo-Techniczne; Oxford, England: Pergamon, 1976. 3rd ed. 2 vols.

A specialist dictionary of Polish and English.

323 Słownik języka polskiego. (The dictionary of the Polish language.)
Editor in chief Witold Doroszewski. Warsaw: Państwowe Wydawnictwo Naukowe, 1958-69. 11 vols.

The largest existing unabridged dictionary of the Polish language which is based on lexical material from the 18th-20th centuries and compiled by a number of experts. The material has been extracted from popular-scientific works, and from the colloquial language used by the mass media. The dictionary includes over 23,000 entries which have never appeared in a dictionary of any kind. In their substantial introduction the compilers explain in detail the methodology used, give a bibliography of sources, list abbreviations, and clarify such pertinent matters as the dictionary's relationship to previously published unabridged dictionaries, the criteria adopted, the definitions and phraseology employed in the work, and the system of qualifiers and cross-references.

324 Słownik poprawnej polszczyzny. (A dictionary of correct Polish language.)
Edited by Witold Doroszewski. Warsaw: Państwowe Wydawnictwo Naukowe, 1973. xl+1,055p. bibliog.

A standard dictionary containing 27,000 entries intended for the widest possible use. Provides information on correct spelling, enunciation, declension, word formation, idioms and syntax. A successor to Stanisław Szober's *Słownik poprawnej polszczyzny* (Warsaw: Państwowy Instytut Wydawniczy, 1958). A 'Polish Webster'.

81

Language. Dictionaries

325 **Nouns from verbs: a contribution to the study of present-day Polish word-formation.**
A. A. Fokker. Amsterdam: Noord Holland, 1966. 122p.

This work, somewhat limited in scope, supports the theory that in most cases verbs preceded other parts of speech.

326 **Recent English loanwords in the Polish language.**
Yvonne Grabowski. *Canadian Slavonic Papers*, vol. 13, no.1 (1971), p. 65-71.

Assesses the increasing influence of English on the Polish word-stock in recent years, especially in science and technology. While English words are quickly integrated, sometimes with modifications, there is also a tendency to develop purely Polish variants. The Polish language adopts words of Latin derivation especially easily.

327 **English-Polish and Polish-English dictionary.**
Tadeusz Grzebieniowski. New York: Hippocrene, 1980. 908p. illus.

A pocket bilingual dictionary also published by Heineman. There are also other earlier editions.

328 **Polish abbreviations: a selected list.**
Janina Hoskins (Wójcicka). Washington, DC: Library of Congress, 1957. 2nd ed. iv+164p.

Contains approximately 2,600 acronyms, mostly of post-1945 derivation. The unabridged Polish equivalent is given for each entry together with the English translation.

329 **A glossary of Polish and English verb forms.**
Stanisław Kaczmarski. Warsaw: Państwowe Wydawnictwo Naukowe, 1979. 3rd ed. 200p.

Juxtaposes English and Polish verb forms. Includes a glossary based on typology and semantic frequency research of Polish learners of English.

330 **201 Polish verbs fully conjugated in all tenses.**
Clara Kaipio. New York: Barron's Educational, 1977. xlix+274p.

Cites the most frequently used Polish verbs in their variety of tenses and aspects.

331 **The great English-Polish and Polish-English dictionary: Wielki słownik angielsko-polski i polsko-angielski.**
Jan Stanisławski, edited and updated by Wiktor Jassem. Warsaw: Wiedza Powszechna, 1979. 6th ed. 2 vols. supplement.

A bilingual dictionary based on 19th and 20th-century literary Polish, containing 180,000 entries. This thoroughly revised edition compares favourably with the

'Kościuszko dictionary' (q.v.), especially as far as the number of idioms and equivalents are concerned. Comprises technological, biomedical terms, as well as regional and colloquial expressions. The supplement includes new idioms, words and meanings. An index of geographical names, abbreviations, and an outline of Polish grammar are included.

A bibliography of Slavic dictionaries; Volume 1: Polish.
See item no. 825.

Religion

Church history

332 Church and society in Catholic Europe of the eighteenth century.
Edited by William J. Callahan, David Higgs. Cambridge, England: Cambridge University Press, 1979. 168p. bibliog.

A collection of essays on the Roman Catholic Church in eight European countries including Poland. The topics treated include religious attitudes and the relations between church and society.

333 The Christian community of Medieval Poland.
Jerzy Kłoczowski. Wrocław: Ossolineum, 1981. 220p.

A volume on Polish socio-religious history comprising essays on: the Christianization of Poland and on the beginnings of Church organization; religious denominations in the Polish-Lithuanian Commonwealth; the clergy; parishes; monasteries; and Church-state relations.

334 Studies on the Roman-Slavonic rite in Poland.
Karolina Lanckorońska. Rome: Pontificium Institutum Orientalium Studiorum, 1961. viii+194p. map. bibliog. (Orientalia Christiana Analecta 161).

According to still prevalent official historiography, Poland was converted to Christianity in 965-66 AD by the Bohemian bishop Adalbert (Wojciech Sławnik). More and more evidence, however, suggests that a Vistulan ('White Croatian') prince was baptized a century earlier, while the diocese of Nitra extended its authority over some parts of Southern Poland. There may also have been contacts between the Slavic missionaries Cyril and Methodius and the Vistulan capital town of Cracow (Kraków).

335 **The Slavic rite in Poland and St. Adalbert.**
Henryk Łowmiański. *Acta Poloniae Historica*, vol. 24
(1971), p. 5-21.
Provides new evidence on the controversial issue of whether a Slavic bishopric and
rite were already present in Poland a century before the Latin rite was introduced
by the Czech bishop Adalbert (Wojciech). Apparently, Poland, like other Slavic
countries, hesitated for a while between the Western and Eastern churches. It is
believed that Svatopolk, Duke of Moravia, compelled a Vistulan duke (not known
by name) to abandon his pagan creed and to accept Christianity from Methodius
around 875.

336 **Freedom of conscience and religion in Poland.**
Adam Piekarski. Warsaw: Interpress, 1979. 220p.
A comprehensive presentation of Church-state relations in Poland from the
government point of view. The book describes the whole course of Polish religious
and ecclesiastical history. It also deals with: Polish-Vatican relations and their
influence on the domestic Polish internal situation; the organization of the Roman
Catholic Church and of other religious denominations in Poland; church-
connected or inspired associations; educational institutions; and the Catholic press
and publishers. The last part of the book considers: the sociology of religion; the
evolution of religious belief in Poland; the relationship between religion and
Marxism; and the official policy towards religious denominations.

337 **Poland's millennium of Catholicism.**
Lublin, Poland: Catholic University of Lublin, 1969. 627p.
A collection of articles in honour of a thousand years of religious life in Poland.
Includes contributions on: the Christianization of the country; sacred art; monas-
tic orders; the study of theology; Church councils; the veneration of the Virgin
Mary and of the saints; Messianism; church organization; union with the Eastern
Orthodox Church; the martyrs of the Second World War; and the role of the
church in contemporary Poland.

338 **Religious change in contemporary Poland: secularization and
politics.**
Maciej Pomian-Srzednicki. London: Routledge, 1982.
xiv+227p.

339 **The Prussian state and the Catholic church in Prussian
Poland, 1871-1914.**
Lech Trzeciakowski, translated by Stanislaus A.
Blejwas. *Slavic Review*, vol. 26, no.4 (Dec. 1967), p.
618-37.
Most of the Polish population in the Kingdom of Prussia was Roman Catholic,
while the majority of the German population was Lutheran, apart from in
Masuria where the situation was the reverse. Relations between the church and
the state were complicated and often strained especially when the government
attempted to suppress the Catholic clergy who supported the Polish national
movement. Mieczysław Cardinal Ledóchowski (1822-1902), Archbishop of
Gniezno, was a conservative and a monarchist, and initially he succeeded in
maintaining good relations with the Prussian king and government. However,
when he became Primate of Poland, he felt he had inherited the historical role of

Religion. Roman Catholicism

'*interrex*', became the spokesman for the Polish cause, defended vigorously his clergy and faithful, and was imprisoned for his pains.

340 The entry of the Slavs into Christendom: an introduction to the medieval history of the Slavs.
Alexis Peter Vlasto. Cambridge, England: Cambridge University Press, 1970. xii+436p. map. bibliog.

One of the four parts of this thorough and well-written book (p. 86-154) deals with Poland, Bohemia and the formerly Slavic territories East of the Łaba (Elbe) and Sala (Saal) rivers. In addition to a discussion of Latin and Byzantine confrontation, the book also deals with Irish and Scottish missionary work among the Slavs.

341 Tolerance and intolerance in old Poland.
Wiktor Weintraub. *Canadian Slavonic Papers*, vol. 13, no.1 (1971), p. 21-44.

Poland in the 18th century had a reputation for religious intolerance. This was partly due to the Counter-Reformation, and partly the result of an influx of foreign invaders in the 17th century, when enemies of the country (including Islamic Turks, Eastern Orthodox Muscovites and Lutheran Swedes) were seen as enemies of the Church. In fact, during the religious wars in Western Europe in the 16th century Poland had remained an oasis of tolerance, continuing the tradition that led her to issue 'tolerance edicts' for Jews persecuted in the 13th century in the West. The author, now retired, was professor of Polish literature at Harvard.

Changes in peasant political and religious attitudes and behaviour in Poland.
See item no. 378.

Antemurale. (The Bullwark.)
See item no. 840.

Catholic life in Poland.
See item no. 843.

Roman Catholicism

342 Religion and atheism in the USSR and Eastern Europe.
Edited by Bohdan R. Baciurkiw, John W. Strong. Toronto: University of Toronto Press, 1975. xviii+412p. tables. bibliog.

These twenty essays by leading scholars constitute a unique work on the subject. The articles deal with relations between church and state and with religious and antireligious movements in each of the states of Eastern Europe during the period since the Second World War. In some cases the articles cut across national boundaries. Chapter twelve by Vincent C. Chrypinski (p. 241-55) deals with Polish Catholicism and social change, while another contribution by Innocentius M. Bocheński is concerned with the Marxist-Leninist treatment of religion. An interesting fact that will surprise many readers and goes some way towards explaining the prominence of Poland within the Catholic world of today, is that, despite all its difficulties, the Roman Catholic Church in Poland is better organized and has more priests (20,000) and churches (14,700) than ever before in its history. Furthermore Sunday church attendance in Warsaw is now double that of Madrid and treble that of Rome.

343 Sources of conflict between church and state in Poland.
Frank Dinka. *Review of Politics*, vol. 28, no.3 (July 1966), p. 332-49.

Since this article was written there have been a number of important developments which have affected the relationship between Church and state in Poland, especially the election of a Polish pope and the declaration of a state of emergency. Nonetheless, this paper provides an account of the unique features determining the relationship between Church and state in Poland. It describes the way in which the late Primate Stefan Cardinal Wyszyński created a pattern of continuity which was based on a tacit understanding of the respective roles of both Church and state. This understanding was maintained despite occasionally explosive, or potentially explosive situations.

344 Church and state behind the Iron Curtain.
Edited by Vladimir Gsovski. New York: Praeger (for the Free Europe Committee), 1955. viii+311p. bibliog.

A collection of essays sponsored by the Mid-European Law Project at a time when relations between church and state were strained in Central-Eastern Europe. The chapter on Poland written by Stefan Posada and Józef Gwóźdź (p. 159-252) covers such topics as the: juridical background (Concordat of 1925); constitutional provisions; People's Republic legislation; nationalization of church-owned land; Roman Catholic Church and the Western recovered territories; church and the family; problem of religious education; and religious minorities. A more recent publication on this subject is *Silent churches: persecution of religions in the Soviet dominated areas* (Arlington Heights, Illinois: Research Publications, 1978. 531p. maps).

345 Communism and religion.
Władysław Kania (*psued.*), translated by R. M. Dowdall. London: Mildner, 1947. 80p.

A critical evaluation of the Communist attitude towards religion and a pessimistic estimate of the possibility of coexistance between the church and a Soviet-type of government. Based on the experiences and research carried out by a member of the Polish Army in the Soviet Union during the Second World War.

346 Pope John Paul II: the life of Karol Wojtyła.
Mieczysław Maliński. New York: Seabury Press, 1979. 283p.

The elevation of the first Pole to the papacy (the first non-Italian since 1523) in the history of the Holy See has had a tremendous impact on the entire life of Poland. Even the ruling communist party found it rather difficult to reconcile national pride with increased political difficulties. It is too early to expect the publication of comprehensive biographical or evaluative works concerning John Paul II's thoughts and actions. Nonetheless several books, mostly superficial and covering only part of the pontiff's life, have appeared. They are either personal recollections, selections of his philosophical and literary writings, or journalistic accounts of his pastoral visits to various countries and places. This book contains a collection of memoirs by a fellow priest from Cracow. Other works include: Francis Xavier Murphy's *Poland greets the Pope* (South Hackensack, New Jersey: Shepherd Press, 1979. 80p. illus.) about the pope's first return trip home; *Polish Review*, vol. 24, no.2 (1979), p. 5-106, a special issue dedicated to the Polish pope and his ties with Poland together with a selection of his writings and pertinent poetry by Juliusz Słowacki and Stanisław Wyspiański; Pope John Paul II's *Return to Poland* (London: Collins, 1979. 190p. illus.), a translated selection of the speeches made by the pope during his visit to Poland; and George Hunt-ston Williams' *The mind of John Paul II: origins of his thought and action* (Somers, Connecticut: Seabury Press, 1981. 415p. map.) which examines the personality of the pope against the background of Polish church traditions and national heritage.

347 The Catholic Church in Poland, 1945-1966.
Ronald C. Monticone. *Polish Review*, vol. 11, no.4 (autumn, 1966), p. 75-100.

This article was written at a time of particularly tense relations between the church and the state in Poland and emphasizes the very special place of the Roman Catholic Church in Poland. The author suggests, that the exceptional position of the Catholic Church in Poland is widely recognized by both historians and the population at large, and that consequently the most the present Polish government can expect is that the church will recognize the socialist reality and the new social structure.

348 Papers on Marxism and religion in Eastern Europe.
Boston, Massachusetts: Reidel, 1976. 181p.

Contains papers on the Roman Catholic Church in Poland, 1918-40, and related subjects including the Roman Catholics in Lithuania and the Ukrainian Uniates. The papers were delivered at the International Slavic Conference held at Banff, Alberta, in 1974.

349 The shrine of the Black Madonna at Częstochowa.
Janusz Pasierb, Jan Samek. Warsaw: Interpress, 1980. 200p. illus.

An art historian's view of the monastery at Jasna Góra, where the image of the Black Madonna, allegedly painted by St. Luke, has been venerated for centuries. The sanctuary's architecture, paintings, sculptures, and decorations form part of Poland's artistic heritage.

350 The Church in Poland: facts, figures, information.
Adam Piekarski. Warsaw: Interpress, 1978. 240p.

A popular handbook which expresses the official view on state-church relations. It discusses such aspects of church activities as ecclesiastical organization, the role of the church in education and culture, the re-Polonization of the northwestern recovered territories, and the relations between believers and non-believers. It also discusses other Christian as well as non-Christian communities in Poland. The author asserts that the church in Poland is not hindered in its activities as long as it does not conflict with the legal order and religious policy.

351 **The cultural heritage of Jasna Góra.**
Zofia Rozanow, Ewa Smulikowska, translated by S.
Tarnowski. Warsaw: Interpress, 1979. 2nd rev. enlarged ed.
180p. illus.
A lavishly illustrated presentation of the art treasures accumulated during the 600
years of this well-known shrine's existence. Besides being a place of worship,
Jasna Góra ('Bright Mountain') monastery has been regarded as a symbol of the
national spirit of independence backed by a profound religious faith ever since it
held out against the Lutheran Swedes in 1655. It is the shrine of the 'Black
Madonna' of Częstochowa (Matka Boska Częstochowska), the patron saint of
Poland and a powerful symbol of indomitable courage.

352 **[The Roman Catholic Church in] Poland.**
B. Stasiewski. In: *New Catholic Encyclopaedia*, New York:
MacGraw-Hill, 1967. vol. 11, p. 471-86. illus. map. bibliog.
Discusses: Polish church history; the church under German occupation; the reor-
ganization of the church after the Second World War; church-state relations; the
state of the Roman Catholic Church in Poland at the beginning of the second
millennium of its existence; and church statistics by diocese (parishes, priests,
congregations). A map is included which shows places of Catholic interest.

353 **A strong man armed.**
Stefan Wyszyński, selected and translated by Alexander T.
Jordan. London: Chapman, 1966. xiii+187p. illus. US
edition appeared as: *The deeds of faith* (New York: Harper,
1966.).
Cardinal Stefan Wyszyński, Primate-Archbishop of Poland, probably commanded
more respect both at home and abroad than almost any other Polish public figure
of recent times. He succeeded in establishing a special kind of *modus vivendi*
between the Roman Catholic Church and the ruling Polish United Workers
Party. He did this without sacrificing any matters of principle and inspite of
Poland's exceptionally inconvenient geopolitical position. Many Poles, and others,
believe that his achievements and reputation constituted an important factor in
the election of a Pole to the highest office in the Christian world.

National Catholic Church

354 **The origin and growth of the Polish National Catholic
Church.**
Stephen Włodarski. Scranton, Pennsylvania: Polish
National Catholic Church, 1974. 239p. bibliog.
This is the most extensive history published so far of the largest single defection
from the Roman Catholic Church in the United States representing approxi-
mately 250,000 faithful. This religious movement was first established among
Polish immigrants in the United States and was later carried back to the 'Old
Country', where it now has several parishes. Originally accused of being more of

a personal protest by its founder (Hodur) against certain rites of the Roman Catholic Church (e.g. celibacy) than a movement determined to achieve a reformation of dogma, this denomination is currently trying hard to gain respectability by establishing theological communion and episcopal succession with Old Catholics.

Protestant churches

355 The Reformation in Poland: some social and economic aspects.
Paul Fox.   Baltimore, Maryland: Johns Hopkins University Press, 1924. 153p. bibliog. Reprinted, New York: AMS Press, 1971. viii + 153p.

A rather general but succint treatment of the subject by a known historian of Polish Protestantism and of the American 'Polonia'.

356 Iron Curtain Christians: the church in communist countries today.
Kurt Hutten, translated by Walter G. Tillmans.   Minneapolis, Minnesota: Augsburg Publishing House, 1967. 495p.

A Lutheran view of the position of the church in Eastern Europe, where only two countries (Latvia and Estonia) are predominantly Lutheran, although there are Protestant minorities in Hungary, Transylvania and the Volga region. In Poland, Augsburg (Augustana) Evangelicals are the largest Protestant denomination with over 100,000 faithful, 190 churches and 100 priests. The largest concentrations of Polish Lutherans are in Masuria and in the Cieszyn district of Silesia.

357 Socinianism in Poland: the social and political ideas of the Polish Antitrinitarians in the Sixteenth and Seventeenth centuries.
Stanisław Kot, translated by Earl Morse Wilbur.   Boston, Massachusetts: Starr King Press, 1957. xxvii + 226p.

An important study of the Polish Brethren by a prominent expert on Polish cultural history and religious reform movements. The author has also been the editor, for many years, of the periodical *Reformacja w Polsce* (now known as *Odrodzenie i Reformacja w Polsce* - Renaissance and Reformation in Poland).

358 **Historical sketch of the rise, progress and decline of the Reformation in Poland and of the influence, which the Scripture doctrines have exercised on that country in literary, moral and political respects.**
Walerian Skorobohaty Krasiński. London: Murray, 1838-1840. xxxi+415p.+xxxii+578p.
Although published in the middle of the 19th century, this book remains the classic work on the history of Protestantism in Poland as a whole. It covers the period of the greatest expansion of the Evangelical churches in Poland, which drew to a close around the middle of the 17th century. The same author also published a general religious history of Slavic countries entitled *Sketch of the religious history of Slavonic nations* (Edinburgh: Johnstone & Hunter, 1851. 2nd ed. xxvi+362p.).

359 **Shapers of religious traditions in Germany, Switzerland and Poland, 1560-1600.**
Edited with an introduction by Jill Raitt. New Haven, Connecticut: Yale University Press, 1981. 256p.
Discusses the Reformation and Counter-Reformation traditions in these countries.

360 **A state without stakes: religious toleration in Reformation Poland.**
Janusz Tazbir, translated by Alexander T. Jordan. Warsaw: Państwowy Instytut Wydawniczy; New York: Kościuszko Foundation, 1973. 232p.
A detailed study of the historical and social roots of this unique phenomenon in European history, examined at two levels: the policy of the authorities and the attitude of the Polish people. The analysis is conducted against the background of Polish cultural and political conditions and covers the period extending from the 15th to the 18th century.

361 **Pacifism in the ideology of Polish Brethren.**
Janusz Tazbir. *Polish Western Affairs*, vol. 15, no.2 (1974), p. 200-23.
The Polish Brethren (also known as Arians, Antitrinitarians, Unitarians, Socinians) condemned all use of force and violence. Like certain other pacifist communities, they attempted to live in isolation and at Raków (Rakov) they founded a community of their own. While some Brethren, and other radical Protestants, accepted defensive wars as a necessary evil, the extremists led by Grzegorz Paweł of Brzeziny, not only opposed any kind of war or military conscription, but further refused to take any active part in political life. Pacifist views at the synods were supported by such leaders as Marcin Czechowic, Szymon Budny, Faustus Socinus, and Benedykt Wiszowaty, to mention only a few. Their major merit is that they established the precursors of the most important issues of international law, which are still awaiting a satisfactory solution: how to avoid waging wars and how to ensure that when they are fought they are conducted in the least harmful way.

362 **The Polish Brethren: documentation of the history and
thought of Unitarianism in the Polish-Lithuanian
Commonwealth and in the Diaspora, 1601-1685.**
Edited and translated by George Huntston
Williams.   Cambridge, Massachusetts: Harvard University
Press, 1980. xxxii+773p.

The Polish Brethren represented the most radical faction of Protestantism and
favoured advanced, progressive social reforms. In 1658 they were expelled from
Poland and found asylum in Transylvania and in the Netherlands.

Eastern Orthodox Church

363 **From Florence to Brest.**
Oskar Halecki.   New York: Fordham University Press,
1958. 444p. Reprinted, Hamden, Connecticut: Archon, 1968.
456p. (Sacrum Poloniae Millenium Series).

Recounts the history of the numerous efforts to reunite Western and Eastern
Christianity. The process of Westernization of those Eastern Orthodox Christians
who remained free both of Byzantine bureaucracy and the Tatar yoke within the
Polish Commonwealth is described here by a distinguished scholar on the basis of
his extensive research in the Vatican Archives.

Society, Social Groups and the Intelligentsia

364 **Social and political transformations in Poland.**
Edited by Stanisław Ehrlich.   Warsaw: Państwowe
Wydawnictwo Naukowe, 1964. ix + 330p.
A collective work which presents the results of a survey on the impact of industrialization on Polish urban and rural life. Industrialization and urbanization in Poland have been so rapid that some of the conclusions of this survey have already been invalidated.

365 **The social structure of Eastern Europe: transition and process in Czechoslovakia, Hungary, Poland, Rumania and Yugoslavia.**
Edited by Bernard Lewis Faber.   New York: Praeger, 1976.
423p. bibliog.
Poland occupied a position midway between socioeconomically advanced Bohemia and rather backward Rumania during the interwar period. During the post-war years Poland's social progress was remarkable although there still exists a degree of nostalgia for the old form of social organization. Surprisingly enough, this feeling sometimes seems stronger among peasants and workers than among those classes that lost their privileged status.

Society, Social Groups and the Intelligentsia

366 **The Russian and Polish intelligentsia: a sociological perspective.**
Aleksander Gella. *Studies in Soviet Thought*, vol. 19 (1979), p. 307-20.

367 **The European nobility in the 18th century: studies of the nobilities of the major European states in the pre-reform era.**
Edited by Albert Goodwin. London: Black, 1954. 201p.

Includes a consideration of the Polish nobility in the 18th century by Alexander Bruce Boswell. It is the author's view that the upper classes played a particularly important role in Poland's history because they formed an unusually large proportion of the population (8-12 per cent). They generally succeeded in sustaining democratic organization within their own group and they also honoured the code of 'noblesse oblige' in response to their privileged position. Today, in People's Poland, the feeling of the population at large towards this formerly privileged class is generally one of respect, sometimes mixed with envy or desire of imitation, and only exceptionally one of resentment.

368 **Native culture and Western civilization: essay from the history of Polish social thought of the years 1764-1863.**
Jerzy Jedlicki. *Acta Poloniae Historica*, vol. 28 (1973), p. 63-85. bibliog.

Discusses Polish traditionalism and Westernization during the period between the partitions and the January 1863 Uprising. The author asserts that the insurrection failed because of the growing influence of Western liberalism, which rekindled a belief in the national heritage and tradition in a spirit of closer community and brotherhood.

369 **The genealogy of Polish intelligentsia.**
Konstanty Aleksander Jeleński. *Soviet Survey*, no.29 (July-Sept. 1959), p. 112-20.

The roots of the Polish intelligentsia are among the poorer gentry, the lower clergy, and the townsfolk. The author is an émigré writer, a literary critic and a sociologist, active in the Paris 'Kultura' milieu.

370 **Polish society and the Insurrection of 1863.**
Stefan Kieniewicz. *Past and Present*, no.37 (1967), p. 130-48.

The January Insurrection affected Polish society and influenced the socioeconomic history of the country up to the end of the 19th century. Agrarian reform weakened the position of the landed gentry, which was largely replaced in the leadership of the country by a new social group - the intelligentsia.

371 **The Polish intelligentsia in the 19th century.**
Stefan Kieniewicz. *Studies in East European Social History*, vol. 1 (1977), p. 121-34.

The process of replacing the nobility by a new class of intelligentsia within the Polish social system began approximately two hundred years ago and was completed in the second half of the 19th century. The author is a prominent Warsaw historian.

372 Social groups in Polish society.
Edited by David Lane, George Kolankiewicz. New York: Columbia University Press, 1973. xvi+380p. illus.

A remarkable book on post-war society in Poland which examines the dynamics and problems of the country as a projection of its social structure rather than its mode of government. The book covers the entire range of Poland's social groups: private sector farmers, industrial workers, the cultural intelligentsia, technological managers, and the political élite.

373 Social change and stratification in Eastern Europe: interpretative analysis of Poland and her neighbors.
Aleksander Matejko. New York: Praeger, 1974. xxv+272p.

A study of the rapidity and depth of social transformations in Poland compared with those of other Central European countries.

374 Polish youth in the thirties.
Andrzej Micewski. *Journal of Contemporary History*, vol. 4, no.3 (July 1969), p. 155-67.

An examination of the ideological and political behaviour of Polish youth during the inter-war period. This generation was influenced either by the ideology of Józef Piłsudski (socialist-orientated, tolerant, and patriotic) or of Roman Dmowski (nationalistic and Catholic). The author discusses the following youth organizations: Związek Polskiej Młodzieży Demokratycznej (Union of Polish Democratic Youth), Legion Młodych (Legion of the Young), Obóz Wielkiej Polski (Camp of Great Poland), Obóz Narodowo-Radykalny (National Radical Camp), and Falanga (Phalanx).

375 A Polish self-portrait.
Stefan Nowak. *Polish Perspectives*, vol. 24, no.2 (1981), p. 13-29.

An essay based on a book of the same title published in Polish in 1979 which deals with the Polish value system, hierarchy of needs, aspirations, expectations, norms of good behaviour, and hopes and fears. An average Pole is a person, who measures prestige by educational status and who still yearns for consumer goods and travel opportunities. He is moderately egalitarian, considers bonds of friendship highly and does not experience a generation gap. A 'common' Pole favours an equal chance in life for everyone and differentiates between the concepts of 'state' and 'nation'. The most interesting consideration of the book is probably the differentiation drawn by Poles between the world of man and the world of institutions. The norms of decency, honesty, and opinion voiced in those two worlds are simply opposite: one can be known as a very respectable, religious and patriotic person in private life, while expressing opportunistic and atheistic opinions in public; one can steal state property while remaining an honest man.

Society, Social Groups and the Intelligentsia

376 **Changing peasantry of Eastern Europe.**
Józef Obrębski, edited by Barbara Halpern, Joel
Halpern. Cambridge, Massachusetts: Schenkman, 1976.
102p. illus.
Reprints some of the works of this well-known Polish ethnographer and sociologist, including some of the papers he delivered at Oxford University. Of special interest are his essays on the peasant community of Polesie (a crossroads between Poland, Belorussia and the Ukraine) which examine the process of social change and the conflicts inherent in modernizing a backward peasant community, and his works connected with the mobility of the younger generation. In this volume the author also applies his findings to the entire peasant community of Poland.

377 **Regional differences and rural change in Poland.**
Donald E. Pienkos. *East Central Europe*, (Summer 1976),
p. 177-94.
Considers the relationships between general rural social and technological transformations, and regional differences in soil, climate and other agricultural conditions with reference to the establishment of eight macroeconomic planning regions.

378 **Changes in peasant political and religious attitudes and behaviour in Poland.**
Donald E. Pienkos. *Polish Review*, vol. 23, no.1 (1978), p. 58-68.
A survey of the extent and depth of ideological orientation in rural areas shows that the communists have still a very limited political base in the countryside. This is due to strong religious feelings and a deepseated loyalty to the Roman Catholic Church. It is also the result of an innate attachment to land ownership and an inclination towards peasant movements.

379 **Polish intelligentsia and the socialist order: elements of ideological compatibility.**
Solomon John Rawin. *Political Science Quarterly*, vol. 83,
no.3 (Sept. 1968), p. 353-77.
The author dwells on the restoration of the traditional role of the intellectual class in Polish society after 1956. Under socialism, according to the author, industrialization provides less of a challenge to the traditional social structure, than it does under capitalism. Also, in spite of its egalitarian aims, socialism does not preclude legitimation of a new elite.

380 **Class structure and social mobility in Poland.**
Edited by Kazimierz Słomczyński, Tadeusz Krauze,
translated by Anna M. Furdyna. White Plains, New York:
Sharpe, 1978. ix+211p. bibliog.
Also published as vol. 7, no.3-4 of the *International Journal of Sociology*. A selection of contributions by leading Polish sociologists on class structure and class consciousness in contemporary Polish society. The topics discussed include: social stratification; social prestige; social mobility; historical background and tradition; rapid transformations; and rising expectations.

381 **Social stratification in contemporary Poland: data and interpretation.**
Konstantin Symmons-Symonolewicz. *Polish Review*, vol. 17, no.3 (Summer 1972), p. 80-88.

The author examines such changes in the class structure as: the steady and rapid growth of the urban population; the increasing number and importance of technocrats, managers and skilled industrial workers; the steady decline of the rural population; the increase in the gainful employment of women; and increased opportunities connected with greater mobility.

382 **The Polish intelligentsia: past and present.**
Jan Szczepański. *World Politics*, vol. 14, no.3 (1962), p. 406-21.

A distinguished Polish sociologist: discusses the traditions of the intelligentsia since the partitions (when that class in Polish society gradually replaced the nobility); reports on their losses during the last war when over one third of them were killed; and finally illustrates their role in the new post-war society, which has been characterized by rapid industrialization and greater egalitarianism.

383 **Polish society.**
Jan Szczepański. New York: Random House, 1970. ix+214p.

This book is written in a style refreshingly free of ideological clichés and is well-balanced and documented. The author advances two main theses: that the egalitarianism resulting from the Second World War brought the image of a classless society closer; and that the totalitarian and monolithic model of communism neither corresponds to Polish reality nor satisfies Polish aspirations. The book is even more worthy of attention, because its author is the director of the Institute of Philosophy and Sociology of the Polish Academy of Sciences, as well as a former president of the International Sociological Association. A committed Marxist, Szczepański is one of the most representative public figures in Poland today, and a high-level advisor to the government. The work is highly informative, intellectually honest and scientifically sophisticated.

384 **Rural socio-cultural change in Poland.**
Edited by Jan Turowski, Lili Maria Szwengrub. Wrocław, Poland: Ossolineum, 1977. 225p.

A study sponsored by the Institute of Philosophy and Sociology of the Polish Academy of Sciences which discusses: social change in the rural areas; the impact of industrialization on the peasantry; and the role of rural cooperatives.

385 **Political socialization in Eastern Europe: a comparative framework.**
Edited by Ivan Völgyes. New York: Praeger, 1975. 200p.

This volume analyses the formation of political views among East European youth. The chapter on Poland, written by Joseph Fiszman, provides solid background information.

Society, Social Groups and the Intelligentsia

386 The peasantry of Eastern Europe.
Edited by Ivan Völgyes. New York: Pergamon, 1979. 2 vols. 208p. 242p.

Volume one describes the 'Roots of rural transformation' and volume two gives an account of '20th century developments'. The editor is a professor at the University of Nebraska.

387 Social structure and change: Finland and Poland: comparative perspective.
Edited by Włodzimierz Wesołowski, Erik Allardt. Warsaw: Państwowe Wydawnictwo Naukowe, 1978. 392p.

Fourteen Polish and fifteen Finnish scholars compare various aspects of social change in their respective countries since the Second World War with reference to: the political system; the socioeconomic structure; demographic mobility; the status of women; the educational system; regional development; the level of welfare; family relations; and community participation.

388 The society of inter-war Warsaw: profile of a capital city in a developing nation, 1918-1939.
Edward D. Wynot, Jr. *East European Quarterly*, vol. 6, no.4 (Jan. 1973), p. 504-19. tables.

After the end of the First World War Warsaw was promoted from a regional capital of 'Russian Poland' to the national capital of a populous state. In addition to being a political and administrative centre, Warsaw became the focal point of growing socioeconomic development and of cultural ferment. The author discusses such subjects as demographic expansion, occupational structure, income brackets, and the ethnic and religious affiliation of the inhabitants of inter-war Warsaw.

389 Conference on women in Eastern Europe and the Soviet Union.
Edited by Tova Yedlin. New York: Praeger, 1980. 229p. bibliog.

Examines: the role of the family in the life of women-revolutionaries; women's economic status; and the political recruitment of women. Also provides biographical and statistical data.

Poland: its people, its society, its culture.
See item no. 1.

The tradition of Polish ideals: essays in history and literature.
See item no. 7.

Poland: the country and its people.
See item no. 10.

Sociological problems of the Western territories.
See item no. 233.

The sociological aspects of demographic changes in Polish western territories.
See item no. 239.

Society, Social Groups and the Intelligentsia

Church and society in Catholic Europe of the eighteenth century.
See item no. 332.

The Green Flag: Polish populist politics, 1867-1970.
See item no. 426.

Wincenty Witos, 1874-1945.
See item no. 431.

The economic and social development of Baltic countries from the 15th to the 17th century.
See item no. 552.

Polish society: studies in methodology; bibliography of sociological works.
See item no. 829.

Płomyk. (The Tiny Flame.)
See item no. 881.

Politics

390 Comparative communist political leadership.
Carl Beck (et al.). New York: MacKay, 1973. xi+319p. tables.

A selection of essays which examines the organization of the communist élite. A relatively small portion of this volume deals with Poland (p. 103-13 and p. 128-38).

391 Gomulka, his Poland and his communism.
Nicholas Bethell. London: Longman; New York: Holt, 1969. 308p. illus. maps.

A journalistic introduction to the complexities of Polish politics and to Poland's relations with the Soviet Union during the time when Władysław Gomułka was a central figure in Poland, ca. 1940s-60s. Of special interest is the story of Gomułka's alleged opposition to Stalin in the late 1940s.

392 The Eastern pretender: Bolesław Piasecki, his life and times.
Lucjan Blit. London: Hutchinson, 1965. 223p.

An account of the political vicissitudes of a highly controversial figure in recent Polish politics: Piasecki was the pre-war leader of a quasi-Nazi splinter group called the 'Falanga'. After the war he became the boss of the 'Pax' movement, which claimed to represent progressive Catholics, but acted independently, and often against the wishes of the church authorities.

393 The origins of Polish socialism: the history and ideas of the first Polish Socialist Party, 1878-1886.
Lucjan Blit. London: Cambridge University Press, 1971. 176p. bibliog.

A succinct account of the development of the Polish workers' movement written for the specialist in political history. It emphasizes the role of the socialist revolutionary party 'Proletariat' after the unsuccessful January 1863 Uprising.

394 From 'Falanga' to 'Pax'.
Adam Bromke. *Survey. Journal of Soviet and East European Studies*, no.39 (Dec. 1961), p. 29-40.

Bolesław Piasecki is unique in recent Polish political history. A self-styled *fuehrer* of a Nazi-like 'Falanga' group in the 1930s, he made an unexpected reappearance after the war as a political figure. He became the leader of the powerful 'Pax' group which was completely divorced from the official Catholic Church authorities but which nevertheless claimed to represent Catholic beliefs. 'Pax' is still very active, for example, in publishing and in marketing sacred objects.

395 Poland's politics: idealism versus realism.
Adam Bromke. Cambridge, Massachusetts: Harvard University Press, 1967. x + 316p. bibliog.

An inquiry into two components of Polish political thought: romantic idealism and positivistic realism. The author also considers their historical conflict. Heroism regardless of any chance of success, and uncompromising opposition to any foreign interference, or any attempt to find a *modus vivendi* with more powerful neighbours as well as the dedication of all national forces to economic development - these are some of the eternal dilemmas of Polish history and politics. Special attention is given here to the place of People's Poland and the Polish United Workers' (communist) Party in the development of this conflict. The author also dwells on the antithesis between realism and idealism as reflected in the national literature, and promotes the thesis that Poles tend to base their behaviour on historical rather than political economic, moral, military or other grounds.

396 The Communist states in disarray, 1965-1971.
Edited by Adam Bromke, Teresa Rakowska-Harmstone. Minneapolis, Minnesota: University of Minnesota Press, 1972. 374p.

A well-edited and comprehensive account of the political developments in individual communist states during this period, which includes an analysis of the influence of nationalism, of internal trends and controversies, and of the effect of the Sino-Soviet conflict on Eastern European countries. The chapter on Poland (p. 95-120) is written by V. C. Chrypiński.

397 Poland: the last decade.
Adam Bromke. Oakville, Ontario: Mosaic Press, 1981. 189p.

A selection of occasional journalistic papers published over a twelve year period by a well-known expert on Polish affairs. The book provides valuable background information to current events.

398 Poland: Communism, nationalism and anti-Semitism.
Michael Chęciński, translated by Tadeusz Szafer. New York: Karz-Cohl, 1982. 289p.

The author, who was the victim of an anti-Jewish purge in the Polish army, blames the Soviet Union for the anti-Semitic slant of the Polish security system. He argues that the present Polish security system is characterized by duplicity and that its real goals are hidden behind a smoke-screen of anti-Zionism.

Politics

399 **Poland since 1956: readings and essays on Polish government and politics.**
Edited by Tadeusz N. Cieplak. New York: Twayne, 1972. 482p.

Provides information concerning the background and consequences of the 'Polish October' of 1956 and presents views of various political currents. Unbiased, and full of exceptional insight.

400 **The role and function of non-communist parties in the Polish People's Republic: the case of the United Peasant Party.**
Tadeusz N. Cieplak. *Canadian-American Slavic Studies*, vol. 6, no.1 (March 1972), p. 92-117.

The United Peasant Party (Zjednoczone Stronnictwo Ludowe) is the successor to that portion of the Polish Peasant Party (Polskie Stronnictwo Ludowe) that accepted a subordinate status in a communist-dominated government. Solidarność Chłopska (Peasant *Solidarity*) extended the activities of the workers' Solidarność to rural areas and has shown a more conciliatory attitude towards the Jaruzelski régime than that advanced by Lech Wałęsa.

401 **Some distinctive characteristics of the communist system in the Polish People's Republic.**
Tadeusz N. Cieplak. *Polish Review*, vol. 19, no.1 (1974), p. 41-66.

Describes Poland's political and socioeconomic system, its national, cultural and social characteristics and the ways in which it differs from its Soviet prototype.

402 **Marxism in our time.**
Isaac Deutscher, edited by Tamara Deutscher. New York: Ramparts, 1971; London: Cape, 1972. 312p.

An anthology of essays by one of the most persuasive rebel Polish-born Marxists. He managed to free himself from blindly following the party line, but maintained till his death a deep conviction that Marxism offers the key to the transformation and improvement of society. One of his essays is entitled 'The tragedy of Polish communism between two wars'.

403 **Dissent in Poland: reports and documents in translation, December 1975-July 1977.**
London: Association of Polish Students in Exile, 1977. 204p.

A collection of petitions and open letters, with a chronology and biographical notes on the Polish protest movement (including youth, students, workers and churchmen). Prefaced by one of the leaders of the intelligentsia protest movement, Adam Michnik.

404 **The mandarins of Western Europe: the political role of top civil servants.**
Edited by Mattei Dogan. New York: Wiley, 1975. 314p.

A collection of essays of a high quality which appraise the political role of top bureaucrats in Europe. Poland is probably included for comparative purposes. For the increasing role of the military in the Polish administration see Andrzej Korboński and R. Kolkowicz's *Soldiers, peasants and bureaucrats: civil-military relations in Communist and modernizing societies* (London: Allen & Unwin, 1982. 340p.).

405 Dualism or trialism? Polish federal tradition.
Marian Kamil Dziewanowski. *Slavonic and East European Review*, vol. 41, no.97 (June 1963), p. 442-66.
The original union (first personal, then organic) between the Crown of Poland and the Grand Duchy of Lithuania had a political rather than an ethnic basis. The awakening of Ukrainian national consciousness subsequently edged the Union towards a tripartite federation. A form of federation with ethnically and culturally related Lithuanians, Ukrainians and Belorussians is still the aspiration of many Poles who wish to strengthen East-Central Europe and to protect the region from both German and Soviet pressure.

406 The Communist Party of Poland: an outline of history.
Marian Kamil Dziewanowski. New York: Columbia University Press, 1977. 2nd ed. 419p. bibliog. (Russian Research Center Studies, no.32).
A pioneering work on the history of the socialist movement in Poland. The work describes the formation of various early leftist factions, and recounts the history of the Social Democratic Party of the Polish Kingdom and of Lithuania (SDKPiL), and of the Communist Party of Poland (KPP) until its dissolution in 1938. After a period of confusion and underground activity a tragic situation followed during which the Polish Workers' (communist) Party became the instrument of Stalinist imperialism and repression. The October 1956 revolt was an attempt to throw off Moscow's determining influence, and to follow a new party line more consonant with Poland's national aspirations and character. The socialist movement among Poles abroad is also described.

407 Poland in the 20th century.
Marian Kamil Dziewanowski. New York: Columbia University Press, 1977. 309p. illus. bibliog.
A lucid presentation of the history of Poland and of conditions in the country in the 1970s. The author explains many of the country's peculiarities: the power of the Roman Catholic Church, the thriving peasantry, the vigorous cultural life, the predisposition to trade with the West and traditionalism.

408 Political leadership in Eastern Europe and the Soviet Union.
Edited by Robert Barry Farrell. Chicago: Aldine, 1971. 359p.
A collection of papers presented at a Northwestern University Conference. The subjects considered include: Marxist theory of leadership; trends in communist leadership; Soviet and Eastern European bureaucracy; the characteristics of Soviet and Eastern European leaders; and decision-making in the Soviet Union and in Eastern Europe. No single paper is specifically concerned with Poland. Some contributors are natives and residents of Eastern Europe. There is no cohesion between the various papers.

409 **A history of the People's democracies: Eastern Europe since Stalin.**
François Fejtö. New York: Praeger, 1971. 380p. Reprinted, London, 1974. 565p.

An in depth analysis of the evolution of Eastern Europe after the death of Stalin. Reference is made to: a gradual transformation from a monolithic bloc into a polycentric association; the new relationship between the Soviet Union and Eastern Europe; the development of Eastern European political and socioeconomic systems; ideological disintegration and modernization; and the attractions of the West. Specifically Polish issues include: finding a successor for Bolesław Bierut, the Moscow imposed head of state, who died in 1956; the Polish 'October Revolution'; the Warsaw Pact; the role of the intellectuals; and anti-Semitism.

410 **The communist parties of Eastern Europe.**
Edited by Stephen Fischer-Galati. New York: Columbia University Press, 1979. 393p.

Contains eight chapters dealing with individual countries including Poland. The editor is a well-known expert on East European affairs, and editor of *East European Quarterly*. The contributors express little hope of liberalization within Eastern Europe as long as the Soviet Union supervizes and limits the freedom of movement of the population.

411 **Roman Dmowski: party, tactics, ideology.**
Alvin Marcus Fountain. Boulder, Colorado: Columbia University Press, 1980. xiii+240p.

The first major analysis in English of the ideas and policies of Dmowski (1895-1907) the founder of modern Polish nationalism. His influence was paramount during the formative period of the National Democratic Party (Narodowa Demokracja), one of the four major political movements of the inter-war period.

412 **Poland: political pluralism in a one-party state.**
Michael Gamarnikow. *Problems of Communism*, vol. 16, no.4 (July-Aug. 1967), p. 1-44.

A discussion of the Polish version of political pluralism, mostly limited so far to intra-party factionalism. The wide spectrum of beliefs existing within the Polish United Workers' Party includes neo-Stalinist dogmatism, nationalistic communism, utopian liberalism and revisionism with social-democratic tendencies. Outside the one-party system there are also a few other political organizations linked to the pro-régime Front of National Unity (Front Jedności Narodowej). They include a collaborationist peasant party, Catholic groups and the leftist non-party intelligentsia.

413 **Civil-military relations in communist systems.**
Dale Herspring, Ivan Völgyes. Boulder, Colorado: Westview Press, 1978. 273p.

A collection of graduate level studies discussing the relationship between the communist party and the armed forces in eight Eastern European countries, including Poland, in terms of opposing theories of conflict and consensus. An inconclusive study.

414 **Poland: bridge for the abyss.**
Richard Hiscocks. London: Oxford University Press, 1963.
368p. maps. bibliog.
An interpretation of political, economic and social developments in post-war
Poland based largely on sources which were researched in Poland itself. A vivid
account of Polish life by a scholar sympathetic to the Polish cause.

415 **The politics of the European communist states.**
Ghita Ionescu. London: Weidenfeld & Nicolson, 1967;
New York: Praeger, 1968. 304p. bibliog.
A stimulating and optimistic book forecasting a gradual pluralization within the
communist states characterized by a step-by-step retreat from the monolithic
approach thus allowing the re-emergent public opinion to be expressed by the
Church, intellectuals, and the labour movement. It is the author's contention that
this trend is irreversible and will eventually bring East European states closer to
the Western European system.

416 **Visa for Poland.**
K. S. Karol (*pseud.*), translated by Mervyn Savill. London:
MacGibbon & Kee, 1959. 260p.
The inside story of communism in Poland as seen by a well-known expert on
communism. 'Karol' was born in Poland but lives in the West. He represents
views to the left of the official communist parties of Western Europe and is close
to a radical, non-orthodox, somewhat Trotskyist position.

417 **East Central Europe and the world: developments in the
post-Stalinist era.**
Edited by Stephen Denis Kertesz. Notre Dame, Indiana:
University of Notre Dame Press, 1962. 386p. bibliog.
An encyclopaedic work centred around countries rather than subjects and present-
ing a useful and reliable account of events (but not of trends). Chapter 3 (p.
45-65) which is on Poland, was written by the well-known Polish historian Oskar
Halecki, while the economy of the country is covered by Jan Wszelaki.

418 **East European perspectives on European security and
cooperation.**
Edited by Robert R. King, Robert W. Dean. New York:
Praeger, 1974. 254p.
A collection of journalistic impressions by analysts of Radio Free Europe.
Includes a chapter on the impact of big power negotiations on the Polish régime.

419 **Eastern Europe's uncertain future: a selection of Radio Free
Europe research reports.**
Edited by Robert R. King, James F. Brown. New York:
Praeger, 1977. xxii+359p.
Selected reports dealing, for example, with international developments, economic
conditions, popular dissent and Church-state relations.

Politics

420 I saw Poland betrayed: an American ambassador reports to the American people.
Arthur Bliss Lane. Indianapolis, Indiana: Bobbs Merrill, 1948. 344p. illus.

An angry analysis of the Soviet pattern of ideological conquest, and a detailed account of political events during the immediate post-war years in Poland. The author, as US ambassador, was expected to offer his support to the establishment of a democratic and freely chosen government. Instead, he witnessed the Soviet imposition of a régime subordinate to the USSR.

421 A case history of hope: the story of Poland's peaceful revolution.
Flora Lewis. Garden City, New York: Doubleday, 1958. xiv+267p. Reprinted as *Polish volcano: a case history of hope*. London: Secker & Warburg, 1959. 267p.

An objective and well-informed work by a journalist of international repute. The author describes the years 1953-57, when Poland moved from despair to qualified optimism, and from subservience to Moscow towards a position in which it solved its problems in a more independent manner.

422 The people's democracies after Prague: Soviet hegemony, nationalism, regional integration?
Edited by Jerzy Łukaszewski. Bruges: College of Europe, 1970. 330p. (Cahiers de Bruges, n.s. no. 25).

A miscellaneous volume containing articles on Eastern Europe in general as well as on Poland itself. The articles examine such subjects as: the place of Eastern Europe in a world dominated by the two superpowers; Comecon; nationalism; and the Soviet and Warsaw Pact invasion of Czechoslovakia in 1968.

423 The captive mind.
Czesław Miłosz, translated by Jane Zielonko. New York: Knopf, 1953. 251p. Reprinted, New York: Octagon, 1981. xvii+251p.

A political treatise in literary form showing how Stalin's cultural policies and methods limited free expression among men of letters. A brilliant analysis of the impact of dialectical materialism upon the intellectual life of Poland in the 1945-50 period and an interpretation of the constraints that a totalitarian régime imposes upon creative forces.

424 The seizure of power (the usurpers).
Czesław Miłosz, translated by Celina Wieniewska. New York: Criterion, 1955. viii+425p.

A fictionalized analysis of the attitude of Polish intellectuals towards the communist take-over. The author ascribes the apathetic behaviour of the intelligentsia to their realization of the overwhelming technological superiority of the Russian military machine. Miłosz, a Nobel Prize winner in literature, is a typical representative of the traditional involvement of Polish men of letters in changes in their country's historical development.

425 **Emigration in Polish socio-political thought, 1870-1914.**
Benjamin P. Murdzek. Boulder, Colorado: East European
Monographs, 1977. xvi+396p. bibliog.
Analyzes the situation which developed in partitioned Poland which led to the
mass emigration of Poles who were searching for a better life. This thoroughly
researched work presents a reliable picture of the political and socioeconomic
situation in occupied Poland despite the ethnic and religious distortions, and
disparities in the available statistical data.

426 **The Green Flag: Polish populist politics, 1867-1970.**
Olga A. Narkiewicz. London: Rowman & Littlefield, 1976.
318p. bibliog.
The peasants, as the largest social group in the country, traditionally claimed a
leading political role, but their numbers have dwindled since the last war due to
rapid urbanization and industrialization. This book covers: the origins and development of various peasant parties and groups from the January Uprising to the
present day; the socioeconomic situation of farmers over the last hundred years;
the peasants' attitude towards other parties; the goals of the peasant movements;
and biographical information on the major leaders of peasant parties. The author
teaches at the University of Manchester.

427 **Rosa Luxemburg.**
Johann Peter Nettl. London: Oxford University Press,
1969. xvii+557p. bibliog.
A very detailed account of the life and achievements of the co-founder of the
SDKPiL (Social Democratic Party of the Polish Kingdom and of Lithuania) and
of the German Communist Party. Rosa Luxemburg, who was born in Zamość in
Southeastern Poland, was one of the top revolutionaries and Marxist theoreticians.
Her role and contribution has been reassessed in recent times and she now occu-
pies a high position in communist hagiography.

428 **Poland today: the state of the republic; reports of a Polish
'Experience and the Future' discussion group forecasting
impending trouble and foreseeable popular unrest.**
White Plains, New York: Sharpe, 1981. 231p.
An analysis of the Polish situation by an intelligentsia-managerial study group
which was first authorized and then dissolved by the Polish authorities. The
group's conclusions found confirmation in real events with surprising rapidity.

429 **Political opposition in Poland, 1954-1977.**
Peter K. Raina. London: Poets' & Painters Press, 1978.
584p. bibliog.
A chronicle and description of internal developments in Poland during the last
quarter of a century. Although it does not contain deep analysis the book paints a
picture of a unique political phenomenon of Eastern Europe: a dissident movement with varied and contradictory components which is not only largely
tolerated by the party in power, but has sometimes actually influenced the course
of events, and in some cases obtained concessions and compromises.

Politics

430 The rise of Polish democracy.
William John Rose. London: Bell, 1944. vii+253p. map.

Discusses the political and social ideas associated with 19th and 20th-century Poland. This book has been written for the general reader by a reputable scholar with a warm understanding of Poland.

431 Wincenty Witos, 1874-1945.
William John Rose. *Slavonic and East European Review*, vol. 25 (1946), p. 39-54.

Witos was the most prestigious leader of the Polish peasant movement, who greatly contributed to the unification of various smaller groups and the foundation of the powerful Polskie Stronnictwo Ludowe (Polish Peasant Party). After the war his name was intentionally left in oblivion by the collaborationist United Peasant Party and his importance has only been recently recognized. A monument to him is currently being erected in Southern Poland. During the inter-war period Witos opposed the Piłsudski administration.

432 Political participation in communist systems.
Edited by Donald E. Schulz, Jan S. Adams. New York: Pergamon, 1981. 334p. bibliog.

In the climate of political détente prevailing in the 1970s, some Western political scientists predicted a possibility of at least limited popular participation in the decision-making process concerning routine matters in some Eastern European countries. Recent events in Poland have placed these predictions in a new perspective.

433 The Eastern European revolution.
Hugh Seton-Watson. New York: Praeger, 1956. 3rd ed. 435p. illus.

A scholarly analysis of the communist seizure of power in Poland in the context of neighbouring countries.

434 Background to crisis: policy and politics in Gierek's Poland.
Edited by Maurice D. Simon, Roger E. Kanet. Boulder, Colorado: Westview Press, 1981. 418p.

An introductory survey by Adam Bromke presents an image of Poland in the 1970s. Other contributions discuss: the role of journalists and the military in policy-making; church-state relations; and the national economy. The final chapter attempts to forecast future developments.

435 Communism, national and international: Eastern Europe after Stalin.
Harold Gordon Skilling. Toronto: University of Toronto Press, 1964. ix+168p. bibliog.

An analysis of political developments in individual Eastern European countries. Poland (with Hungary) is treated in a chapter entitled 'Two unorthodox satellites'. The author affirms that since 1956 Poland has followed a separate course from the other Eastern European countries. Within the context of recent events this view now appears to be something of an understatement.

436 **The governments of communist Eastern Europe.**
Harold Gordon Skilling. New York: Crowell, 1966. 256p.
maps. bibliog.

A penetrating analysis of the similarities and diversities of the governmental structure and process in Poland, and other East European countries as compared with the national traditions and socioeconomic background of each area. Individual chapters deal with: ethnic problems; constitutional and administrative organization; the communist ascent to power; party bureaucracy and decision making; regional autonomy; public opinion; economic planning; and the interdependence and integration of Eastern European countries.

437 **Poland 1944-1962: the Sovietization of a captive people.**
Richard Felix Staar. New Orleans, Louisiana: Louisiana
State University, 1962. 320p. illus. maps. bibliog. Reprinted,
Westview, Connecticut: Greenwood Press, 1975.

This work sets out to prove the thesis of the title. The author, a well-known 'Kremlinologist', discusses: the various phases and changes in Polish communism; the structure of the government; the activities of the ruling party; the prospects for liberalizing the régime; the government's attitude towards the intelligentsia; and the chances of reaching a compromise between the Polish national character and the established ideology effectively imposed by the Soviet Union.

438 **Profile of Poland.**
Richard Felix Staar. *Current History*, vol. 44, no.261
(May 1963), p. 257-320.

The author contends that the present Polish régime seized power with Soviet political and military support and consequently all future governments of that derivation will necessarily be dependent on the Soviet Union for their very survival.

439 **Communist regimes in Eastern Europe.**
Richard Felix Staar. Stanford, California: Hoover
Institution Press, 1970. 4th ed. xiv+375p. bibliog.

Chapter six of this book entitled 'Captive Eagle' discusses Polish elections, and Poland's constitution, party system, economy, religion, minorities, as well as its frontier with Germany and its relations with other East European countries.

440 **Eastern Europe since Stalin.**
Edited by Jonathan Steele. London: David & Charles;
New York: Crane, Russak, 1974. 216p. bibliog.

An excellent introduction to the period of deStalinization, the consumer revolution and some of the more liberal trends in Eastern Europe. This volume written with insight by a British journalist, contains a good selection of source readings and critical evaluations, reflecting both the hopes and the malaise of East European society. Includes an examination of developments in Poland during the period 1956-58.

Politics

441 **The independent satellite: society and politics in Poland since 1945.**
Hansjakob Stehle. New York: Praeger, 1965. 350p. bibliog.; London: Pall Mall Press, 1965. 361p.

A thorough, scholarly and readable account of Western attitudes towards contemporary Poland. The author, a German journalist who spent several years in Warsaw as a news correspondent, displays a clear understanding of Poland's problems.

442 **Invitation to Moscow.**
Zbigniew Stypułkowski. London: Thames & Hudson; New York: MacKay, 1951. xvi+359p. Reprinted, New York: Walker, 1962. 360p.

The author was invited to Moscow for consultations by the Stalinist régime together with a group of Polish leaders, and was the only one to survive. He exposes Soviet methods of political terror including the extraction of phoney confessions, and discusses the perfidious treatment of the anti-Soviet underground.

443 **The new regime: the structure of power in Eastern Europe.**
Marek Tarniewski. London: Allison & Busby; New York: Schocken, 1981. 224p.

The author gives special attention to the structure of power in Poland, and the upheavals in Poland since 1956.

444 **Opposition in Eastern Europe.**
Edited by Rudolf L. Tökes. Baltimore, Maryland: Johns Hopkins University Press, 1979. 336p.

An anthology of selected, well-researched essays on dissent and opposition trends among intellectuals, workers and peasants in Central Eastern European countries since 1968. Some studies deal with individual countries, while others cross boundaries and attempt a general assessment. Intellectual discontent seems to centre on the bureaucratic nature of socialist society, and in addition rural workers demand a standard of living comparable with that of the urban population.

445 **The changing face of communism in Eastern Europe.**
Edited by Peter A. Toma. Tucson, Arizona: University of Arizona Press, 1970. xv+413p.

Since the last war there has been a gradual change from a monolithic party line dictated by Moscow to a step-by-step adaptation of Comintern communism to local conditions and national traits. This change has taken place in all of Eastern Europe, with a parallel although more limited, development in the Soviet Union itself. The chapter on Poland, 'Continuity and change' (p. 39-88) is by Joseph R. Fiszman.

446 **Talking to Eastern Europe: a collection of the best readings from the broadcasts and background papers of Radio Free Europe.**
Edited and introduced by G. R. Urban. London: Eyre & Spottiswoode, 1964. 304p.

Although the source material for this book implies a definite opinion slant, this volume offers a surprisingly clear and dispassionate view of the impact of communism on the life and thought of Eastern European countries.

447 **The communists of Poland: a historical outline.**
Jan B. de Weydenthal. Stanford, California: Hoover Institution Press, 1978. xv+217p. bibliog.

This volume considers the history of the communist movement in Poland from its foundation in 1893. The author discusses various aspects of the subject and refers to the development of: the SDKPiL (Social Democratic Party of the Polish Kingdom and of Lithuania), the KPP (Communist Party of Poland), the PPR (Polish Workers' Party), and the PZPR (Polish United Workers' Party). This is a well-documented account which presents an impartial evaluation of the difficulties and efforts of the present Polish authorities. Prior to 1981 the population seemed to accept the limitations imposed on citizens and government alike by both Soviet control and the necessity to find a *modus vivendi* within the East European reality. On the other hand the government curbed its interference into religious life, adopted a fairly permissive attitude towards criticism by intellectuals, allowed the private ownership of land and property, encouraged the private initiative of craftsmen and shopkeepers, and even tried to employ advanced Western technology to replace outdated Eastern European machinery. Recent events have shown that even this limited programme was full of errors, inadequacies and contradictory decisions.

448 **Policy and politics in contemporary Poland: reform, failure, crisis 1970-1981.**
Edited by Jean Woodall. New York: St. Martin's Press. 1982.

449 **Poland, Eagle in the East, a survey of modern times.**
William Woods. New York: Hill & Wang, 1968. 272p. illus.

A fascinating travelogue through the complexities of Polish political economic, ethnic and religious problems. The author is somewhat superficial and naive, when discussing such matters as the 'Pax' organization and Polish-Jewish relations.

450 **Polish politics in transition: the Camp of National Unity and the struggle for power.**
Edward D. Wynot, Jr. Athens, Georgia: University of Georgia Press, 1974. xiii+294p. maps. bibliog.

After the death of the Grand Marshal, Józef Piłsudski, whose personal charisma had maintained a degree of stability in Poland in earlier years, there was a transitional period (1935-39) characterized by international difficulties and a

Politics

search for identity in internal politics. Poland was squeezed between two totalitarian superpowers and Piłsudski's heirs attempted to assure internal cohesion by creating a new party Obóz Zjednoczenia Narodowego (Camp of National Unity). However, the party had no recognized leadership and a confused ideology.

Poland from inside: a symposium.
See item no. 5.

The Soviet bloc: unity and conflict.
See item no. 87.

Tensions within the Soviet captive countries.
See item no. 98.

Polish politics and national reform, 1775-1788.
See item no. 110.

The government of Poland.
See item no. 111.

Social and political transformations in Poland.
See item no. 364.

British Broadcasting Corporation, Monitoring Service: Part 2-Eastern Europe.
See item no. 842.

Radio Free Europe: Polish Press Survey.
See item no. 863.

Kultura. (Culture.)
See item no. 875.

Polityka. (Politics.)
See item no. 882.

Trybuna Ludu. (People's Tribune.)
See item no. 889.

Law, Institutions and Administration

451 **Parliament of the Polish People's Republic.**
Andrzej Burda, translated by Stanisław
Tarnowski. Wrocław, Poland: Ossolineum, 1978. 176p.
A brief account of the structure, activities and role of the parliament (Sejm) in
People's Poland, which also outlines parliamentary traditions and the electoral
system. In addition the author compares the status of the members of the legislat-
ive branch with that of the executive branch. The author is the director of the
Institute of Public Administration and Law at the State University of Lublin.

452 **Codification in the communist world: a symposium.**
Edited by F. J. M. Feldbrugge. Leiden, Netherlands:
Sijthoff, 1975. xv + 363p.
This collection of papers contains an essay by Dominik Lasok on the codification
of Polish law which analyzes the areas of constitutional, civil, private, international and family law, and concludes that after 1945 the Polish government broke
away from the country's legal tradition in favour of a Marxist juridical approach.

453 **Man, state and society in Eastern Europe.**
Stephan Fischer-Galati. New York: Praeger, 1970. 343p.
bibliog.
Provides selections from the constitutions, declarations of independence, decrees
and other basic laws of Eastern European countries. This documentary collection
covers the modern and contemporary periods, and has both a comparative and a
national approach. Chapters dealing specifically with Poland are: 'The Polish
crisis in the 18th century' by Robert H. Lord (p. 106-120), 'Socialism and nationalism in Poland' by Konstanty Srokowski (p. 235-38), and 'Reflections on dictatorship' by Józef Piłsudski (p. 282-86).

Law, Institutions and Administration

454 The origins of the Polish Sejm.
Karol Górski. *Slavonic and East European Review*, vol. 44 (1966), p. 122-38.
The beginnings of the Polish parliament called the *sejm* (meaning 'gathering') go back to the *sejmiki ziemskie* (territorial or land congresses) and to the *sejmiki generalne* (general regional congresses) which both date back to the 15th century. The author is professor of history at the University of Toruń.

455 Polish elections, 1918-1928.
Alexander J. Groth. *Slavic Review*, vol. 24, no.4 (Dec. 1965), p. 653-65.
Polish parliamentary elections between the wars took place in the years 1919, 1922, 1928, 1935, and 1938. All political parties took part in the first three elections and therefore they are more representative than the remaining two. An explanatory note on Polish political parties indicates their place in the political spectrum.

456 Government, law and courts in the Soviet Union and Eastern Europe.
Edited by Vladimir Gsovski, Kazimierz Grzybowski. New York: Praeger, 1959. 2,067p. bibliog.
Contains contributions on Polish constitutional, administrative, civil, criminal, labour, economic and agrarian law by various authors including K. Grzybowski and Piotr Siekanowicz. Other contributions deal with: the Sovietization of law in Eastern Europe; the concepts of law and justice promoted by the Soviet Union; and the function of the courts and the legal procedure that the Soviet Union is attempting to impose on Poland.

457 Polish civil law.
Dominik Lasok. Leiden, Netherlands: Sijthoff, 1975. 2 vols. 242p.+239p.
The author has also written *Polish family law* (Leiden, Netherlands: Sijthoff, 1968. 304p.).

458 Civil code of the Polish People's Republic.
Edited by Ewa Łętowska, Józef Piątowski, translated by A. Makowski. Warsaw: Wydawnictwa Prawnicze, 1981. 284p.
This book was sponsored by the Institute of State and Law of the Polish Academy of Sciences.

459 Administation in People's Poland.
Edited by Janusz Łętowski. Wrocław, Poland: Ossolineum, 1980. 275p.
A collection of articles dealing with: the public administration system; the civil service; the administrative procedures; the organization of the national economy; and the state apparatus, management and supervision.

Law, Institutions and Administration

460 **Legal problems under Soviet domination.**
Edited by Zygmunt Nagórski. New York: Association of
Polish Lawyers in the US, 1956. 132p.
Contains contributions by prominent Polish lawyers residing in the West including: Kazimierz Grzybowski; Tytus Komarnicki; Władysław Kulski; Marek Korow-
icz; Krystyna Marek; and Arnold Zurcher. The volume as a whole applies to the
earliest period of communist domination in Poland.

461 **Communist administration in Poland within the framework of
input-output analysis.**
Jarosław A. Piekałkiewicz. *East European Quarterly*, vol.
6 (July 1972), p. 230-58.
Polish public administration is considered within the pattern of Marxist political
behaviour. The author discusses central versus local administration in a communist system.

462 **Communist local government: a study of Poland.**
Jarosław A. Piekałkiewicz. Ohio: Ohio University Press,
1975. xiv+282p. illus. bibliog.
Discusses the role of local government in a socialist state and how that model has
been adapted to suit Poland. The author considers some of the problems of public
participation in local government, and changes in the size and organization of
socioeconomic microregions.

463 **Principles of Polish law.**
Warsaw: Państwowe Wydawnictwo Naukowe, 1979. 640p.
A survey of contemporary Polish legislation, jurisprudence, and law by well-
known Polish experts.

464 **The constitutions of the communist world.**
Edited by William Simons. Leiden, Netherlands: Sijthoff
& Noordhoff, 1980. xvii+644p.
A consideration of the constitutions of Poland and fourteen other communist
countries. The work includes background historical information concerning the
evolution of the fundamental laws of each country.

465 **Studies in Polish law.**
Leiden, Netherlands: Sijthoff, 1963. (Law in Eastern Europe
Series, no.6-7).
Contains contributions on civil, criminal, administrative, international and private
law by prominent émigré scholars including: Kazimierz Grzybowski, Bronisław
Hełczyński, Zygmunt Nagórski Sr., and Dominik Lasok.

Law, Institutions and Administration

466 Constitutions of the communist party states.
Edited by Jan F. Triska. Stanford, California: Hoover
Institution Press, 1968. 541p.

A meticulously edited study of the constitutional laws of all communist states
including Poland (in English translations).

**467 Polish law throughout the ages: 1,000 years of legal thought
in Poland.**
Edited by Wieńczysław Józef Wagner. Stanford,
California: Hoover Institution Press, 1970. xii+476pp.

This volume is the most important single contribution to the history of Polish law
available in English. The work consists of fourteen essays on the entire spectrum
of the Polish legal system throughout the country's history which examine the:
historiography of Polish juridical studies and institutions of Polish law; legal
system in Poland during the partition period; Polish theories of international law;
criminal, private, constitutional and administrative law in post-war Poland; Polish
contributions to legal theory; psychological school of law of Leon Petrażycki; and
biographies of prominent legal scholars. The editor is a well-known US university
professor, of Polish origin, who now teaches in Detroit.

Poland: the country and its people.
See item no. 10.

Polish politics and national reform, 1775-1788.
See item no. 110.

The government of Poland.
See item no. 111.

The institutions of Comecon.
See item no. 557.

Legal sources and bibliography of Poland.
See item no. 831.

Law in Eastern Europe.
See item no. 847.

Polish Yearbook of International Law.
See item no. 862.

Foreign Relations

General

468 **Final report: diplomatic memoirs.**
Józef Beck. New York: Robert Speller, 1957. 278p.
Examines Polish foreign policy during the period 1926-39. The author was
Poland's Foreign Minister between 1932 and 1939 and took over entire responsibility for the conduct of Poland's foreign affairs after the death of Józef Piłsudski
in 1935. Beck's reliance on bilateral agreements and on Poland's own forces
rather than on broader alliances had already become controversial in the pre-war
period, and was severely criticized by his adversaries after the Second World
War.

469 **Poland and the coming of the Second World War: diplomatic
papers.**
Anthony Joseph Drexel Biddle. Columbus, Ohio: Ohio
State University Press, 1976. 358p. illus. map.
A stimulating account of the nature, intent, scope, tactics and impact of the
initial phase of Nazi aggression in Europe based on the vast documentation
housed in the Roosevelt Library at Hyde Park, New York, and covering the
period 1937-39. The author was the last US ambassador in Warsaw before the
Second World War.

470 **East-West relations and the future of Eastern Europe: politics and economics.**
Morris Bornstein (et al.). Boston: Allen & Unwin, 1981. x+301p.

471 **Poland and the Western powers 1938-1939: a study in the interdependence of Eastern and Western Europe.**
Anna M. Cienciała. London: Routledge; Toronto: Toronto University Press, 1968. x+310p. maps. bibliog.
A valuable and well-documented book on a short but eventful period in European diplomatic history. The author sums up the guiding principles behind Polish efforts to preserve freedom of action (and hopefully political freedom as well). Poland tried to maintain a balance between the two neighbouring superpowers, Germany and the USSR, and to establish alliances with France and Rumania. The author discusses Polish foreign policy during the anschluss, the Munich betrayal, the Czechoslovak crisis and the 'Corridor' issue.

472 **The Warsaw Pact: political purpose and military means.**
Robert W. Clawson (et al.). Wilmington, Delaware: Scholarly Resources, 1982.
A study of the political aims of the Warsaw Pact and its role in providing support for Soviet foreign policy. This book was sponsored by Kent State University Center for NATO Studies.

473 **The diplomats.**
Edited by Gordon Alexander Craig. Princeton, New Jersey: Princeton University Press, 1953. x+700p. illus.
An appraisal of the leading diplomats of the inter-war period, including a chapter entitled 'The diplomacy of Colonel Beck' by H. L. Roberts (p. 579-614). The Polish Foreign Minister Józef Beck, who endeavoured to continue Piłsudski's policy of bilateral pacts, of reliance primarily on Poland's own strength and of maintaining equal distances from major European powers, is presented here as a statesman of good will but limited capacities.

474 **Foreign policy of Poland, 1919-1939: from the rebirth of the Polish Republic to World War II.**
Roman Dębicki, foreword by Oskar Halecki. London: Pall Mall Press; New York: Ungar, 1962. xi+192p. bibliog.
A brief but well-organized and clear survey of recent Polish diplomatic history. This work is a chronological account of European political events as seen from Warsaw, based on official archives and private sources. The author, formerly a Polish ambassador, surveys Poland's quest for security and its efforts to preserve its national identity.

475 **Between war and peace: the Potsdam Conference.**
Herbert Feis.   Princeton, New Jersey: Princeton University
Press, 1960. 367p. maps. bibliog.

Considers the effects of the Polish issue on inter-allied relations towards the end
of the Second World War. At the Potsdam Conference a decision was made to
move Poland's Western frontier to the Odra-Nysa Line, and the Eastern border
to a modified Curzon Line (with the inclusion of the Białystok district).

476 **Poland's international affairs 1919-1960: a calendar of**
treaties, agreements, references and selections from
documents and texts of treaties.
Stephan Horak.   Bloomington, Indiana: Indiana University
Press, 1964. xviii + 284p.

This book covers treaties of the Polish Republic 1919-39, the Polish government-
in-exile 1939-44, the Polish Committee of National Liberation (1944-45) and the
Polish People's Republic. Selected declarations, proclamations, protocols and
decrees are also included.

477 **The foreign policies of Eastern Europe: domestic and**
international determinants.
Edited by James A. Kuhlman.   Groningen, Netherlands:
Sijthoff, 1978. 322p. tables.

Chapter six of this work deals with Poland, and more specifically with the domi-
nant themes and assumptions of Polish foreign policy, the institutions involved in
its formulation, and Poland's relations with the West and with the Communist
International.

478 **Bear and foxes: the international relations of the Eastern**
European states.
Ronald Haly Lindon.   Boulder, Colorado: East European
Monographs, 1979. vii + 328p. illus.

The most common mistake of Western European observers is to presume that the
Central European neighbours of the Soviet Union form a homogenous unit. In
reality they present a similar diversity to that exhibited by the Romance or
Germanic countries. Their most important unifying factor is probably their common effort to outwit the Russian bear but even here the ways they camouflage
their attempts differ considerably.

479 **The foreign policies of East Europe: new approaches.**
Edited by Ronald Haly Lindon.   New York: Praeger, 1980.
322p.

A volume of essays that begins with emphasizing the difference between political
science and practical politics, and which covers a wealth of factual data. Poland's
principal objective, which is to gain uncontrolled independence, is discussed at
great length. Ironically, the success of that undertaking depends largely on the
willingness of Western powers to accept Poland as their partner.

480 **The foreign policy of People's Poland in the last thirty years.**
Stefan Olszowski. *Acta Poloniae Historica*, vol. 31 (1975),
p. 33-58.

Asserts that peace and security are the two goals of Polish foreign policy and that
socialist transformations have helped to raise Poland's standing in the international community. The author, considered to be the most prominent advocate of
close collaboration between Poland and the Soviet Union, again became foreign
minister in Wojciech Jaruzelski's military junta.

481 **The great powers and the Polish question 1941-1945: a
documentary study of cold war origins.**
Edited by Antony Polonsky. London: London School of
Economics and Political Science, 1976. 282p. maps.

An analysis of the complexity of inter-Allied relations over the Polish question
during the Second World War. It documents the radical change in attitude in
British circles from pre-war coolness towards the French-dominated security
system in Central-Eastern Europe to a close alliance and warm friendship with
the Poles in spite of their 'stubbornly unrealistic attitude towards Russia'.
Includes a collection of documents from various US, British, Polish and Russian
sources, many of them published for the first time.

482 **The foreign policy of the Polish People's Republic.**
Mieczysław F. Rakowski. Warsaw: Interpress, 1975. 211p.

A concise examination of Poland's participation and role in international politics
during the thirty years following the end of the Second World War. The author,
the longstanding editor-in-chief of Poland's leading political journal, *Polityka*,
rose to a very influential position in the government and became vice-premier.

483 **Allied war-time diplomacy: a pattern in Poland.**
Edward J. Rożek. New York: Wiley, 1958. xviii+481p.
maps. bibliog.

A well-documented study of the Polish question during the Second World War,
and its relationship to inter-Allied relations. The author takes three main positions: that Stalin tried to reduce Poland to the status of a Soviet satellite; that
the Western powers abandoned Poland to her fate; and that Polish émigré leaders
Sikorski and Mikołajczyk conducted an uphill struggle to preserve Poland's
independence and integrity.

484 **Poland in international politics.**
Piotr Stefan Wandycz. *Canadian Slavonic Papers*, vol. 14,
no.3 (Autumn 1972), p. 401-20.

Discusses Poland's role in Eastern European international relations and pays
particular attention to the period since the last war. The author deals with: the
problem of a Polish doctrine in foreign relations; the 'Polish question' in European
history; and *Ostpolitik* and Poland.

485 **On the border of war and peace: Polish intelligence and diplomacy in 1937-1939, and the origins of the ultra secret.**
Richard Andrew Woytak. New York: Columbia University Press, 1980. 168p.
A group of brilliant young Polish mathematicians succeeded in breaking the German secret code named 'Enigma' thus making a great contribution to Allied intelligence and to the Allies' war effort.

Poland: the country and its people.
See item no. 10.

The international relations of Eastern Europe: a guide to information sources.
See item no. 830.

Studies on International Relations.
See item no. 868.

Polish-Canadian

486 **The Maple Leaf and the White Eagle: Canadian-Polish relations 1918-1978.**
Aloysius Balavylder. Boulder, Colorado: East European Monographs, 1980. viii+300p.
This chronological survey is based on thorough archival research, but the book reflects official documents and views more than the author's own critical evaluation.

Polish-Czech

487 **Poland and Czechoslovakia: the hesitant alliance.**
Adam Bromke. *Central European Federalist*, vol. 15, no.1 (June 1967), p. 9-20.
Historically, relations between Czechoslovakia and Poland have resembled those of two sisters with old grudges. Once in a while far-sighted statesmen have attempted to transform outdated resentments into an organic alliance, to give both nations greater political security and increased bargaining power with their powerful neighbours. The last such attempt was made during the Second World War by the governments-in-exile of the two countries.

Foreign Relations. Polish-Czech

488 Polish-Czechoslovak relations, 1918-1926.
Zygmunt Jerzy Gąsiorowski. *Slavonic and East European Review*, vol. 35, no.84 (Dec. 1956), p. 172-93.
The Cieszyn (Těšín) question was probably the most important territorial dispute between the two countries during these years. The area has a very strong Polish minority (which at one time represented the majority of the population), and is of great importance economically and as a railway junction. The author is professor of history at the University of Georgia.

489 Slovak nationalists and Poland during the interwar period.
Thaddeus V. Gromada. *East European Quarterly*, vol. 11, no.3 (Autumn 1977), p. 293-304.
Czech failure to grant Slovakia autonomous status within the Czechoslovak Republic, and Polish claims to the border districts of Spisz, Orawa and Czadca were largely responsible for Slovak friendliness towards Germany at the outset of the war.

490 Poland and Czechoslovakia.
Frederick G. Heymann. Englewood Cliffs, New Jersey: Prentice Hall, 1966. viii+181p. Reprinted, Westport, Connecticut: Greenwood Press, 1979. 181p. maps.
It is the author's thesis (shared by many Poles, Czechs and Slovaks) that Poland and Czechoslovakia can only gain if conflict is replaced by cooperation. This chronological account shows no nationalistic bias even though it displays a more informed appreciation of the Czech point of view.

491 Influences of Czech culture in Poland.
Stanisław Kolbuszewski. *Slavonic and East European Review*, vol. 18, no.52 (1939), p. 155-69.
This article together with Karel Krejčí's 'Polish influences on Czech culture' in the *Slavonic and East European Review*, vol. 19 (1940), p. 110-22 are parallel essays which examine the reciprocal influences of the Czech and Polish cultures. Krejčí was a prominent expert on Polish literature and civilization, while Kolbuszewski was a professor of Slavic studies who specialized in Czech literature, as well as in Silesian culture which can be considered a *trait d'union* between Polish and Czech.

492 Czechoslovak-Polish confederation and the Great Powers, 1940-1943.
Piotr Stefan Wandycz. Bloomington, Indiana: Indiana University Press, 1956. iii+152p. bibliog.
This book surveys the history of the attempts to reorganize Central-Eastern Europe as a federal state and considers the future possibilities for such endeavours. It shows how the Czech-Polish impasse over Cieszyn was resolved through personal contacts between Beneš and Sikorski and why, in spite of their common ancestry, Poland and Czechoslovakia clashed on many fronts, including foreign relations, internal government and religion. The author also outlines the intransigent opposition of the USSR to any closer ties between these two cognate nations.

493 **Recent traditions of the quest for unity: attempted Polish-Czechoslovak and Yugoslav-Bulgarian confederations, 1940-1948.**
Piotr Stefan Wandycz. *Cahiers de Bruges*, new series no.25 (1970), p. 35-93.

Outlines plans for a federation or confederation between Poland and Czechoslovakia within the post-war new order of Europe. The author considers the attempts to reconcile the heritage of historical misunderstandings, territorial problems, and contrasting national characteristics, and efforts to overcome Soviet opposition.

494 **Polish military intervention into Czechoslovakian Teschen and Western Slovakia in September-November 1938.**
Richard Andrew Woytak. *Eastern European Quarterly*, vol. 6, no.3 (Sept. 1972), p. 376-87.

The Czech occupation of Cieszyn after the First World War, when Poland was preoccupied with defending herself against Russia in the East, was followed by an equally unfortunate Polish occupation of the area when Czechoslovakia was threatened by Germany.

Czechoslovak-Polish relations, 1918-1939: a selected and annotated bibliography.
See item no. 828.

Polish-French

495 **The Polish-British and Polish-French alliance treaties of 1939.**
Henryk Batowski. *Polish Western Affairs*, vol. 14, no.1 (1973), p. 78-98.

The above alliance (the Polish-British Treaty of April 6, the agreement of 25 August 1939, and the Polish-French Treaty of 4 August 1939 supplementing Polish-French protocols of 1921 and 1925) had little immediate value: Poland did not receive any assistance after the German invasion, nor did the Western Allies form a second front to relieve the Polish armed forces from the enormous pressure of the Wehrmacht. Notwithstanding this, the announcement of the Polish-British-French alliance brought immense moral support not only in September 1939 but during the entire period of the Second World War. The Poles felt that they had the support of their distant allies, and this fact in itself strengthened their traditionally Western orientation.

496 **Diplomat in Paris, 1936-1939: papers and memoirs of Juliusz Łukasiewicz, ambassador of Poland.**
Edited by Wacław Jędrzejewicz. New York: Columbia University Press, 1970. xxvi+408p.

A documentary record of Polish-French relations at a time of growing European crisis, when the Polish-French alliance was weakened by the efforts of the Polish

Foreign Relations. Polish-German

Foreign Minister Józef Beck, who hoped to avoid military conflict through bilateral contacts with all the great powers.

497 The Franco-Polish alliance and the remilitarization of the Rhineland.
George Sakwa. *Historical Journal*, vol. 16, no.1 (1973), p. 125-46.

The military occupation of the Rhineland by Germany on 7 March 1936 offered France her last chance of containing Nazi expansion and reinforcing her alliances in Eastern Europe. By accepting the remilitarization, and by not opening a second front in the West after the German invasion of Poland, France handed hegemony over Central-Eastern Europe to Germany.

498 France and her Eastern allies, 1919-1925: French-Czechoslovak-Polish relations from the Paris Peace Conference to Locarno.
Piotr Stefan Wandycz. Minneapolis, Minnesota: University of Minnesota Press, 1962. ix+454p.

A very detailed and thorough study of France's efforts to form a barrier that would keep the USSR and Germany apart. France's gradual withdrawal from her Eastern European sphere of interest, and the British policy of appeasement towards Germany were, in the author's opinion, jointly responsible for the outbreak of the Second World War.

Napoleon's campaign in Poland, 1806-1807.
See item no. 117.

La Pologne en France: essai d'une bibliographie raisonnée. (Poland in France: an attempt at an annotated bibliography.)
See item no. 827.

Polish-German

499 The German-Polish non-agression pact of 1934.
Zygmunt Jerzy Gąsiorowski. *Journal of Central European Affairs*, vol. 15, no.1 (April 1955), p. 3-29.

The non-agression pact was meant to postpone all controversial issues for a decade and in the meantime there was to be a policy of gradual rapprochement and good neighbourly relations. Unfortunately, as Polish Foreign Minister Beck discovered too late, Hitler did not feel bound by any agreements and only used them as a means of deception.

500 The Polish plan for a 'preventive' war against Germany, 1933.
Wacław Jędrzejewicz. *Polish Review*, vol. 11, no.1 (1966), p. 62-91.
Polish proposals for a preventive war against Germany following Hitler's rise to power were rejected by the Western Allies. Piłsudski's objective was to strengthen the Versailles Treaty and to stop German rearmament.

501 Poland between East and West: Soviet and German diplomacy toward Poland, 1919-1933.
Josef Korbel. Princeton, New Jersey: Princeton University Press, 1963. xi+321p. bibliog.
A lucid and well-organized study of German and Soviet diplomacy towards Poland during the inter-war period and to a lesser extent Polish foreign policy during these years. The author considers German and Soviet attempts to collaborate at Poland's expense, and the largely unsuccessful efforts of Polish diplomacy to exploit differences between Moscow and Berlin to Poland's advantage. Based on impressive research into primary and secondary sources.

502 Germany and Poland: from war to peaceful relations.
Władysław Wszebór Kulski. New York: Syracuse University Press, 1976. 336p. illus. bibliog.
An in-depth analysis of a thousand years of mutual hostility between Germany and Poland. Beginning with prehistoric settlements, the book leads up to the most recent developments including: the Hallstein doctrine, *Ostpolitik* as applied to Poland, and the impact of German-Polish relations on European security.

503 The territorial, ethnical and demographic aspects of Polish-German relations in the past (X-XV centuries).
Gerard Labuda. *Polish Western Affairs*, vol. 3, no.2 (1962), p. 223-60. maps.
An analysis of the origin of Polish-German antagonism and conflict which deals with: the German extermination of Poland's Western 'cousins' - the Polabians and Lusatians as well as the Baltic Prutenians (Old Prussians); German colonization of Polish towns; 19th-century Germanization policy in Prussia; German cultural and religious penetration; social persecution of Polish peasants; and the German Eastward expansion (*Drang nach Osten*) followed by an exodus from the East (*Ostflucht*).

504 A historiographic analysis of the German *Drang nach Osten.*
Gerard Labuda. *Polish Western Affairs*, vol. 5, no.2 (1964), p. 221-65.
Discusses German penetration into Eastern Europe as seen by German and Slavic historians. The German claim of a cultural mission among ethnic groups at a lower level of civilization, and of the Christianization of pagan tribes, is counterposed by evidence of: forced assimilation or military extermination; using church organization for Germany's own political goals; spreading the racist ideology of ethnic superiority; social subordination of local peasants to German landlords; and of atrocities justified as an unavoidable historical process.

505 **Diplomat in Berlin, 1933-1939.**
Józef Lipski. New York: Columbia University Press, 1968.
xxxvi+679p. bibliog.

Reproduces the papers of the Polish ambassador to Berlin during the crucial pre-war period (including 163 Polish, British, German and French documents). Lipski is regarded as the architect of the Polish-German Non-agression Pact of 26 September 1934. Lipski favoured efforts to negotiate with Germany on a bilateral basis and in the context of formulating an anti-Soviet policy. He adopted his stance partly because of the appeasent policies being pursued by Western powers. The documents have been arranged chronologically by Wacław Jędrzejewicz, a former member of the Polish cabinet who became a US university professor.

506 **Conflict, compromise and conciliation: West German-Polish normalization 1966-1976.**
Louis Ortmayer. Denver, Colorado: University of Denver, 1976 (Monograph Series in World Affairs).

It took Poland two decades to overcome the resentment generated by German atrocites in Poland during the Second World War. During the following decade a *modus vivendi* was gradually developed that created a basis for normal diplomatic relations, economic exchange, travel facilities and the repatriation of ethnic Germans (and of persons of mixed parentage) to the Federal Republic.

507 **Poland between Germany and the USSR 1929-1939: the theory of two enemies.**
Polish Review, vol. 20, no.1 (1975), p. 3-63.

A report on a symposium promoted by the New York Piłsudski Institute. The symposium analyzed recent Polish history in an attempt to ascertain whether Poland could have allied herself in 1939 with a neighbouring power, and what would have been the effect of such an alliance on the outcome of the Second World War. The discussions concerned German policy towards Poland, Soviet policy towards Poland, and Polish foreign policy.

508 **German-Polish relations, 1918-1933.**
Harald von Riekhoff. Baltimore, Maryland: Johns Hopkins University Press, 1971. xi+421p.

A definitive study of German-Polish relations during the Weimar Republic and of German policy towards Poland at the time, presented in a broader European setting. The work is based on thorough research in German, as well as French and Polish archives, and shows a high degree of objectivity. The author's principal thesis is that Germany and Poland complement each other economically, and that they should have sought closer ties.

509 **German and Pole: national conflict and modern myth.**
Harry Kenneth Rosenthal. Gainesville, Florida: University Presses of Florida, 1976. viii+175p. Reprinted, Ann Arbor, Michigan: University Microfilms, 1978.

An account of the development of German attitudes to Poland, which takes into consideration the differing views of West and East Germany. The author notes, but does not support, the view, that the shortcomings in the Polish character and behaviour justify German attempts to subjugate Poland. Similarly he refers to the notion that a sense of guilt on the part of the Germans led them to blame the Poles for their own misdeeds during the Second World War.

One thousand years of history of the Polish Western frontier.
See item no. 20.

The Polish-German frontier in the system of international agreements.
See item no. 21.

The stabilization of the Polish Western frontier under Casimir the Great, 1333-1370.
See item no. 22.

The logic of the Oder-Neisse frontier.
See item no. 23.

The Oder-Neisse boundary and Poland's modernization: the socio-economic and political impact.
See item no. 24.

Poland's return to the Baltic and the Odra and Nysa in 1945: historical and current conditions.
See item no. 25.

Polish conceptions of the Polish-German frontier during World War II.
See item no. 26.

Germany's Eastern neighbours: problems relating to the Oder-Neisse and the Czech frontier regions.
See item no. 28.

Slavic civilization through the ages.
See item no. 88.

Teuton and Slav: the struggle for Central Europe.
See item no. 96.

German colonization in medieval Poland in the light of the historiography of both nations.
See item no. 101.

Tannenberg 1410: 1914.
See item no. 102.

National solidarity and organic work in Prussian Poland, 1815-1914.
See item no. 122.

Germanizing Prussian Poland: the H.K.T. society and the struggle for the Eastern marches in the German Empire, 1894-1919.
See item no. 134.

The German campaign in Poland.
See item no. 151.

Nazi rule in Poland, 1939-1945.
See item no. 154.

Hans Frank's diary.
See item no. 155.

Genocide 1939-1945.
See item no. 156.

Fighting Auschwitz.
See item no. 159.

Commandant at Auschwitz.
See item no. 160.

Anus mundi: 1,500 days at Auschwitz/Birkenau.
See item no. 161.

The death camp Treblinka: a documentary.
See item no. 162.

Treblinka.
See item no. 163.

The Black Book of Poland.
See item no. 182.

Documents concerning German-Polish relations and the outbreak of hostilities between Great Britain and Germany on 3rd September 1939.
See item no. 184.

The German Fifth Column in Poland.
See item no. 185.

The German New Order in Poland.
See item no. 186.

The Polish White Book: official documents concerning Polish-German and Polish-Soviet relations, 1933-1939.
See item no. 190.

The Teutonic Order in Prussia.
See item no. 219.

The German exodus: a selective study on the post World War II expulsion of the German population and its effects.
See item no. 234.

The expulsion of the German population from the territories east of the Oder-Neisse Line.
See item no. 238.

The number of Germans in Poland in the years 1931-1959 against the background of German losses in the Second World War.
See item no. 263.

The Polish Germans, 1919-1939: national minority in a multinational state.
See item no. 264.

The Prussian state and the Catholic church in Prussian Poland, 1871-1914.
See item no. 339.

Polish Western Affairs.
See item no. 861.

Polish-British

510 Postscript to victory: British policy and the German-Polish borderlands, 1919-1925.
Patricia A. Gajda.   Washington, DC: University Press of America, 1982. 246p. bibliog. illus.

511 Anglo-Polish relations in the past.
Oskar Halecki.   *Slavonic and East European Review*, vol. 12, (1934), p. 659-69.
A summary of the history of English-Polish relations by a prominent historian of the inter-war period.

512 England and Poland in 16th and 17th centuries.
Józef Jasnowski.   London: Oxford University Press, 1948. 56p.
An outline of English-Polish relations during the first two centuries of modern times by an émigré historian.

513 Poland in the British parliament, 1939-1945.
Wacław Jedrzejewicz, Pauline C. Ramsey. New York: Józef Piłsudski Institute, 1946-63. 3 vols. map. bibliog.
The titles of the three volumes are: vol. 1 *British guarantees to Poland: the Atlantic Charter (March 1939-August 1941).* (xxix+495p.); vol. 2 *Fall 1941-Spring 1944* (xviii+607p.); and vol. 3 *Summer 1944-Summer 1945* (vii+732p.). These volumes provide stenographic records (Hansard) of the British parliamentary debates on Polish-British relations and on British attitudes and reactions to the Polish question during the Second World War. As well as reproducing the texts the authors provide comments and background information. The *Polish Fortnightly Review,* a London journal, also published in 1944 a similar, though differently arranged, collection entitled *British Parliament on Poland 1939-1944: verbatim reports of parliamentary debates on Poland* (252p.). This work contains a preface by Stephen King-Hall.

514 March 1939: the British guarantee to Poland: a study in the continuity of British foreign policy.
Simon K. Newman.   New York: Oxford University Press, 1976. 253p. bibliog.
An attempt to explain why the British chose to oppose Germany at that particular time and on the particular issue of Poland. The author also clarifies the origins of Britain's fateful decision. He also argues that the British government, in switching from appeasement to a new commitment to Poland, was simply following Britain's traditional line on the continental balance of power.

129

515 **Poland, Russia and Great Britain 1941-1945: a study of evidence.**
Roman Umiastowski. London: Hollis & Carter, 1946. 544p. maps.
An assessment of Britain's attitude towards the Polish-Russian conflict. The author was a former colonel in the Polish army, who was responsible on 7 September 1939 for issuing the controversial order that the civilian population must evacuate Warsaw.

Poland, S.O.E., and the Allies.
See item no. 195.

In Allied London.
See item no. 201.

Great Britain, the Soviet Union and the Polish government in exile (1939-1945).
See item no. 209.

Papers relating to the Scots in Poland, 1575-1793.
See item no. 266.

The Poles in Great Britain, 1914-1919.
See item no. 296.

Polish guide to London. (Polski Londyn: Informator przewodnik.)
See item no. 297.

Between two cultures: migrants and minorities in Britain.
See item no. 298.

Polish immigrants in Britain: a study of adjustment.
See item no. 299.

The Polish-British and Polish-French alliance treaties of 1939.
See item no. 495.

England's Baltic trade in the early seventeenth century: a study in Anglo-Polish commerical diplomacy.
See item no. 575.

Polish-Lithuanian

516 **The Polish-Lithuanian war scare 1927.**
Alfred Erich Senn. *Journal of Central European Affairs,* vol. 21, no.3 (Oct. 1961), p. 267-84.
The compromise achieved during the brief meeting at Geneva between Józef Piłsudski and Augustinas Valdemaras was hailed as a success for the League of Nations. However, the agreement was limited to a normalization of neighbourly relations, while the possibility of a more durable solution through a federation between these two states with their long-lasting political, military, economic and cultural ties, was not achieved, mainly because of German and Russian opposition.

517 **The great powers, Lithuania and the Vilna question, 1920-1928.**
Alfred Erich Senn. Leiden, Netherlands: Brill, 1966.
xii+239p.

A well-researched and well-written book by a scholar, who offers an impartial view of Polish-Lithuanian relations during the period following the Polish-Soviet war, even though his personal sympathies are with Lithuania. The question of Wilno (Vilnius, Vilna) is one of the most inflammable and intricate of Central-Eastern Europe. Wilno, the capital city of the former grand duchy of Lithuania, was predominantly Polish with a strong Jewish minority, but surrounded by a mixed Lithuanian-Polish-Belorussian rural population.

L'Union de Lublin: ses origines et son rôle historique. (The Lublin Union: its origins and its historical role.)
See item no. 106.

Polish federalism 1919-1920 and its historical antecedents.
See item no. 138.

The seizure of Vilna, October 1920.
See item no. 224.

The Polish minority in Lithuania, 1918-1926.
See item no. 300.

Dualism or trialism? Polish federal tradition.
See item no. 405.

Polish-Russian/Soviet

518 **Polish-Soviet relations, 1932-1939.**
Bohdan Budurowycz. New York: Columbia University Press, 1963. xi+229p. bibliog.

An extensively researched and scholarly contribution to this critical period in Eastern European diplomatic history. The author, who is of Ukrainian origin and therefore less emotionally engaged, provides an objective account of the long periods of distrust and conflict and short flashes of collaboration between these two neighbouring Slavic countries. The author also analyzes Polish efforts to maintain a balanced relationship with her powerful Eastern neighbour.

519 **Documents on Polish-Soviet relations, 1939-1945.**
London: Heinemann, 1961-68. 2 vols.

Volume 1 (1939-April 1943) covers diplomatic negotiations, agreements and correspondence between the Polish government-in-exile and the Soviet government. The preface is by Edward Raczyński, long-term Polish ambassador to the court of St. James (xl+625p.). Volume 2 (May 1943-August 1945) deals with Soviet policy towards the Polish government-in-exile against the background of US-British-Soviet relations, including Soviet efforts to develop a rival Polish administration in the homeland (lvi+868p.). In addition in 1944 the Polish embassy in Washington published a collection of official documents entitled: *Polish-Soviet relations, 1918-1939* (xi+251p.) which covers the Soviet-Polish war

Foreign Relations. Polish-Russian/Soviet

1920, the Riga peace treaty of 1921, the Sikorski-Maisky agreement of 1941, and the Katyń Woods massacre.

520 The Soviet domination in Eastern Europe in the light of international law.
Jerzy August Bolesław Gawenda.   London: Foreign Affairs Publishing Co., 1974. 224p. bibliog.

An examination of the implications of limited national sovereignty prevailing in Eastern Europe under Soviet supremacy, and of the states in which Communist Party laws have ultimate authority over state laws.

521 Conversations with the Kremlin and dispatches from Russia.
Stanisław Kot, translated by Harry C. Stevens.   London: Oxford University Press, 1963. xxx+285p.

Professor Kot is a well-known scholar of Polish cultural history, who turned diplomat during the Second World War and was Sikorski's ambassador to Moscow after the relations between the two governments were established in 1941. He was regarded as the *enfant terrible* of Polish diplomacy, who succeeded in having strained relations with both the Soviet Foreign Office and Polish high command and with Molotov and Anders.

522 Stalin and the Poles: an indictment of the Soviet leaders.
Bronisław Kuśnierz, foreword by August Zaleski.   London: Hollis & Carter, 1949. xx+317p. Reprinted, Hyperion, 1980.

This book, written and foreworded by two of the top Polish émigré leaders, is yet another 'j'accuse' publication directed against the Stalinist régime and its treatment of Poland.

523 Russia, Poland and the West: essays in literary and cultural history.
Wacław Lednicki.   New York: Roy; London: Hutchinson, 1954. 419p. Reprinted, Port Washington, New York: Kennikat Press, 1966. 419p.

An erudite and penetrating collection of essays on Russo-Polish cultural relations, and on 19th-century literary relations in particular, written by a one-time authority on Slavic literatures and civilizations. The main contention of this book is that throughout history Russia has failed to establish any institution capable of defending the rights of an individual and/or community from the autocracy of its rulers, and that the long-standing Polish-Russian conflict is basically a conflict of ideologies (liberty versus totalitarianism, faith in individual abilities and rights versus institutional impositions), rather than one of interests, territorial claims or ethnic animosities. According to the author, many Russians have been morally disturbed by their country's attitude towards Poland and consider Poland's partitions to be Russia's original sin committed against the soul of another Slavic nation.

132

524 **Poland and Russia, 1919-1945.**
James Thomson Shotwell, Max M. Laserson.   New York:
King's Crown Press, 1945. vi+114p. map. bibliog.
Reprinted, Westview, Connecticut: Greenwood Press, 1976.

A brief attempt at an impartial presentation of Polish-Soviet relations in the
inter-war and Second World War periods. The work was sponsored by the Carnegie Endowment for International Peace.

525 **Soviet-Polish relations, 1917-1921.**
Piotr Stefan Wandycz.   Cambridge, Massachusetts:
Harvard University Press, 1969. ix+403p. maps.

A clear and objective book on Polish-Russian frontier and borderland problems,
with an emphasis on diplomatic history. The work also provides good background
reading for the history of the Soviet-Polish war of 1919-1920. Poland wanted
strategic guarantees and was sponsoring the 'Intermarium' federation as protection against the Russian and/or German threat. The Soviet Union considered
Poland the principal obstacle in the Westward expansion of both the Bolshevik
revolution and the Russian state. The author, professor of history at Yale University, also offers introductory remarks on Polish-Russian cultural and institutional
relations.

Kresy: the frontier of Eastern Europe.
See item no. 18.

Poland's Eastern frontiers, 981-1939.
See item no. 19.

**Polish political thought and the problem of the Eastern borderlands of
Poland, 1918-1939.**
See item no. 27.

**East-West relations and the future of Eastern Europe: politics and
economics.**
See item no. 86.

Slavic civilization through the ages.
See item no. 88.

**Antecedents of revolution: Alexander I and the Polish Kingdom,
1815-1825.**
See item no. 120.

White Eagle, Red Star: the Polish-Soviet war 1919-1920.
See item no. 137.

The eighteenth decisive battle of the world: Warsaw, 1920.
See item no. 140.

The inhuman land.
See item no. 204.

Katyn: crime without parallel.
See item no. 205.

A world apart.
See item no. 206.

Poles in the European resistance movement 1939-1945.
See item no. 208.

Foreign Relations. Polish-Scandinavian

Great Britain, the Soviet Union and the Polish government in exile (1939-1945).
See item no. 209.

Katyn Forest massacre: final report of the select committee to conduct an investigation and to study the facts, evidence and circumstances... pursuant to H. Res. 390 and H. Res. 539. (82nd Congress, 2nd Session, House of Representatives report no. 2505).
See item no. 210.

The Polish Army in the battle of Berlin 1945.
See item no. 213.

Death in the forest: the story of the Katyń Forest massacre.
See item no. 214.

The Poles in the Soviet Union.
See item no. 301.

Poland between Germany and the USSR 1929-1939: the theory of two enemies.
See item no. 507.

Poland, Russia and Great Britain 1941-1945: a study of evidence.
See item no. 515.

The road to Gdańsk: Poland and the USSR.
See item no. 622.

Russia, the USSR and Eastern Europe: a bibliographical guide to English-language publications 1964-1974.
See item no. 818.

Polish-Scandinavian

526 **Polish-Scandinavian relations in the years of the Second World War.**
Tadeusz Cieślak. *Polish Western Affairs*, vol. 10, no.1 (1969), p. 63-80.
Sweden and other Scandinavian countries were neutral during the Second World War and were therefore able to offer humanitarian aid to Poles seeking shelter through the Red Cross organization.

527 **Swedish contribution to the Polish resistance movement during World War Two (1939-1942).**
Józef Lewandowski, translated by T. Szafer. Uppsala, Sweden: University of Uppsala, 1979. 114p.
Considers the Swedes in the Polish resistance and Polish-Swedish war-time connections. Also includes documentary material.

528 **Poland at the XI International Congress of Historical
Sciences in Stockholm.**
Warsaw: Polish Academy of Sciences, 1960. 336p.
A collection of studies dedicated to the historical relationship between Poland and
the Baltic and Scandinavian countries which examine: early mediaeval relations
between Pomerania and Scandinavia; Poland's Baltic trade in the 15th-18th centuries; Poland's relations with Denmark and Sweden in 16th-17th centuries; immigration from Sweden into Poland in the 16th-17th centuries; Gdańsk, Poland and
Sweden in the inter-war period; and a bibliographical essay concerning Polish
literature on the Baltic and Pomerania since 1945. The book was sponsored by
the Institute of History, University of Uppsala.

529 **Ten centuries of Polish-Scandinavian cultural contacts.**
Kazimierz Ślaski. *Polish Western Affairs*, vol. 18, no.2
(1977), p. 293-312.
A review of architectural, artistic, musical, intellectual, literary and religious contacts between Poland and the other countries around the Baltic Sea.

Polish-Ukrainian

530 **Poland and Ukraine past and present.**
Peter J. Potichnyi.   Edmonton, Canada: Canadian Institute
of Ukrainian Studies, 1980. 364p.
A Ukrainian view of the historical relationship between these two very closely
related Slavic nations. Because of its geopolitical position, the Ukraine (known
also as Ruthenia and Lesser Russia) often changed her alliances between Poland,
Muscovy, Turkey, and more recently between Germany and Sweden. Such Ukrainian leaders as John Wyhowski or Simon Petlura favoured an alliance and a
federation with Poland. After the Ukraine became incorporated into the Soviet
Union, Ukrainian national consciousness was greatly reinforced and the attitude
towards Poland became generally speaking more friendly.

Polish federalism 1919-1920 and its historical antecedents.
See item no. 138.

Dualism or trialism? Polish federal tradition.
See item no. 405.

Polish-United States

531 Woodrow Wilson and the rebirth of Poland, 1914-1920: a study in the influence on American policy of minority groups of foreign origin.
Louis L. Gerson.   New Haven, Connecticut: Yale University Press, 1953. xx + 166p. illus. bibliog.
President Wilson's efforts on Poland's behalf are presented as a case study to illustrate that ethnic groups often have a detrimental influence on US national interests. The author considers the attitudes towards Poland of both the Allies and Central Powers, and the role played by Wilson and by Colonel House, as well as by American Poles, during the clash of views and policies that took place between Piłsudski and Paderewski.

532 The fate of East Central Europe: hopes and failures of American foreign policy.
Edited by Stephen Denis Kertesz.   Notre Dame, Indiana: University of Notre Dame Press, 1956. xii + 463p.
Presents sixteen papers delivered at a symposium on American diplomatic history and US foreign policy in Central Eastern Europe. Hungarians, Czechs and Poles question the sincerity of US foreign policy when the encouragement of dissent and protest movements in those countries is not supported by tangible aid in times of need. Nationals of those countries wonder whether some US governments exploit freedom movements for their own purposes in a way similar to the Soviet Union's exploitation of leftist groups for its own goals.

533 Herbert Hoover and Poland.
George Jerzy Lerski.   Stanford, California: Hoover Institution Press, 1977. xvi + 124p. illus.
Herbert Hoover headed the US aid mission to Poland immediately after the First World War, and was present in Warsaw during the difficult times of the Polish-Soviet war of 1920. His mission was sponsored by the Society of Friends (Quakers).

534 The strange allies: United States and Poland, 1941-1945.
Richard C. Lukas.   Knoxville, Tennessee: University of Tennessee Press, 1978. 230p. bibliog.
A clear, well-documented and objective presentation of the US attitude towards Poland in the Second World War. A chronicle of facts and events enlivened by the addition of little known, intimate details. Although Roosevelt had committed himself to support Poland for reasons of both electoral strategy and personal sympathy, little tangible support was forthcoming. Under the threat of a separate German-Soviet peace treaty, the US (whose main objective was to keep the USSR fighting Germany) did not hesitate to sacrifice Poland. Meanwhile, Polish Americans were trying to secure territorial integrity and real independence for their 'old country'. The author describes the gradual erosion of Poland's special moral and political position following the German invasion of the USSR and the showdown between the Soviet and Polish governments over the Katyń affair.

535 **The United States and Poland.**
Piotr Stefan Wandycz. Cambridge, Massachusetts:
Harvard University Press, 1980. v+465p. maps. bibliog.
A history of US-Polish relations which is intended to enhance understanding
between the two nations. The author tries to explain to Americans the 'old
country' approach, and to the Poles the American failure to fulfil their hopes for
support and deeper involvement. The subject is placed against the broader background of Polish history, with special reference to developments during the last
hundred years.

Kościuszko and Puławski.
See item no. 114.

Poles in the history and culture of the United States of America.
See item no. 278.

**Who's who in Polish America: a biographical directory of
Polish-American leaders and distinguished Poles resident in the Americas.**
See item no. 279.

**For God and country: the rise of Polish and Lithuanian ethnic
consciousness in America, 1860-1910.**
See item no. 280.

Poles in the United States of America, 1776-1865.
See item no. 281.

Polish past in America, 1608-1865.
See item no. 282.

Polish pioneers in California.
See item no. 283.

**Jamestown pioneers from Poland... in commemoration of the arrival of
the first Poles in America, 1608-1958.**
See item no. 284.

My name is million: an illustrated history of the Poles in America.
See item no. 285.

Poles in America: bicentennial essays.
See item no. 287.

**The transplanted family: a study of social adjustment of the Polish
immigrant family to the United States after the Second World War.**
See item no. 288.

The Polish Americans: whence and whither.
See item no. 289.

The Poles in America, 1608-1972: a chronology and fact book.
See item no. 290.

Polish-American community life: a survey and research.
See item no. 291.

Poles in American history and tradition.
See item no. 292.

Polish Americans: status competition in an ethnic community.
See item no. 293.

Polish-American history and culture: a classified bibliography.
See item no. 837.

Economy and Economic History

536 **Polish post-war economy.**
  Thad Paul Alton. New York: Columbia University Press,
  1955. xv+357p. bibliog. Reprinted, Westview, Connecticut:
  Greenwood Press, 1974.
An introductory review of the inter-war period followed by a comprehensive
account of Polish economic policy and planning during the first decade of the
Polish People's Republic. Considers the aims and effects of Polish economic policy
concerning industry, trade, finance and agriculture. The work also discusses: the
future objectives of long-range economic policy; the achievements and errors of
investment policy; and the social price paid by the labour force under the economic rule of Hilary Minc.

537 **Economic development in East-Central Europe in the 19th
  and 20th centuries.**
  Ivan T. Berend, György Ránki. New York: Columbia
  University Press, 1974. 402p. bibliog.
A translation of a Hungarian book first published in 1969. A brief summary of
16th-18th century conditions in Austro-Hungary, Poland and the Balkans is followed by an account of the later economic development of the Central
European-Danubian region with special emphasis on economic institutions. The
authors argue that the economic development of the area was retarded by an
archaic socioeconomic structure and by over-reliance on Western European investment. The book pays special attention to the period betwen 1850 and 1940.

538 **Economic planning East and West.**
  Edited by Morris Bornstein. Cambridge, Massachusetts:
  Ballinger, 1975. x+334p. illus.
A theorectical anlysis and empirical comparison of economic planning in various
countries. Some studies of individual countries are included, among them a
chapter on Poland.

138

539 **Socialist economic integration: aspects of contemporary economic problems in Eastern Europe.**
Jozef M. van Brabant. Cambridge, England: Cambridge University Press, 1980. 275p. illus. bibliog. (Soviet and East European Studies).
Considers economic integration in Eastern Europe in the context of the Soviet model of growth and the doctrinaire approach of communist economic planning.

540 **The economics and politics of socialism.**
Włodzimierz Brus. London: Routledge, 1973. 117p.
A collection of essays by this well-known Polish economist (now teaching in England) which deal with the role of economic planning and its relationship to the market. Although not specifically dealing with Poland, but with socialist countries in general, this book is based mostly on the author's past experiences and research in Poland.

541 **Transitional economic systems: the Polish-Czech example.**
Dorothy Sybil Douglas. New York: Monthly Review, 1972. viii+375p.
This book discusses Poland's pre-war and war-time economies, as well as the first decade of post-war socioeconomic change. The topics examined include: the nationalization of industry; output and the labour force; wages and social welfare; the cooperative movement; land reform; and the nationalization of commerce.

542 **The crisis in East European economics: the spread of the Polish disease.**
Edited by Jan Drewnowski. London: Croom Helm, 1982. 192p.

543 **The economics of a socialist enterprise: a case study of the Polish firm.**
George R. Feiwel. New York: Praeger, 1965. 398p. illus.
A pioneering attempt to investigate the performance of a specific socialist enterprise within a planned economic system which also considers working conditions.

544 **Industrialization and planning under Polish socialism: 1. Poland's industrialization policy: a current analysis and 2. Problems of Polish economic planning.**
George R. Feiwel. New York: Praeger, 1971. xviii+471p.
Analyzes Polish planning and industrialization policies at the beginning of the 1970s. The policies were supposed to guarantee Poland a great leap forward but instead they brought social unrest and economic disaster.

Economy and Economic History

545 **Economic reforms in Eastern Europe.**
Michael Gamarnikow. Detroit, Michigan: Wayne State
University Press, 1968. 205p.

A thorough analysis of the Eastern European situation based on a wealth of facts
However, because of changes that have taken place during the last decade this
volume is largely of historical value. The author discusses conflict between a
dogmatic and a pragmatic approach to economic reality, and one chapter deals
exclusively with Polish economic reforms, and with the bureaucratic resistance to
their implementation.

546 **New economic systems of Eastern Europe.**
Edited by H. H. Hohmann. London: Hurst, 1975. 585p.

The work contains individual chapters on nine East European states, including
Poland, and this allows the reader to compare their respective economic systems.

547 **The energy situation in Eastern Europe: problems and
prospects.**
Christopher C. Joyner. *East European Quarterly*, vol. 10,
no.3 (Winter 1976), p. 495-516.

This article analyzes the energy situation in Eastern Europe during the 1970s
The author covers: the energy capacity of the area as a whole; the requirements
of the individual coutries; the implications of the energy situation on economic
growth; the supply of sources of energy to Eastern Europe by the USSR and
other potential internal and external energy sources; and energy production prospects. Includes a breakdown of energy resources by commodity and country.

548 **Poland and the Council of Mutual Economic Assistance,
1949-1971.**
Andrzej Korboński. *Central European Federalist*, vol. 19,
no.1-2 (1971), p. 40-51.

Analyzes the tasks assigned to Poland by the *Soviet Ekonomicheskoi Vzaimopo-
moshchi* within the framework of Eastern European economic cooperation, and
Comecon's impact upon Polish economic development. The author also examines
the controversy regarding the benefits deriving from participation in the Council
and charges of Soviet exploitation of other participating countries.

549 **National income and outlay in Czechoslovakia, Poland, and
Yugoslavia.**
Jaroslav Krejci. New York: St. Martin's Press, 1982. 256p.
bibliog.

550 **An economic theory of the feudal system: towards a model of
the Polish economy, 1500-1800.**
Witold Kula, translated by L. Garner. New York:
Humanities, 1976. 192p. illus. map.

A well-researched book by a leading Marxist economic historian. The author
provides an account of the later feudal period in Poland on the basis of a
preconceived theoretical model.

551 **Economic problems of the early feudal Polish state.**
Henryk Łowmiański. *Acta Poloniae Historica*, vol. 3
(1960), p. 7-32.

The unification of the ethnically Polish area into one state extinguished tribal conflicts, and brought closer contacts between various local groups. It also facilitated the penetration of advanced technologies, and created better conditions for the growth of production, for larger urban settlements and for the accumulation of resources.

552 **The economic and social development of Baltic countries
from the 15th to the 17th century.**
Marian Małowist. *Economic History Review*, Series 2, vol.
12, no.2 (1959), p. 127-89.

This paper deals with the socioeconomic history of Poland and the other countries bordering on the Baltic Sea during the period corresponding to the rule of the Lithuanian-Polish Jagellonian dynasty and Swedish-Polish Vasa (Waza) house. The author is a professor of Eastern European economic history at the University of Warsaw.

553 **Crisis in socialist planning: Eastern Europe and the USSR.**
Jean Marczewski, translated by N. Lindsay. New York:
Praeger, 1974. xvii+245p. bibliog.

The volume covers: agricultural, industrial, trade, and financial planning; planning coordination; and future planning prospects. The Polish models of agricultural and industrial planning are discussed on ps. 23-30 and 75-82 respectively. The author is professor of economics and politics at the Sorbonne, Paris.

554 **Central planning in Poland.**
John Michael Montias. New Haven, Connecticut: Yale
University Press, 1962. xv+410p. illus. Reprinted, Westview,
Connecticut: Greenwood Press, 1974.

A consideration of: the theory and practice of Polish economic planning, pricing policy, and investment; and Polish efforts to set up a national economic model, which would not duplicate the Soviet experience nor constitute such a radical divergence from the latter as to provoke political consequences. The author believes that it is possible to modify the economic situation in Poland through reforms from within.

555 **Poland's progress, 1919-1939.**
Michael Murray, introduction by Ernest Barker. London:
J. Murray, 1944. xii+152p. illus.

An overview of Poland's economic progress during the inter-war period, with reference to progress in other areas.

Economy and Economic History

556 **The Polish upswing, 1971-1975.**
Edited by Mieczysław F. Rakowski. Warsaw: Interpress, 1975. 152p.

A brief assessment of the economic policy pursued in Poland during these years. This period was characterized by an attempt to make a 'great leap forward' through massive investment, the purchase of Western know-how, the liberalization of private enterprise, the encouragement of joint ventures, and the abandonment of dogmatism in the national economy.

557 **The institutions of Comecon.**
Giuseppe Schiavono. New York: Holmes & Meier, 1980. 160p. bibliog.

The present Polish economic crisis is often blamed on the Eastern European Economic Common Market's (Comecon) imposition of assigned fields of specialization for each country. The process is dictated by the Soviet Union and includes, for example, providing compulsory assistance to some revolutionary régimes and movements.

558 **Changes in the economic structure of Poland in the past fifty years (1918-1968).**
Kazimierz Secomski. *Review of the Polish Academy of Sciences*, vol. 14, no.4/54 (April-June 1969), p. 42-60.

A consideration of structural change and growth in the Polish economy during the inter-war and post-war periods. The author is one of Poland's top economists.

559 **Economic devolution in Eastern Europe.**
Ljubo Sirc. London: Longman, 1969. 180p.

A simplified and abridged analysis of economic problems and trends in East European countries. The author emphasizes the frustrations caused by the conscious awareness that, within the existing political framework, the final goal cannot include relinquishing communism.

560 **Soviet price discrimination against the satellites.**
Stanisław Skrzypek. *Slavic and East European Studies*, vol. 7 (Spring-Summer 1962), p. 81-92.

Although this article reports on a situation which existed about twenty years ago, the validity of its conclusions is confirmed by the USSR's current attitudes towards its East European partners.

561 **Sources of the conflict.**
Artur Starewicz. *Polish Perspectives*, vol. 23, no.11-12 (1980), p. 23-27.

The editor-in-chief of this monthly journal discusses the economic policy of the Gierek administration during the period 1970-80. The author emphasizes the excessive investment drive which went far beyond the country's capacities. Instead of overcoming past backwardness, Poland acquired an increasing trade deficit, and an economy characterized by a growing gulf between the purchasing power of the population and the supply of consumer goods. In addition imported technology was not utilized correctly. Consequently, national income dropped sharply, as did supplies of foodstuffs, energy and raw materials. Moreover, the economic situation brought about a confidence crisis and general stagnation which in turn led to a sharp drop in both industrial and agricultural production and in living standards.

562 The economic development of Poland, 1919-1950.
Jack Taylor. Ithaca, New York: Cornell University Press, 1952. xiv+222p. bibliog. Reprinted, Westview, Connecticut: Greenwood Press.

A concise but well-documented analysis of Poland's economic development during these years which pays particular attention to the inter-war and Nazi-Soviet occupation periods. Especially interesting are the comments on mixed economy experiments.

563 The economies of the Soviet Bloc: a study of decision-making and resources allocation.
Stanisław H. Wellisz. New York: MacGraw-Hill, 1960. 245p.

An introductory handbook on socialist planning with examples derived largely from Poland.

564 Polish post-war economic growth from the viewpoint of Soviet experience.
John Whalley. *Soviet Studies*, vol. 25, no.2 (April 1973), p. 533-40.

An analysis of output and investment in the centrally administered economies of Poland and the USSR. This article, which is only suitable for specialists, concludes that although they operate within the same theoretical system the Soviet and Polish economies are substantially different. The author asks if the Soviet economic system is more typical of a communist economy in general than the Polish economy.

565 Socialist economic development and reforms: from extensive to intensive growth under central planning in the USSR, Eastern Europe and Yugoslavia.
Joseph Wilczyński. New York: Praeger, 1972. 350p.

A study of the changes in the East European economic system since 1950. The volume covers: reforms in planning; management; incentives for labour and enterprises and their influence on productivity; structural changes; production and distribution; the quality of output; and technological progress.

566 Profit, risk and incentives under socialist economic planning.
Joseph Wilczyński. New York: Harper, 1973. 231p.

The author discusses such subjects as: ideological conflicts; the relevance of economic incentives to productivity; and the effects of financial reforms on economic improvements in eight countries, including Poland.

Economy and Economic History

567 Changing economic thought in Poland.
Peter J. D. Wiles. *Oxford Economic Papers*, new series,
vol. 9 (June 1957), p. 190-208.

An analysis of the economic situation in Poland in 1956, with an introductory
note. The themes discussed in detail include: pricing policy; self-sufficiency and
Comecon relations; and long-term economic planning. The article is followed by
the views of two well-known Polish economists (Józef Pajestka and Włodzimierz
Brus) on the Polish pricing system and on the rationality of central planning (p.
209-24).

568 Poland's maritime economy.
Czesław Wojewódka. *Polish Western Affairs*, vol. 18, no.2
(1977), p. 213-32.

Provides an overall view of the rapid growth (in both absolute figures and percen-
tages) of Polish shipyards and seaports and Poland's merchant marine and deep-
sea fishing fleet, as well as her processing, passenger, container and transit facilities. Poland now occupies a prominent place among shipbuilding nations specializing in certain categories of vessels, and the 'Hipolit Cegielski Works' in Poznań
are Europe's largest producers of ship engines. The Polish fishing fleet has left
the Baltic fishing grounds and now operates all over the world. Bulky cargoes (coal,
ore, oil, sulphur, timber) are handled at Gdańsk and Szczecin, while Gdynia is a specialized passenger and container terminal. In addition, Swinoujście
acts as a ferryboat harbour, while Kołobrzeg and other smaller Western Pomeranian ports operate as fishing bases.

**569 Poland between two wars: a critical study of social and
economic changes.**
Ferdinand Zweig. London: Secker & Warburg, 1944. 176p.
bibliog.

A good outline of Polish inter-war economic history written by a well-known
economist.

Poland from inside: a symposium.
See item no. 5.

Politics and economics in Congress Poland, 1815-1865.
See item no. 123.

Facts about Poland.
See item no. 628.

Polish economy of the years 1918-1939 in Polish post-war publications.
See item no. 824.

Oeconomica Polona. (Polish Economics.)
See item no. 849.

Polish Economic Survey.
See item no. 854.

Ekonomista. (The Economist.)
See item no. 873.

Finance

570 **The monetary crisis of the 17th century and its social and psychological consequences in Poland.**
Maria Bogucka. *Journal of European Economic History*, vol. 4, no.1 (Spring 1975), p. 137-52.
Considers the influences of monetary perturbations in the 17th century upon the socioeconomic situation with reference to the hoarding of goods and investment in landed property as remedies against market insecurity. All social classes were affected with the sole exception of speculators. The author also examines the role of the mints and the flooding of the currency market with foreign currencies which resulted in a wave of xenophobia. The author is a professor in the Polish Academy of Sciences.

571 **Financing foreign trade in Eastern Europe: problems of bilateralism and currency convertibility.**
John S. Garland. New York: Praeger, 1977. 168p. bibliog.
Discusses the: patterns of Comecon foreign trade; obstacles to intrabloc economic integration; financing of socialized enterprises; and East-West trade.

572 **The influence of foreign capital upon the Polish economy, 1918-1939.**
Zbigniew Landau. In: *Poland at the 12th International Congress of Historical Sciences at Vienna*, 1965, p. 113-45.
Analyzes the role of international finance in the development of Polish resources and industry.

573 **Foreign capital in Poland.**
Leopold Wellisz. London: Allen & Unwin, 1938. 281p. tables.
Examines the history of the penetration of foreign (mostly West European) capital into the Polish economy prior to the outbreak of the Second World War. Heavy industry including mining, textiles and chemicals, as well as transport and

communications and insurance companies were largely owned by French, German, English, Belgian, Swedish, and Italian capital.

574 Money, banking and credit in the Soviet Union and Eastern Europe.
Adam Zwass, translated by Michel C. Vale. White Plains, New York: Sharpe, 1979. x+233p.

An analysis of the trading and financial imbalances between East and West based partly on the personal experience of the author.

Trade

575 **England's Baltic trade in the early seventeenth century: a
study in Anglo-Polish commerical diplomacy.**
J. K. Fedorowicz.   Cambridge, England: Cambridge
University Press, 1980. xiii+334p.

576 **The Polish Baltic trade in the 15th-18th centuries.**
Stanisław Hoszowski.   In: *Poland at the 11th International
Congress of Historical Sciences in Stockholm.* Warsaw:
1960. p. 117-54.
An examination of Polish maritime trade mostly through Gdańsk (Danzig) at a
time when timber exports were the main wealth of the country, and when the
Teutonic Order tried to control navigation along the Lower Vistula against the
interests of the most important Polish harbour.

577 **Information for businessmen trading with Poland.**
Warsaw: Polish Chamber of Foreign Trade, 1975. 168p.
map.
Provides general information on Polish foreign trade, followed by a detailed list
of: export-import enterprises; commerical agents; trade fairs; banking facilities;
details concerning the transport and port system; insurance services; and Polish
commercial representatives abroad.

578 **Poland's trade through the Black Sea in the Eighteenth
century.**
Henryk Klimesz.   *Polish Review,* vol. 15, no.2 (Spring
1970), p. 55-80.
An outline of the economic regeneration that took place during the reign of
Stanislaus Augustus Poniatowski, and an account of the attempt to divert Polish trade
routes from the Baltic to the Black Sea.

Trade

579 **Export of grain and the problem of distribution of national income in Poland in the years 1550-1650.**
Antoni Mączak. *Acta Poloniae Historica*, vol. 18 (1968), p. 75-98.
This article examines: the transport of grain on the Vistula river; the social origin of grain exporters; regional differences in the price of grain; and the export of the grain surplus and its impact on the gross national income.

580 **East European integration and East-West trade.**
Edited by Paul Marer, John Michael Montias. Bloomington, Indiana: Indiana University Press, 1980. 432p.
Studies the relationship between the fulfillment of production quotas and the necessity to comply with the decisions of the East European Common Market on the one hand, and the preference on the other hand of individual countries to secure through bilateral trade the hard currency for the purchase of Western know-how and products.

581 **The psychology of East-West trade: illusions and opportunities.**
Zygmunt Nagórski, Jr. New York: Mason & Lipscomb, 1974. 228p. bibliog.
An analysis of economic reforms in Poland and in other East European countries in the early 1970s and the switch to the importation of Western rather than Eastern technology. The East attempts to import technological know-how for purely economic reasons but the West hopes to achieve political liberalization through free trade.

582 **East-West trade and the technology gap: a political and economic appraisal.**
Edited by Stanisław Wąsowski. New York: Praeger, 1970. xvi+214p.
A consideration of the technical backwardness of the Comecon nations and their need for more trade with technologically advanced countries. The author also discusses: the role of East-West trade in bridging the technology gap and in technology transfer; and the impact of Western patents, licenses, joint ventures, up-dated equipment and product design.

583 **The economics and politics of East-West trade.**
Joseph Wilczyński. New York: Praeger, 1969. 416p.
A clearly written and readable book dealing with the interrelation of trade and politics. The work focuses on such issues as: trade embargoes; strategic export controls; equal trading opportunities; and dumping and discriminatory trade arrangements.

Poland from inside: a symposium.
See item no. 5.

Industry

584 Tracing the development of Polish industry.
Aleksander Bocheński.   Warsaw: Interpress, 1971. 112p.
A brief history of Polish heavy industry preceded by an essay on the relationship
between social change and technological growth. Other chapters deal with scientific research in Poland and with Poland's place in the world of technology. The
author is an official economic and political commentator.

585 Poland's industrialization policy: a current analysis.
George R. Feiwel.   New York: Praeger, 1971. 2 vols.
748p.+454p.
Volume one deals with the causes of economic growth and recession, and volume
two examines continuity, change and the prospects for Polish industry. More
recent publications on the state of Polish industry now enable the reader to
compare these forecasts with actual achievements and failures.

586 Industry in Poland.
Irena Fierla.   Warsaw: Interpress, 1980. 300p. illus.
A brief industrial history of Poland which covers: the industrialization process; the
development of various branches of industry; the progress achieved since the
Second World War; and Polish industrial growth compared with contemporary
developments in other countries. The author teaches economic history at the
Higher School of Planning and Statistics in Warsaw.

587 The industrial enterprise in Eastern Europe.
Edited by Ian Jeffries.   Eastbourne, Sussex; New York:
Praeger, 1981. ix+165p. illus.
Nine articles on as many East European countries. The chapter on Poland by
Domenico Mario Nuti is entitled 'Industrial enterprises in Poland, 1973-1980'.

Industry

588 **Problems of socialist industrialization in Poland.**
Andrzej Karpiński. Warsaw: Państwowe Wydawnictwo
Ekonomiczne, 1963. 255p.

An attempt to evaluate Poland's economic policy during the five-year period
1950-55, which was designed to ensure the rapid industrialization of the country.
Both the positive and the negative results are discussed. Several problems are
illustrated including those concerning investment policy, employment, raw
materials, production and consumption levels, new technologies and industrial
geography.

589 **Polish ship-building industry.**
Włodzimierz Korchot. *Polish Western Affairs*, vol. 3, no.1
(1962), p. 193-213. tables.

A brief history of Polish shipbuilding between the wars, together with an account
of the spectacular expansion of the industry that has occurred during the post-war
period. Reference is made to: the number of vessels built; the dead weight ton-
nage delivered; the percentage of ships exported; the major shipyards at Gdańsk,
Gdynia and Szczecin; docks and repair bases; Poland's place in the world ship-
building industry; skilled manpower; and advanced research.

590 **The industrial development of Poland.**
Rosa Luxemburg, translated by Tessa
DeCarlo. Campaigner, 1977. 190p.

A survey of 19th-century Polish industry by a Polish-born Marxist theoretician
and leader.

591 **Polish-US industrial cooperation in the 1980s: findings of a
joint research project.**
Edited by Paul Marer, Eugeniusz
Tabaczyński. Bloomington, Indiana: Indiana University
Press, 1982. 409p.

A collection of twelve seminar papers on industrial cooperation followed by summaries of project discussions, conclusions and recommendations and analyses of
case studies. Also includes a synopsis of the Polish approach to joint ventures.
This is an excellent research manual which is relevant to industrial cooperation in
Eastern Europe.

592 **Oil and gas in Comecon countries.**
Daniel Park. New York: Nichols; London: Kegan Paul,
1979. 240p. bibliog.

The book is primarily concerned with Soviet oil and gas production, consumption
and exports. However, some attention is also given to Poland's: energy resources;
its energy sources and consumption; its supplies of oil and natural gas; and to the
country's general energy policy and planning which takes into account the
resources and needs of other Comecon countries.

593 **Industrial progress in Poland, Czechoslovakia and East Germany, 1937-1962.**
Alfred Zauberman. New York: Oxford University Press, 1964. xiv+338p. bibliog.

A comparative study of industrial growth in these three states which rank as the most developed of Eastern Europe. The comparative evaluations are made with reference to each country's past industrial progress and to the performance of other European countries.

594 **Planning in East Europe: industrial management by the state.**
Janusz G. Zieliński, Michael Charles Kaser. London: Bodley Head, 1970. 184p.

This is the only study of its kind. Although the book discusses some theoretical issues, it is orientated towards planning practice and discusses such aspects as: central versus regional and local planning; autonomy of management; the formulation of targets and prices; access to finance; and labour-management relations. It also describes the limited efforts of some East European countries to establish their own economic patterns of development.

595 **Economic reforms in Polish industry.**
Janusz G. Zieliński. New York: Oxford University Press, 1973. ix+333p.

An important study of the economic theory and practice of socialist planning in Poland. The effectiveness of Polish economic reforms and the tendency of socialist enterprises to avoid risk and innovation is also discussed. According to the author, there was no consistent attempt to carry out structural changes in the Polish economy and its overall performance was improved neither quantitatively nor qualitatively.

Industrialization and planning under Polish socialism: 1. Poland's industrialization policy: a current analysis and 2. Problems of Polish economic planning.
See item no. 544.

The energy situation in Eastern Europe: problems and prospects.
See item no. 547.

Agriculture and Fishing

596 **The Soviet agricultural model in Eastern Europe.**
Arthur E. Adams. *East European Quarterly*, vol. 8, no.4
(Jan. 1975), p. 461-77.
Compares the Soviet model of agriculture with systems operating in other Eastern
European countries. The Polish system (dealt with specifically on p. 463-65) is
defined as a state-directed model even though the vast majority of land remains
privately-owned.

597 **Polish revolutionary populism: a study in agrarian socialist
thought from the 1830s to the 1850s.**
Peter Brock. Toronto: University of Toronto Press, 1977.
125p. bibliog.
A pioneering work that centres on the second (conspiratorial and revolutionary)
phase of Polish populism, which followed a period of sporadic outbursts of
peasant anger against the landlords. The book considers: Kostka Napierski in the
17th century; the Humań massacre in the 18th century; and the Austrian-inspired
Galicia massacre of 1846. This was followed after the 1870s by a more pragmatic
approach. Polish populists at home and abroad maintained contact wih the Russian intelligentsia and inspired the Russian populism that followed a generation
later.

598 **Agricultural policies in the USSR and Eastern Europe.**
Ronald A. Francisco, Betty A. Laird, Roy D.
Laird. Boulder, Colorado: Westview Press, 1980.
xvi+332p.
The continual failures of state and collective farming mean that even today the
anachronistic and inefficient smallholder system of farming is widespread in
Poland. This system is capable of yielding a satisfactory supply of crops despite
heavy taxation and the low priority given to the delivery of agricultural
machinery, tools and fertilizers.

152

599 **The organization of agriculture in the Soviet Union and Eastern Europe.**
Everett Jacobs, Alec Nove. Montclair, New Jersey: Allanheld, Osmun, 1980. 500p. bibliog.

An examination of the relationship between state farms, collective farms and private farms. Reference is made to agricultural machinery service stations and to the compulsory delivery of agricultural products.

600 **Soviet and East European agriculture.**
Edited by Jerzy F. Karcz. Berkeley, California: University of California Press, 1967. xxv+445p.

A collection of articles on the historical, economic, geographical and political aspects of agricultural problems in various East European countries. Includes 'Peasant agriculture in socialist Poland from 1956: an anternative to collectivisation' by Andrzej Korboński (p. 411-35).

601 **Politics of socialist agriculture in Poland: 1945-1960.**
Andrzej Korboński. New York: Columbia University Press, 1965. 330p. bibliog.

Considers the interplay of politics and agriculture and covers in succession: land reform; the defeat of the independent peasant movement; the attempt at collectivization and its collapse; and the 'new course' of cooperation between the nationalized, cooperative and private agricultural sectors.

602 **Polish agriculture: characteristics, types and regions.**
Jerzy Kostrowicki, Roman Szczęsny. Budapest: Hungarian Academy of Sciences, 1972. 120p.

This work deals with the structure of Polish agriculture and refers to: the small-holdings in Southern Poland; the relatively large number of cooperatives in the Westernmost territories; the larger farms in Greater Poland; and the backwardness of agricultural technology in Eastern Poland. Polish agriculture is characterized by: mostly private ownership; a limited reliance on animal breeding; the regional distribution of crops; and agricultural labour problems. The author is director of the Institute of Geography and Environmental Studies of the Polish Academy of Sciences.

603 **Polish sea fisheries development.**
Andrzej Niegolewski. *Polish Western Affairs*, vol. 4, no.2 (1963), p. 264-94.

Outlines the development of the Polish fishing industry before and since the Second World War. The author discusses: improved methods of catching fish; coastal and seagoing fishing; fishing ports and the fishing fleets; fish consumption in Poland; and fish processing including salting, freezing, smoking, canning, and pickling. The author teaches at the Maritime Fishing Institute at Gdynia.

Agriculture and Fishing

604 **Agriculture in Poland's Western territories: under Prussian rule and in People's Poland.**
Wacław Radkiewicz. *Polish Western Affairs*, vol. 4, no.2 (1963), p. 295-329.

Considers such aspects of agricultural development as the 'Ostflucht' (flight from the East) of German farmers during the Prussian administration and the gradual development of crops and livestock after 1945.

605 **Agricultural policies in Poland.**
Stanisław Skrzypek. *Journal of Central European Affairs*, vol. 16, no.1 (April 1956), p. 45-70.

For centuries Poland was an agricultural country with a large grain and dairy surplus. During the period 1920-39 there were attempts at agrarian reform including: the integration of scattered land lots; the elimination of tiny uneconomical farms; and the division of large estates. After the Second World War agriculture was a weak spot in the Polish economy and emphasis was placed on making agricultural production more efficient. However, in spite of mechanization and massive government support the most efficient farms supplying vegetables, fruit and poultry to the major cities continued to be the small private properties.

606 **Agriculture in Eastern Europe and the Soviet Union: comparative studies.**
Karl-Eugen Wadekin, Alec Nove. Montclair, New Jersey: Allanheld, Osmun, 1980. 450p. bibliog.

607 **Recent developments in Polish agriculture.**
Augustyn Woś. Warsaw: Interpress, 1979. 156p.

Analyzes Polish agriculture and agricultural policy from 1944 to 1976. The author examines: changes in socioeconomic structure in the rural areas; the part played by agriculture in the national economy; and the prospects for the future.

Economic-demographic interrelations in developing agricultural regions: a case study of Prussian Upper Silesia, 1840-1914.
See item no. 35.

The vegetation of Poland.
See item no. 67.

Transport

608 Poland and the Baltic: the problem of Poland's access to the sea.
Henryk Bagiński, introduced by Alan Graham, translated by Peter Jordan. London: Polish Institute for Overseas Problems, 1946. 2nd rev. ed. xvi+232p. maps. bibliog.

The topics discussed in this book, which was written before Poland's access to the Baltic sea was extended to its present length, include: Poland's position between the Baltic and the Black Seas; her maritime strength; overseas trade; inland waterways and hydrography; the German ethnic assimilation policy of the Polish seaboard population; and the incorporation of Polish maritime provinces into Germany.

609 Polish aircraft 1893-1939.
Jerzy B. Cynk. London: Putnam, 1971. 760p.

A definitive study of the history of the Polish aircraft industry and of aircraft construction design up to the outbreak of the Second World War. During this period Poland specialized in producing small passenger planes and won several international competitions including the Challenge International. Poland also started to produce medium-sized military aircraft. The PZL Works still continue their pre-war tradition, but Comecon regulations limit the production of planes to those for agricultural and related use.

610 Communist ships and shipping.
John D. Harbron. London: Adlard Coles, 1962. 262p.

The second part of this book deals with Poland (p. 27-122), and contains chapters on: the Polish maritime tradition; the organization of shipping; administration and operations; shipbuilding and wharves; and seaports. Poland is now a major ship-building nation and Polish yards concentrate on producing merchant, passenger and fishing vessels. The warships for Eastern European countries are built at Soviet wharves.

Transport

611 The Polish seaports.
Bolesław Kasprowicz. *Polish Western Affairs*, vol. 4, no.1 (1963), p. 51-90. diags.

A brief history of Polish ports and their relationship with the economic hinterland. The article also considers the areas serviced by various ports as part of Poland's economic geography. Reference is made to the Vistula and Odra River basins; the inland waterways and their estuaries at Gdańsk-Gdynia; to the Szczecin-Swinoujście twin harbour cities; to the utilization of Polish ports by other countries; and to long-range development plans. Statistics are provided concerning: cargo turnover; the types of goods handled; and the number of ships.

612 East European transport: regions and modes.
Edited and introduced by Bogdan Mieczkowski. The Hague: Nijhoff, 1980. xiv+353p. illus.

A consideration of national and international transport in Eastern Europe which pays particular attention to planning and investment. The editor has authored a book on a similar subject entitled *Transportation in Eastern Europe: empirical findings* (Boulder, Colorado: East European Monographs, 1978. 221p. maps. bibliog.).

613 Polish merchant navy, 1926-1939.
Donald Steyer. *Acta Poloniae Historica*, vol. 23 (1971), p. 119-35.

The author shows that after a period of slow growth between 1918 and 1925 the Polish merchant navy began to develop quickly in the years after 1926. Regular passenger and cargo lines were opened, proper training facilities for personnel were organized, a new port was opened at Gdynia, and Poland's overseas trade, shipbuilding industry and sea routes began to expand.

The Oder river: transport and economic development.
See item no. 41.

Road atlas of Poland.
See item no. 48.

The Odra: an album.
See item no. 216.

Employment, Labour and *Solidarity*

614 Employment policies in the Soviet Union and Eastern Europe.
Edited by Jan Adam. New York: St. Martin's Press, 1982.
240p.

615 The Polish August: the self-limiting revolution.
Neal Ascherson. London: Allen Lane, 1981. 351p. illus.

This publication, which appeared simultaneously in a paperback edition (Penguin
Books), examines the *Solidarity* movement in Poland and associated developments. Also of interest is a volume introduced by Neal Ascherson entitled *The
book of Lech Wałęsa: a collective portrait by Solidarity members and critics*
(London: Allen Lane, 1982). Several other works on this subject have also
appeared including: Kevin Ruane's *The Polish Challenge* (London: British Broadcasting Corporation, 1982); Jean-Yves Potel's (translated by Phil Markham) *The
summer before the frost: Solidarity in Poland* (London: Pluto Press, 1982); Denis
MacShane's *Solidarity: Poland's Independent Trade Union* (Nottingham,
England: Spokesman, 1981); *Gdańsk 1980: pictures from a strike* (London: Puls
Publications, 1980); Stewart Steven's *The Poles* (London: Collins/Harvill, 1982);
and A. Touraine et al. *Solidarity, the analysis of a social movement: Poland
1980-81* (Cambridge University Press, 1983). See also Michael Dobbs, Dessa
Trevisan and K. S. Karol (*pseud.*) *Poland/Solidarity/Walesa* (q.v.) and Daniel
Singer's *The road to Gdańsk: Poland and the USSR* (q.v.).

616 Poland/Solidarity/Walesa.
Michael Dobbs, Dessa Trevisan, K. S. Karol (*pseud.*). New
York: MacGraw-Hill, 1981.

The name of Lech Wałęsa and that of 'Solidarność' (NSZZ Solidarność-
Independent Self-governing Trade Union *Solidarity*) are known world-wide for
what they stand for: the fearless struggle of Polish workers to gain recognition for
civil and labour rights similar to those enjoyed in Western countries. Other works
on the *Solidarity* movement include: W. Szymański's *Candle for Poland: 469 days
of Solidarity* (Borgo Press. 128p.) and C. Barker's *Solidarność: from*

Employment, Labour and *Solidarity*

Gdańsk to military repression (International Socialism. 154p.). See also Daniel Singer's *The road to Gdańsk: Poland and the USSR* (q.v.) and Neal Ascherson's *The Polish August: the self-limiting Revolution* (q.v.).

617 **The Polish worker: a study of a social stratum.**
Feliks Gross, translated by Norbert Guterman. New York: Roy, 1945. 274p. bibliog. Reprinted, New York: AMS Press.
An analysis of: the history and structure of the Polish labour movement; the Polish proletariat within a European framework; the standard of living of the Polish workers in the 20th century; Polish labour legislation; and the sufferings of the Polish workers under the Nazi occupation.

618 **Employment in Poland in 1930-1960: dynamics and structure.**
Hanna Jędruszczak. *Acta Poloniae Historica*, vol. 18 (1968), p. 250-63.
Discusses the size of the Polish workforce in 1930, 1950 and 1960 and the impact of the planned economy, social change and the investment rate on the labour supply. The author also considers: the demographic background to employment patterns; and the transformation of Poland from an agricultural into an agricultural-industrial and then an industrial-agricultural country.

619 **A Polish factory: a case study of workers' participation in decisions in industry.**
Jiri Thomas Kolaja. Lexington, Kentucky: University Of Kentucky Press, 1960. xviii+157p.
A pioneering and unprejudiced work on labour-management relations and on workers' participation in management in Poland. The report is based both on printed sources and on first-hand experience. The author concludes that the reduction of areas of conflict is now the goal of both management and the labour unions, both in free market and in planned economies.

620 **Education and youth employment in Poland.**
Barbara Liberska. Berkeley, California: Carnegie Council on Policy Studies in Higher Education, 1979. viii+83p. illus.
Provides the results of a research project designed to investigate ways of adjusting educational policies to the demands of the labour market. In addition to Poland the work also refers to five other European countries, Mexico, Japan, and Southern Asia. The volume deals with: the principles of educational policy; the accessability of education; employment policy; young people's value systems; attitudes toward work; and the use of free time.

621 **Workers' self-management in Poland.**
Anna Michalska. *Polish Western Affairs*, vol. 12, no.2 (1971), p. 385-402.
An essay on workers' self-management and on workers' participation in the management of state enterprises. The article discusses the connection between Poland's socioeconomic system, the state ownership of the means of production, and the extent of the workers' influence on management. Other subjects which are studied include: workers' councils and workers' self-management; the council's scope, functions and limitations; group sharing of profits; individual rewards for

Employment, Labour and *Solidarity*

efficiency; the relationship between workers' councils, trade unions and party authorities; the handling of controversies and management control over workers' recommendations; the legal basis of workers' self-management, -the regulations of December 1956 and December 1958; and Poland's workers' self-management system compared with the systems in other socialist countries.

622 The road to Gdańsk: Poland and the USSR.
Daniel Singer. New York: Monthly Review, 1981. 256p.
The glorious name of the old Hanseatic port of Gdańsk is now generally associated in Poland with the constitution of the 'Solidarność' labour movement, which soon had a membership of 10 million Polish workers.

623 The workers' councils in Poland.
Adolf Sturmthal. *Industrial and Labor Relations Review*, vol. 14, no.3 (April 1961), p. 379-96.
The author outlines the organization and function of workers' councils in Poland, which are designed to appease those of the working class who have aspirations of participating in industrial management. In addition the councils help to make the production process more efficient. Unlike Yugoslavia, worker participation in Poland has so far seemed little more than a formality. Moreover, General Jaruzelski's government, while dissolving 'Solidarność', also stipulated that a return to pre-Solidarność labour unions was out of the question.

624 Blue-collar workers in Eastern Europe.
Edited by Jan F. Triska, Charles Gati. London: Allen & Unwin, 1981. 302p.
A selection of essays dealing with: the deterioration of living and working conditions; workers' self-management; wages; the chances for promotion; and economic and political reality as compared with Marxist theory. These papers were originally presented at a conference at Stanford University in May 1980.

625 The workers' dilemma of Polish politics: a case study.
John B. de Weydenthal. *East European Quarterly*, vol. 13, no.1 (Spring 1979), p. 95-125.
An almost prophetic article which discusses workers and the political system in contemporary Poland. The author shows how the dissent of factory workers can manifest itself in a constitutional way despite the lack of formal channels. Economic scarcity is not the main cause of discontent, even though it might act as a spark. Workers particularly resent political manipulation, and the fact that the process of government is performed in their name but without their participation.

Employment-seeking emigrations of the Poles world-wide.
See item no. 267.

Polish emigrants in Europe.
See item no. 268.

The Polish peasant in Europe and America.
See item no. 270.

Emigration from Poland in the nineteenth and twentieth centuries.
See item no. 271.

Statistics

626 **Concise statistical yearbook of the Polish People's Republic.**
Warsaw: Główny Urząd Statystyczny, 1947- . maps. graphs.
tables.
An abridged edition of this originally unabridged statistical yearbook which was
first published in 1930. The book provides statistical data concerning political,
demographic, social, economic, cultural and artistic developments and also supplies comparative data on Poland and other countries.

627 **Polish maritime economy: facts and figures.**
Izabella Dzieduszycka (et al.). Gdańsk, Poland:
Wydawnictwo Morskie, 1965. 160p. illus.
A brief descriptive and statistical publication on Polish maritime facilities, the
merchant marine, ports, ocean fishing and overseas trade.

628 **Facts about Poland.**
Warsaw: Interpress Agency, 1980. 206p.
Provides concise general information and statistical data (revised at irregular
intervals) about all aspects of Polish life including: economic conditions and planning; population; the constitution; public administration; the armed forces; political parties; family life; youth; the cooperative movement; trade unions; employment;
sport; tourism; education; art; the mass media; the environment; mining; industry;
agriculture; foreign policy; and Poles abroad. The loose-leaf format enables individual
pages to be updated and replaced as needed. The 1980 edition covers sixty-three
topics.

629 **The East European and Soviet data handbook: political,
social and developmental indicators, 1945-1975.**
Paul S. Shoup. New York: Columbia University Press for
the Hoover Institution, 1981. 482p.
An overview of social change and the development of élites in the period 1945-
1978. Data is provided on: population; party membership; nationalities; education;
classes; and party leaders and their background. The bulk of the information is

derived directly from East European censuses, original documents and biographical dictionaries. Poland is considered in each of the crossnational chapters.

Environment, Planning and Urbanization

630 Selected problems of urban ecology.
Tadeusz Bartkowski. Poznań, Poland: Uniwersytet im.
Adama Mickiewicza, 1979. 191p. illus.

This volume deals with city and regional planning and specifically with: the ecological bases of urban settlements; ecological elements in regional planning; old and new conurbations; protected areas within industrial zones; rural tourism (agrotourism); and the relationship between man and the biosphere. The authors are professors of environmental and regional planning at the University of Poznań.

631 The urbanization of Poland in the years 1870-1970.
Marian Marek Drozdowski. *Studia Historiae Oeconomicae*,
vol. 9 (1974), p. 223-44.

Considers Poland's transformation from a rural agricultural country into first a rural-urban and later an urban-rural nation.

632 Urbanisation in contemporary Poland.
Kazimierz Dziewoński. *Geographia Polonica*, no.3 (1964), p.
37-56. map.

Describes the: past and present growth of the urban population in Poland; the process of urbanization; the effectiveness of planning policy for urban growth; urbanization and regional factors; and centralized versus decentralized planning of urban development. This is an article for specialists only.

162

Environment, Planning and Urbanization

633 **Transformations of the rural landscape of Poland during the last two centuries.**
Kazimierz Dziewoński. *Geographia Polonica*, vol. 38 (1978), p. 83-88.
The present rural landscape of Poland reflects successive agrarian reforms. This truism is particularly reflected by the patterns of human settlements and field cultivation. The author is professor of economic geography and environmental planning at the University of Warsaw.

634 **City and regional planning in Poland.**
Edited by Jack C. Fisher. Ithaca, New York: Cornell University Press, 1965. xxvi+491p. illus. maps.
Publishes twenty papers by Polish specialists including economists, geographers and administrators on planning in Poland at the city, regional and national levels. Consideration is given to microregions and major conurbations: the Warsaw capital district; the Silesia-Cracow coal and steel basin; the Gdańsk-Sopot-Gdynia tri-city seaboard area; and the Łódź textile industry district. Attention is also paid to urban conservation and renewal; the pariticpation of the private and the cooperative sectors in housing programmes; the establishment of new urban centres which conform with local resources; and environmental impact studies. The contributors openly admit that there have been errors and shortcomings in planning and in the actual implementation of plans.

635 **Urban development in east central Europe: Poland, Czechoslovakia and Hungary.**
Edited by Erwin Anton Gutkind. New York: Free Press; London: Collier-Macmillan, 1972. 475p. maps.
This book is volume 7 of the International History of City Development Series. The chapter on Poland has been written by Wojciech Kalinowski, professor of historical monuments preservation at the University of Toruń.

636 **Urban system in Poland: its development and functional organization.**
Marek Jerczyński. *Geographia Polonica*, vol. 37 (1977), p. 73-88. map.
Examines the size, structure and development of Polish towns, the growth of the urban population, and population density.

637 **Urbanization and East-Central Europe after World War II.**
Leszek A. Kosiński. *East European Quarterly*, vol. 8, no.2 (June 1974), p. 129-53. map. bibliog.
A comparative study of urban development in eight East European countries during the last three decades. The article also assesses the percentage of the population living in the largest national and regional centres; the demographic concentration in the metropolitan areas; and the rate of growth of the urban population. The author foresees a more intense growth of medium-sized cities and the consolidation of metropolitan conurbations. It is shown that the largest multi-city metropolitan concentration of population in Eastern Europe is to be found in Upper Silesia which has a population of over 3.2 million.

Environment, Planning and Urbanization

638 **The influence of industrialization and urbanization on land use and agriculture in Poland.**
Jerzy Kostrowicki. *Geographia Polonica*, no.3 (1964), p. 175-92.

This article concentrates on a discussion of the agricultural potential of a region and the desirable level of industrialization and residential construction.

639 **Poland builds new towns.**
Bolesław Malisz. Warsaw: Polonia, 1962. 173p. illus. maps.

A prominent Polish expert on town and regional planning deals with urban problems of dimensional and social growth. The work concentrates on the Polish-post-war policy of urban transformation, and includes three case studies, two concerning new Polish towns established in the inter-war period (Stalowa Wola, Nowe Tychy) and one during the post-war period (Nowa Huta).

640 **Concept of regional planning.**
Bolesław Malisz. *Polish Perspectives*, vol. 15, no.3 (March 1972), p. 18-24.

A discussion of regional development plans for Poland as a whole. The author, professor of environmental planning at the Polish Academy of Sciences, took part in the development of eight economic planning regions in Poland in the 1970s.

641 **Regional development: experiences and prospects in Eastern Europe.**
Kosta Mihailović. The Hague: Mouton, 1972. 225p. bibliog.

Compares the Yugoslav experience of regional development with the theory and practice of regionalization in seven other East European countries. The Yugoslav government was obliged to take into account the complicated ethnic composition of the country. However, Poland has established eight regions of economic planning which are arranged according to economic considerations and which often cut across historical regions and subdivisions.

642 **Socialist city planning: a re-examination.**
American Institute of Planners Journal, vol. 31, pt. 1 (Feb. 1965), p. 31-42.

A comparative study of town planning in Poland and Yugoslavia, the two countries considered to be most advanced and most autonomous in this field in Eastern Europe.

643 **Environmental deterioration in the Soviet Union and Eastern Europe.**
Edited by Ivan Völgyes. New York: Praeger, 1974. 168p. maps.

Argues that state ownership of the means of production and of the land produces lax environmental controls because the same authority supervises industrial establishments and natural resources.

Education

644 Comparative method in education.
George Beraday, Zygmunt Fijałkowski. New York: Holt, 1964. 302p.

A chapter in this book entitled: 'Indoctrination in schools in one country' (p. 55-69) includes an essay on political indoctrination in Polish schools and on the resulting conflicts between communist ideology on one side and the country's religious heritage on the other.

645 History of education in Europe.
Edited by T. G. Cook. New York: Methuen, 1975. 100p.

A collection of papers delivered at a conference sponsored by the History of Education Society. R. Szreter's paper on education and nation-building in Poland is judged by many to be the best in this volume of miscellanea.

646 Revolution and tradition in People's Poland: education and socialization.
Joseph R. Fiszman. London: Oxford University Press, 1973. xxii+382p. bibliog.

This work asserts that the Polish people preserve entrenched traditional values, and that the Catholic Church and the intelligentsia contribute to those conservative tendencies. The author poses the basic question: if the Polish teacher upholds the existing power structure what chance is there of defeating the old humanistic and anti-vocational bias in Polish education. It appears that the educational aims of both the church and the state have a puritanical tendency while, from the ideological point of view, Polish teachers have a long tradition of leftist orientation. The author discovers some surprising facts, for example, in spite of the great expansion of the educational system since the war, the offspring of the intelligentsia still retain their privileged position. He also concludes that leftist ideology is more deeply rooted among older teachers than among young ones; the latter are more conservative and religious. Finally, he shows that the largest percentage of students of peasant extraction can be found in theological academies.

Education

647 **The history of the education of Polish immigrants in the U.S.**
Józef Miąso, translated by Ludwik Krzyżanowski. New
York: Kościuszko Foundation, 1977. 294p. illus. (Library of
Polish Studies).
An overview of various educational and cultural institutions serving Polish Americans and Americans of Polish descent.

648 **National Education Commission: product of the Polish
Enlightenment period.**
Jerzy Topolski. *Polish Western Affairs*, vol. 15, no.1
(1974), p. 107-16.
The author, who is a professor of history at the University of Poznań, believes
that the most important product of the Enlightenment was the growing number of
people thinking in community (state, nation, society) terms rather than limited
(town, estate, village) terms. The creation in Poland of the first European ministry of education resulted from the realization that human action depends on
man's knowledge, an idea which prompted various groups to promote school
reform according to their own ideas and models. The new Polish educational
system, one of the crowning achievements of the Stanislavian era, replaced a
religious programme by a patriotic one. It also brought the school curriculum
closer to practical life and expanded the social base of youth participation.

Poland: the country and its people.
See item no. 10.

Education and youth employment in Poland.
See item no. 620.

**Eastern European education: a bibliography of English-language materials
on Poland.**
See item no. 812.

Universities and
Learning

649 **Nicolaus Copernicus and his epoch.**
Jan Adamczewski. Warsaw: Interpress, 1972. 152p. illus.
Reprinted, New York: Scribner, 1974. 160p. illus.

A consideration of the life and work of the Polish astronomer Nicolaus Copernicus (1473-1543) as well as the places connected with his activities and achievements. This book is beautifully illustrated with photos, prints and woodcuts. It is
one of the publications which appeared to mark the 500th anniversary of Copernicus' birth and is well documented. Another volume published on the same occasion is *The world of Copernicus* by Henryk Bietkowski and Włodzimierz Zonn
(Warsaw: Arkady, 1973. 167p.) which provides a biography of Copernicus and an
album of townscapes of the Polish and Italian towns where he lived and created
his major works. Charlotte B. and Howard V. Evans discuss Copernicus as a
product of the Renaissance and as an encyclopaedic scholar and humanist who
foreshadowed the approaching epoch of the Enlightenment (see *East European
Quarterly*, vol. 7, no.3, fall 1973, p. 231-49.). Hermann Kesten in his *Copernicus
and his world* (New York: Roy, 1945. ix+408p. illus.) offers a vivid biography of
the great astronomer told against the background of humanism and the Renaissance. Kesten emphasizes Copernicus' lifelong struggle against the forces of
obscurantism and his quest to establish a new vision of the world.

650 **Madame Curie.**
Eve Curie, translated by Vincent Sheean. New York:
Garden City, 1943. Reprinted, London: Heinemann, 1945.
xi+396p.

One of the daughters of Marie Curie, (neé Marysia Skłodowska) the great Polish
scientist, recounts her memories of her mother. Another highly readable life story
of Marie Curie, the only woman to win the Nobel Prize twice, is Robert Reid's
Marie Curie (New York: Dutton, 1974. 349p. illus. bibliog.).

Universities and Learning

651 **Polish scholars: their contribution to world science.**
Marian Dobrowolski. Warsaw: Polonia, 1960. 208p. illus.
A brief general survey of the history of Polish learning. Individual chapters are arranged according to historical periods and specific disciplines.

652 **The Collegium Majus of the Jagellonian University in Cracow.**
Karol Estreicher. Warsaw: Interpress, 1973. 168p. illus.
A richly illustrated book on the history and collections of the most distinguished university college in Poland, the mediaeval seat of the most ancient university of Central-Eastern Europe. The author, who writes in a lively and colourful style, is a famous art historian, bibliographer and historian of Polish civilization, whose ancestors have been prominently associated with the university for three generations.

653 **Polish civilization: essays and studies.**
Edited by Mieczysław Giergielewicz. New York: New York University Press, 1979. 318p.
This anthology, sponsored by the Polish Institute of Arts and Sciences in the United States is designed to cover the millennium of Poland's cultural achievement. The thirteen essays selected for this volume of miscellanea deal with Polish learning, civilization, social classes, religious minorities and literature, and include the following articles: 'Peasant rituals and seasonal customs' by Cezaria Jędrzejewiczowa; 'Towns in mediaeval Poland' by Jan Ptaśnik; 'Polish humanism' by Stanisław Kot; 'Protection of Jewish rights in Poland' by Isaac Lewin; 'Recollections from Sachsenhausen extermination camp' by Stanisław Pigoń; and 'Reformation in Poland' by Aleksander Brückner.

654 **Aesthetics in twentieth-century Poland: an anthology.**
Edited by Jean Gabbert Harrell, Alina Wierzbiańska. New York: Bucknell, 1973. 285p.
The beginnings of the development of aesthetics in Poland go back to the middle of the 19th century. A chair of aesthetics was established at the University of Warsaw in 1957. Roman Ingarden has carried out important research on aesthetic phenomenology, Jan Białostocki has produced valuable aesthetical analysis in the methodology of art history, and Władysław Tatarkiewicz has made significant contributions to the history of aesthetics.

655 **Polish philosophy.**
George Herburt-Krzywicki, edited by Paul Edwards. In: *The encyclopaedia of philosophy*, New York: Macmillan, 1967. vol. 6, p. 363-70.
The author is a professor at the City University of New York.

656 **An outline of Polish science.**
Maciej Iłowiecki. Warsaw: Interpress, 1980. 520p. illus.
Discusses the origin and development of individual disciplines in Poland in a clear and lively way. Various branches of learning are examined against the general background of Polish cultural and intellectual life.

657 **Philosophy and ideology: the development of philosophy and Marxism-Leninism in Poland since the Second World War.**
Zbigniew A. Jordan. Dordrecht, Netherlands: Reidel, 1963. xii+600p. bibliog.

Another work of interest on this subject is a book published by the American Marxist Institute (1968) entitled *Humanistic philosophy in Poland and Yugoslavia today* by Howard L. Parsons.

658 **For your freedom and ours: Polish progressive spirit through the centuries.**
Edited by Manfred Kridl, Władysław Malinowski, Józef Wittlin, prefaced by Malcolm W. Davis, translated by Ludwik Krzyżanowski. New York: Ungar, 1943. 360p.

This volume was also published under the title *The democratic heritage of Poland: for your freedom and ours; an anthology* (London: Allen & Unwin, 1944. 236p.) and a second enlarged edition, revised by Krystyna Olszer was published by Ungar in 1981 (xiii+367p.). The book provides a somewhat subjective selection of documents, excerpts and writings by prominent Polish scholars and men of letters. The anthology covers six hundred years of Polish democratic thought.

659 **A half century of Polish mathematics.**
Kazimierz Kuratowski. Warsaw: Państwowe Wydawnictwo Naukowe, 1979. xviii+204p. illus.

A history of Polish mathematics which refers to the achievements of such famous scholars as Wacław Sierpiński, Stefan Banach, Stefan Mazurkiewicz, and the author of this book himself. The Polish school of mathematics was mainly based in Warsaw, and its findings were published in *Fundamenta Mathematicae*.

660 **Economic sciences in Poland.**
Oskar Lange. *Polish Perspectives*, vol. 7, no.4 (April 1964), p. 29-35.

The development of economic sciences in Poland since the Second World War is outlined by the late chief theoretician of Polish economic planning.

661 **Six centuries of geography at the Jagellonian University in Cracow.**
Stanisław Leszczycki. *Geographia Polonica*, vol. 11 (1967), p. 5-28. illus.

A discussion of the 600-year history of earth sciences at the oldest Polish university, which reflects *ipso facto* the history of geography in all of Poland. The author is the retired director of the Institute of Geography of the Polish Academy of Sciences, a professor at the University of Warsaw, as well as a former President of the International Geographical Society.

Universities and Learning

662 **Polish logic, 1920-1939.**
Storrs McCall, edited and translated by B. Gruchman (et al.). Oxford, England: Clarendon Press, 1967. 406p. bibliog.

This volume contains contributions by some of the best known Polish scholar including Tadeusz Kotarbiński and Kazimierz Ajdukiewicz.

663 **Fifty years of Polish sociology.**
Władysław Markiewicz. *Polish Western Affairs*, vol. 10, no.2 (1969), p. 354-77.

An outline of Polish sociology since the early 19th century including the inter-wai period, the Nazi occupation and postwar developments. Especially interesting and tragic was the period from 1952 to 1955, when sociology was treated as a reac tionary and deviationist discipline, and chairs of sociology were in most case abolished although they were later reinstated and combined with those of philoso phy. The author discusses the present trends in Polish sociology, its vitality and current research in theoretical, practical and methodological fields. Reference is also made to the education of sociologists and the activites of the Polish Sociolog ical Society.

664 **Political sciences in Poland.**
Warsaw: Państwowe Wydawnictwo Naukowe, 1979. 420p.

A collection of twenty-two essays designed to acquaint foreign specialists and the interested general public with the state of political science in Poland. The leading theme is the development of a socialist society in specifically Polish conditions Essays of particular merit include: 'The history of the Polish United Workers Party' by Andrzej Werblan; 'The Polish party system' by Wiesław Skrzydło; 'The political culture' by Włodzimierz Wesołowski; 'The international peace problems by Marian Dobrosielski; 'The unity of the world working class' by Janusz Gołębiowski; and 'State of research of modern Marxist theory' by Kazimier Opałek. Other essays deal with the nature of socialist democracy, the role of law the future of the socialist movement, and the socialist concept of human right and liberties.

665 **Present-day philosophy: anthology.**
Warsaw: Państwowe Wydawnictwo Naukowe, 1979. 640p.

A selection of representative studies of Polish contemporary philosophy and socia thought. All the major trends and centres of learning are included and historica aspects are discussed as well as current problems.

666 **Higher education in Poland.**
Seymour Rosen, Nellie M. Apanasiewicz. Washington, DC Office of Education, 1963-64. 2 vols. vi+38p. 81p. maps. diagrams. illus.

Volume one is entitled *Organization and administration* and volume two *Rules o admissions, student activities and curriculum*. The work includes charts and stat istics, and is useful for both the researcher and the prospective student in Poland.

667 **Polish analytical philosophy: a survey and comparison with British analytical philosophy.**
Henryk Skolimowski. London: Routledge & Kegan Paul; New York: Humanities Press, 1967. ix+275p.

A comparative analysis of Polish philosophy 1895-1960, which concentrates on the writings of Ajdukiewicz, Kotarbiński, Łukasiewicz, Tarski, Tatarkiewicz and Twardowski.

668 **The Sovietization of culture in Poland.**
Paris: Mid-European Research and Planning Centre, 1953. xiv+207p.

An English translation of the special issue of the Paris émigré Polish monthly *Kultura* published in 1952, and entitled *Ramy życia w Polsce* (The framework of life in Poland). Individual articles written by Polish émigré experts deal with several topics including: learning and education by Tadeusz Sulimirski; family life by Jan Szułdrzyński; publishing by Maria Danilewicz; agriculture by Stanisław Gryziewicz; public administration; justice; and finance. The Stalinist period which is covered in this publication is now known in Poland as the 'period of errors and distortions'.

669 **The Jagellonian University: a historical sketch.**
Wanda Stachiewicz. *Polish Review*, vol. 9, no.2 (1964), p. 89-112. bibliog.

A brief history of the oldest Polish university. The work was published on the occasion of the sixth centenary of the university's foundation by Casimir the Great. The same issue contains other contributions on various aspects of the activities of the university: memoirs; contacts with Bohemia; and biographies of prominent scholars.

670 **Bronisław Malinowski: an intellectual profile.**
Konstanty Symmons-Symonolewicz. *Polish Review*, vol. 3, no.3 (fall 1958), p. 55-76.

This article is the first of three papers published in the *Polish Review* which present a scholarly and human profile of this famous Polish social and cultural anthropologist. Malinowski was a professor at London University and founder of the functionalist school of social anthropology. The other two articles are entitled 'Bronisław Malinowski: formative influences and theoretical evolution' (vol. 4, no.4, fall 1959, p. 17-45) and 'Bronisław Malinowski: individuality as a theorist' (vol. 5, no.1, winter 1960, p. 53-65).

671 **The development of social sciences in Poland.**
Jan Szczepański. *Polish Perspectives*, vol. 23, no.1 (Jan. 1980), p. 13-17.

Summarizes the expansion of social science research in Poland during the last thirty five years. Major accomplishments have been recorded in several fields including: the changing class structure of Polish society under the impact of socialist ideology; the processes of transformation during the resettlement of the former German Northwestern territories; and industrialization and urbanization, and their demographic effects. The author also notes the trend towards a greater emphasis on the socioeconomic aspects of history.

672 **The state of sociology in Eastern Europe today.**
Edited by Jerzy J. Wiatr. Carbondale, Illinois: Southern Illinois Press, 1971. xiv+273p. bibliog.

An introductory guide to East European sociology which discusses: scholars; research centres; publications; the present state of sociology; and future prospects for the discipline. Controversial opinions are presented without any attempt to achieve unanimity. The sections on Poland (p. 97-137 and p. 249-254) were written by Władysław Markiewicz. The editor of this miscellaneous volume also wrote a pamphlet entitled *Past and present of Polish sociology* (Wrocław, Poland: Ossolineum, 1974. 23p.) as part of the series of reports of conferences (no.64) organized by the Polish Library in Rome. This pamphlet deals with: the development of Polish sociology in relation to the cultural tradition of the nation; the development of sociological methods reflecting political changes; and forecasts of future developments.

Poland: its people, its society, its culture.
See item no. 1.

Poland from inside: a symposium.
See item no. 5.

Poland: the country and its people.
See item no. 10.

Polish research guide.
See item no. 809.

The Review of the Polish Academy of Sciences.
See item no. 865.

Literature

Literary history and criticism

673 Under pressure: the writer in society; Eastern Europe and the USA.
A. Alvarez. Baltimore, Maryland: Penguin, 1965. 189p.
Assesses the current position of writers in Poland compared with those in Czechoslovakia, Hungary, Yugoslavia, and the United States.

674 Fiction and drama in Eastern and Southeastern Europe: evolution and experiment in the post-war period.
Edited by Henrik Birnbaum, Thomas Eekman. Los Angeles: University of California Press, 1980. 463p.
A collection of papers dealing in particular with the relationship between tradition and innovation (connection versus contraposition) in literature in East European countries.

675 For Wiktor Weintraub: essays in Polish literature, language, and history presented on the occasion of his 65th birthday.
Edited by Victor Erlich. The Hague: Mouton, 1975. (Slavistic Printings and Reprintings Series).

676 Polish poetry during the last war.
Zbigniew Folejewski. *Slavic Review*, vol. 10, no.3 (1951), p. 216-25.
In spite of difficulties of communication during the Second World War, Polish language and literature retained its basic unity in the homeland and in the lands of the diaspora.

677 **Socialist realism in Polish literature and criticism.**
Zbigniew Folejewski. *Comparative Literature*, vol. 12, no.1 (1959), p. 565-76.

The first decade of the existence of the Polish People's Republic was characterized by a strong Soviet influence in the fields of literary and artistic creativness
and criticism. This trend, represented by such authors as Stefan Żółkiewski, was
short-lived, however, and only had a limited long-term impact on Polish literature.
The author is professor of Polish literature at the University of British Columbia.

678 **Notes on the novel in contemporary Poland.**
Zbigniew Folejewski. *Canadian Slavonic Papers*, vol. 13, no.4 (1971), p. 299-313.

The achievements of Polish prose during the decade 1960-70 were considerably
less spectacular than those of poetry or drama. The themes which are especially
considered in this article are the experiences of the Second World War and the
sociopolitical transformations which took place in the post-war period and the
influence of both on Polish literature. Reference is also made to the impact of
Soviet realism and Western literary prose on the Polish novel.

679 **Polish historical novel.**
Xenia Gąsiorowska. *Comparative Literature*, vol. 9 (winter 1957), p. 17-32.

The genre of the historical novel represents one of the main veins of Polish
literature, and in the late 19th century its major representative was without any
doubt the Nobel Prize Winner, Henryk Sienkiewicz (1846-1916). In the 20th
century the struggle and suffering in Poland during the Second World War
offered a theme for post-war Polish historical prose which was fully developed
during the period 1945-55.

680 **Polish exile poetry and Polish exile prose.**
Mieczysław Giergielewicz, Alexander Janta. *Queens Slavic Papers*, vol. 1 (1973), p. 8-24 and p. 25-52.

Many prominent poets and writers escaped from Poland after the German inva-
sion and after the end of the Second World War either returned to their home-
land or remained (and often died) abroad. The most prominent of these were: Jan
Lechón, Maria Jasnorzewska, Antoni Słonimski, Julian Tuwim, Kazimierz Wie-
rzyński, Józef Wittlin, Czesław Miłosz, Józef Łobodowski, Jerzy Pietrkiewicz,
Ferdynand Goetel, Zygmunt Nowakowski, Wacław Grubiński, Arkady Fiedler,
Maria Kuncewiczowa, Melchior Wańkowicz, Gustaw Herling-Grudziński, Witold
Gombrowicz and Tymon Terlecki.

681 **A survey of Polish literature and culture.**
Manfred Kridl, translated by Olga Scherer-Virski. New
York: Columbia University Press, 1956. viii+525p. bibliog.
Reprinted, Hague: Mouton, 1967.

A history of Polish literature from the earliest times to the Second World War by
the one-time professor of Polish literature at Columbia University.

682 A history of Polish literature.
Julian Krzyżanowski, translated by Doris
Ronowicz. Warsaw: Państwowe Wydawnictwo Naukowe,
1979. 809p. illus. bibliog.

A definitive history of Polish literature by an erudite and versatile writer, whose lively style ensures pleasant reading. The volume represents the work of a lifetime and contains a wealth of information which is carefully appraised. Polish literature is discussed against the background of changing cultural and social conditions, which in each period influenced language and literature. The author considers Poland's literary contribution to world civilization and the place of Polish literature within the European family of *belles lettres*. In addition to being a professor of Polish literature at the University of Warsaw, the author taught this subject at the University of London, and at Columbia University in New York.

683 Life and culture of Poland as reflected in Polish literature.
Wacław Lednicki. New York: Roy, 1944. xi+328p.

The author presents Polish literature as a mirror reflecting the national character, and political and socioeconomic ideas as well as cultural and religious beliefs. This work consists of a series of lectures delivered by this prominent Polish and Slavic scholar and is valuable both for the specialist and the general reader.

684 Contemporary Polish poetry, 1925-1975.
Madeleine G. Levine. Boston, Massachusetts: Twayne,
1981. 195p. bibliog.

A lucid discussion of ten well-chosen poets representative of this period (Baczyński, Białoszewski, Gajcy, Grochowiak, Harasymowicz, Herbert, Miłosz, Przyboś, Różewicz and Szymborska). According to the author the importance of Polish poetry is wide-ranging and indeed it conditions the understanding of the Polish national spirit and ideological identity.

685 Literary studies in Poland.
Wrocław, Poland: Ossolineum, 1978-1980. 6 vols.

This multi-volume work was sponsored by the Institute of literary research of the Polish Academy of Sciences and is in English and French. Vol. 1, *Theory of literature in Poland* (1978. 181p.) contains articles on past and present Polish literature, and research in the fields of literary folklore, literary history, and the history of ideas; vol. 2, *Sociology of literature in Poland* (1978. 170p.) is a collection of essays on the wide appeal of Polish writers and the sociology of literature in Poland; vol. 3, *Renaissance-Baroque* (1979. 186p.) examines Renaissance literature in Poland, theatre and drama in the Baroque period, and the poetry of Mikołaj Sęp Szarzyński; vol. 4, *The Age of Enlightenment* (1979. 161p.) contains contributions on the literary aspects of the Polish Enlightenment, the writer and the literary culture of the Enlightenment period and Rococo literature in Poland; vol. 5, *Romanticism* (1980. 194p.) contains outline articles on the place of Polish Romanticism in the European literature of the period, and on the Romantic history, epic and style of life; and vol. 6, *Positivism* (1980. 132p.) discusses the dialectics of Polish positivists, Polish literary realism and naturalism in Polish literature.

686 Contemporary Polish writers.
Ryszard Matuszewski. Warsaw: Polonia, 1959. 290p. ports. bibliog.

Provides literary portraits of twenty-four Polish writers who were active during the inter-war and post-war periods. The volume also includes an introductory essay containing a brief characterization of Polish literature in the past. The last chapter draws a picture of the post- and inter-war periods as a whole.

687 The history of Polish literature.
Czesław Miłosz. New York: Macmillan, 1969. xviii+570p.

A readable, vividly written book, full of surprising curiosities. It includes a discussion of Polish literature in Latin as well as sections on the Lithuanian, Belorussian and Ukrainian literatures within the Polish Commonwealth of Nations. The work is organized according to traditional period subdivisions and by genre. The author, a Nobel Prize winner for literature, is a poet and an essayist as well as a historian of literature and a professor of Polish literature at the University of California at Berkeley. In this volume, he also discusses the Polish literary tradition, its significance in the world context, its peripheral and anachronistic characteristics and its artistic and aesthetic values.

688 Polish literature and the 'Thaw'.
Lawrence L. Thomas. *American Slavic and East European Review*, vol. 18, no.3 (Oct. 1959), 395p.

The Polish national character, and consequently Polish literature, display certain permanent features. These ensure the continued existence of at least some unbroken minds and free spirits in the face of political repression.

The tradition of Polish ideals: essays in history and literature.
See item no. 7.

The literatures of the world in English translations: a bibliography; Volume 2: the Slavic literatures.
See item no. 826.

Pamiętnik Literacki: Czasopismo kwartalne poświęcone historii i krytyce literatury polskiej. (Literary Diary: a quarterly journal devoted to the history and criticism of Polish literature.)
See item no. 880.

Przegląd Humanistyczny. (Humanities Review.)
See item no. 884.

Twórczość: Miesięcznik Literacko-Krytyczny. (The Creativeness: a monthly journal of Literary Criticism.)
See item no. 890.

Życie Warszawy. (The Life of Warsaw.)
See item no. 894.

Individual writers

689 Wacław Berent, his life and work.
Joachim T. Baer. *Antemurale*, vol. 18 (1974), p. 75-239.
An analysis of the artistic craftsmanship of the Polish fiction writer Wacław Berent (1873-1940). The author also discusses Berent's method of presentation, his symbolic use of the language, and his approach to life. This article comprehensively assesses Berent's place in Polish literature and among contemporary writers.

690 Selected writings of August Cieszkowski.
Edited and translated with an introduction by André Liebich. Cambridge, Cambridge University Press, 1979. 173p.
Cieszkowski, a 19th-century Polish philosopher, historian and statesman, interpreted history as an organic whole, and not as an agglomeration of accidental events. His concept of history was deeply religious and he also assigned an important role to religion in social life and in his attempt to anticipate future events in the light of the past.

691 Maria Dąbrowska.
Zbigniew Folejewski. New York: Twayne, 1963. 123p.
A portrait of Maria Dąbrowska, the contemporary grande dame of Polish literature, who is a prosaist, essayist, translator, and author of children's books. Folejewski's emphasis is on Dąbrowska's most valuable accomplishment - her novels and stories. He places this in the broader context of world literature, relating her achievements to the Polish national tradition but also to the European realism of the turn of the century. In her works Dąbrowska glorifies individual values as opposed to historical determinism and makes aesthetics coexist with morality. Includes a critical analysis of her language and style.

692 Alexander Fredro and his anti-Romantic memoirs.
Wiktor Weintraub. *Slavic and East European Review,*. vol. 12, no.4 (1953), p. 535-48.
Fredro (1793-1876), a co-founder of the Polish theatre, came before the Romantic poets, and in his writings he avoided direct involvement in the controversy between the Classicists and the Romantics. Unlike the three great Romantic poets, he actively participated in the Napoleonic wars in the army of the Duchy of Warsaw, and then in the French imperial army itself.

693 Witold Gombrowicz.
Ewa Thompson (Majewska). New York: Twayne, 1979. 171p. bibliog.
A balanced biographical account of this widely-known contemporary Polish author. Gombrowicz does not belong to any single literary school, but is generally considered to be a master of paradox. Although he spent many years in Argentina and France he has exercised a great influence on Polish literature. His pre-existentialist prose, grotesque and colourful, assures him a unique place in Polish literature and attracts increasing attention both in Poland and abroad.

694 Jan Kochanowski.
David Welsh. New York: Twayne, 1974. 160p.

A brief portrait which discusses the life and works of Kochanowski (1530-84) the most prominent Polish poet of the Old Polish-Renaissance era. He was the most important literary figure of his period among the Slavs and the first to elevate the Polish literary language to the Western European level of expression.

695 Joseph Conrad: a critical biography.
Jocelyn Baines. New York: McGraw-Hill, 1960. 523p. bibliog. Reprinted, Chester Springs, Pennsylvania: Dufour, 1965. 507p. and London: Weidenfeld & Nicolson, 1969. 507p.

A well-written, detailed and accurate biography which makes use of many hitherto untapped sources. The author provides a full account of the life and creative work of the great Anglo-Pole Joseph Conrad-Korzeniowski (1857-1924). Gerard Jean-Aubry has produced another biography of Conrad entitled *The sea-dreamer: a definitive biography of Joseph Conrad* (Hamden, Connecticut: Shoe String Press, 1967. 321p.) but although this work is the result of a lifetime's devotion to the subject it is a rather dry and unromantic book full of facts but lacking literary criticism. The *Polish Review* (vol. 20, nos.2-3, 1975, p. 5-222) published the proceedings of the International Conference of Conrad Scholars at the University of California at San Diego, August-September 1974 under the title *Joseph Conrad: commemorative essays*. This volume contains 'Conradiana' by British, US, French and Russian writers. In addition Józef Hieronim Retinger has written *Conrad and his contemporaries* (New York: Roy, 1943. 182p.) which contains admirable pen and ink sketches by Feliks Topolski.

696 Ignacy Krasicki.
David Welsh. New York: Twayne, 1969. 150p.

Krasicki (1735-1801), the prince-bishop of Warmia, was the most important figure of the Stanislavian period in Polish literature (at the end of the 18th century), and one of the outstanding personalities of his age. He made the first attempt to reconcile positive native traditions with the progressive, imported innovations of the Enlightenment.

697 Zygmunt Krasiński, romantic universalist: an international tribute.
Edited by Wacław Lednicki. New York: The Polish Institute of Arts and Sciences, 1964. 228p.

A profile of Krasiński (1812-59) one of the greatest poets of the Romantic period. This book is edited by a once prominent Polish Slavist, who used to teach at the University of California at Berkeley.

698 Bolesław Leśmian: the poet and his memory.
Rochelle Heller Stone. Berkeley, California: University of California Press, 1976. xi+364p.

A monograph about one of the greatest 20th-century Polish poets, whose creative genius has been more fully recognized during the last few decades. This is a study of his poetic magic, his motifs, and his remarkable ability to transform single words rendering them richer and more powerful. Leśmian's rhythm and verse, his use of paradox and the grotesque, and his adaptations of folk motives are also discussed. The reader of this thorough analysis must be impressed by Leśmian who is justly considered to be Poland's number one symbolist, and a master of the written word.

699 Adam Mickiewicz, poet of Poland: a symposium.
Edited by Manfred Kridl. New York: Columbia University Press, 1951. xii+292p. illus.

A collection of papers delivered at a symposium to mark the hundredth anniversary of Mickiewicz's death. The symposium was organized by Columbia University.

700 Adam Mickiewicz in world literature: a symposium.
Edited by Wacław Lednicki. Berkeley, California: University of California Press, 1956. xvi+626p. plates.

The essays brought together in this volume concern Mickiewicz's poetry and his place in the world of literature. Echoes and influences of Mickiewicz's (1798-1855) creative art are reported by prominent scholars from France, Italy, Switzerland, Germany, Belgium, Britain, the Netherlands, Scandinavia, the United States, Russia, Lithuania, the Ukraine, Czechoslovakia, Yugoslavia, Hungary, Romania and China.

701 The poetry of Adam Mickiewicz.
Wiktor Weintraub. The Hague: Mouton, 1954. 302p. bibliog.

A detailed analysis of the poetical work of Mickiewicz supplemented by biographical and historical data. The author is a retired professor of Polish literature at Harvard.

702 Adam Mickiewicz.
David Welsh. New York: Twayne, 1966. 168p.

This compact volume is one of a very useful universal biography series. The individuality and the literary art of Poland's greatest poet are presented here in the most concise manner possible.

703 Adam Mickiewicz, 1798-1855: in commemoration of the centenary of his death.
Paris: Unesco, 1955. x+295p. bibliog.

An officially sponsored publication containing selections from Mickiewicz's own writings, a brief biographical sketch, and contributions from prominent French, Italian, Russian, and other Slavic scholars dealing with Mickiewicz's fortunes in their respective countries. A bibliography of the principal translations of Mickiewicz's work into the major European languages is appended.

704 Czesław Miłosz: Nobel Prize winner.
Jerzy Lisowski. *Polish Perspectives*, vol. 24, no.1 (1981), p. 55-57.

After thirty years of ostracism the deep sociopolitical transformations that are taking place in Poland restored Miłosz to his natural audience: the Polish nation.

Literature. Individual writers

In addition to being a poet, an essayist and literary critic, Miłosz is also a translator, and his recent venture in that field is a new Polish translation of the Bible.

705 **Andrzej Frycz Modrzewski (1503-1572) and his book on war and peace.**
Waldemar Voisé. *Polish Western Affairs*, vol. 15, no.2 (1974), p. 188-99.

Modrzewski's *Commentatiorum de Republica emendanda libri quinque* contains an explicit condemnation of war, which he describes as the greatest calamity of mankind, bringing only suffering and death. In the third part of his work, 'The Book of War', however, he makes a distinction between agressive hostilities and defensive or just wars. It is worth noting that, unlike Modrzewski, other prominent writers like Krzysztof Warszewicki or Stanisław Trembecki did not consider offensive wars against non-Christians to be just. The author also includes a general discussion of the ideas on war expounded by such thinkers as Paweł Włodkowic, Stanisław of Skarbimierz and Biernat of Lublin.

706 **Adam Naruszewicz: a 'committed' poet.**
David Welsh. *Antemurale*, vol. 19 (1975), p. 85-90.

Considers the work of Adam Naruszewicz (1733-96) in the context of both the milieu of the Stanislavian era and the Polish literature of the Enlightenment.

707 **Cyprian Norwid.**
George Gömöri. New York: Twayne, 1974. 162p. bibliog.

A fascinating study of this complex and perplexing Romantic poet, misunderstood and forgoetten by his contemporaries and restored to well-deserved greatness by Zenon Miriam Przesmycki in the 20th century. His use of the Polish language was ahead of his time, and the symbolism of his poetry was obscure and hard to grasp.

708 **Stanisław Orzechowski: the uneasy years, 1550-1559.**
Hanna Świderska. *Polish Review*, vol. 8, no.3 (summer 1963), p. 3-45.

This article forms part of an Oxford University dissertation on this well-known Polish writer who, although an ordained priest, spent most of his life at variance with the church. This challenge, the author points out, was limited to ritual and external matters, while Orzechowski remained doctrinally faithful.

709 **Jan Parandowski.**
George Harjan. New York: Twayne, 1971. 160p.

A brief account of the life and literary creativeness of this prominent writer and translator who was president of the Polish section of PEN Club. Parandowski's work was characterized by faith in man and the permanent values which have emerged during the course of history. He was particularly enchanted with the Mediterranean civilization and with the classics.

710 **Pasek as a historian.**
Maria A. J. Święcicka. *Antemurale*, vol. 20 (1976), p. 25-31.

The interesting, colourful and sincere memoirs of Jan Chryzostom Pasek, covering the period 1656-1688, are generally regarded as the best example of their kind in Polish literary history. In addition, they are also a valuable source of historical information. Pasek's memoirs have been published in two translations: by Maria Święcicka (Kościuszko Foundation, 1978), and by Catherine Leach (University of California Press, 1977).

711 **A Polish satanist: Stanisław Przybyszewski.**
Maria Kuncewicz. *Polish Review*, vol. 14, no.2 (spring 1969), p. 3-20.

A brief essay on this controversial leader (1868-1927) of Polish modernism who was known for his Bohemian way of life, and his dissolute behaviour. He considered sex to be the only motive of human actions, and claimed that an artist should be free from any duty or service, and responsible to no one.

712 **Władysław Stanisław Reymont.**
Jerzy R. Krzyżanowski. New York: Twayne, 1972. 170p. bibliog.

A popular monograph for the general reader. Reymont's literary work is placed in its historical and social context and the author also provides plot summaries and descriptions of major characters. Reymont won the Nobel Prize for literature in 1924 for his peasant saga *Chłopi*.

713 **Henryk Sienkiewicz.**
Mieczysław Giergielewicz. New York: Twayne, 1968. 192p. bibliog.

A highly recommended, objective and informative monograph on this leading prose writer. The author attempts to maintain a balance between the conservative view which considers Sienkiewicz (1846-1916) a national monument, and the revisionistic bid to belittle his art.

714 **Aleksander Świętochowski, 1848-1938.**
Zygmunt Szwejkowski. *Slavonic and East European Review*, vol. 19 (1940), p. 228-36.

Świętochowski was a prominent writer, critic, philosopher and historian of the Positivism period who was a theoretician of the 'work from the foundations' trend.

715 **The author of *Anhelli*.**
Francis J. Whitfield. *Slavic and East European Review*, vol. 8, no.4 (1949), p. 317-27.

An essay on the great Romantic poet, Juliusz Słowacki (1809-49), who is considered to be the principal adversary of Adam Mickiewicz in both art and life. The author is a distinguished professor of Polish and Slavic studies at the University of California at Berkeley. The Polish Research Center in New York published a memorial volume in honour of Słowacki entitled: *Juliusz Słowacki: the centenary volume, 1849-1949; a symposium* (1951. 448p.).

716 Witkacy: Stanislaw Ignacy Witkiewicz as an imaginative writer: criticism and interpretation.
Daniel Charles Gerould. Seattle, Washington: Washington University Press, 1981. 380p. illus. bibliog.

This is the first comprehensive critical study in English of one of Europe's outstanding modern playwrights who was one of the precursors of the theatre of the absurd. The *Polish Review* published a special issue (vol. 18, no.1-2, 1973. 157p.) containing contributions to a symposium held to 'explore Witkiewicz's place in the history of drama, his relationship to some of his famous contemporaries, his ideas and theories as expressed in his plays, and the interpretation of his works on the contemporary stage by American directors'. This special issue also contains a chronology of Witkiewicz's life and works.

717 The greatness and ill-fortune of Stanisław Wyspiański.
Tymon Terlecki. *Antemurale*, vol. 14 (1970), p. 259-77.

Wyspiański has a reputation as one of the most esoteric Polish writers, but his greatness lies in the fact that he is a prominent representative of Symbolism and he therefore deserves to be considered in a broader context. The same writer authored another article on Wyspiański entitled 'Wyspiański in two perspectives' (*Antemurale*, vol. 15, 1971, p. 299-315) in which he both explores the difficulties connected with translating Wyspiański works into foreign languages, and stresses that the scope of his writings is European and not merely Polish.

718 An analytical study of the early literary work of Stefan Żeromski, its cultural background and its critical reception in Poland.
Danuta Irena Bieńkowska. *Antemurale*, vol. 16 (1972), p. 187-316. bibliog.

Evaluates the ideological trends and aesthetical values of Żeromski's (1864-1925) works. Although generally regarded as one of the major representatives of Young Poland, Żeromski, in the author's view, remained a Romantic at heart. A chronological list of Żeromski's more important works is appended. In 1943 Edmund I. Zawacki published (*Slavic Review*, no. 56, p. 96) an article entitled 'The Utopianism of Stefan Żeromski' in which he expresses the opinion that the entire creative activity of Zeromski is permeated with Utopian hopes for a radical change in the social conditions of the working classes and for national liberation.

English translations

719 Tales by Polish authors.
Else Benecke. New York: Longman-Green, 1915. viii+198p.

Provides translations of Sienkiewicz, Sieroszewski, Szymański and Żeromski. The same translator also published *More tales by Polish authors* (Oxford: Blackwell,

1916. viii+288p.) containing English versions of works by Prus, Reymont, Siero-szewski, Szymański and Żeromski, and *Selected Polish tales* (Oxford: Blackwell, 1921. x+348+viiip.) with translations of Kaden-Bandrowski, Nałkowska, Prus, Reymont and Żeromski.

720 Specimens of Polish poets..
John Bowring. London: Baldwin, Cradock & Joy, 1827. xxi+227p.

Covers the entire Old Polish period from Bogurodzica to Niemcewicz.

721 The Polish land.
Marion Coleman (Moore). Trenton, New Jersey: White Eagle, 1943. xiii+127p. Rev. ed. Alliance College, Pennsylvania, 1974.

Reproduces poems and legends on various Polish regions, cities, rivers and mountains.

722 Bloods of their blood: an anthology of Polish American poetry.
Edited by Victor Contoski. New York: New Rivers Press, 1980. 126p.

This volume was published on the initiative of the American Council of Polish Cultural Clubs.

723 A Polish anthology.
T. M. Filip (*pseud.*). London: Duckworth, 1944. 405p.

Translations of Kochanowski, Krasiński, Malczewski, Mickiewicz, Norwid, Pawli-kowska-Jasnorzewska, Słowacki, Tuwim, Wyspiański and Żeromski.

724 Introduction to modern Polish literature: an anthology of fiction and poetry.
Adam Gillon, Ludwik Krżyzanowski. New York: Twayne, 1964. 480p.

An ambitious and comprehensive anthology of 20th-century Polish prose and verse. The quality of the translations is uneven and frequently there is undue emphasis on second-rate authors. Forty-seven writers are represented.

725 The new Polish poetry.
Milne Holton, Paul Vangelisti. Pittsburgh: University of Pittsburgh Press, 1978. xv+117p.

A bilingual anthology of fifty-five poems by Bursa, Grochowiak, Herbert, Różewicz and Szymborska. This work reflects the poetry of the 1970s generation, one of the most vital in Europe. The authors stress the disparity between poetry and reality.

Literature. English translations

726 **The modern Polish mind: an anthology.**
Maria Kuncewiczowa (Szczepańska). Boston,
Massachusetts: Little, Brown; London: Secker & Warburg,
1963. viii+440p. bibliog.
This volume represents a panorama of experiences of Polish intellectuals (émigré
writers not included). Translations of thirty-seven stories and essays by writers
and scholars are provided and every effort is made to reveal, without bias, what
Polish authors remember, how they see life, what they believe in and what they
laugh about.

727 **The broken mirror: a collection of writings from
contemporary Poland.**
Paweł Mayewski, introduction by Lionel Trilling. New
York: Random House, 1958. x+209p.
Reproduces the writings of Polish intellectuals, mostly living in Poland but including some émigrés, which reflect their struggle to correct creative distortions
caused by the need to adapt themselves to Polish reality.

728 **Postwar Polish poetry.**
Czesław Miłosz. Garden City, New York: Doubleday,
1965. 150p.
A highly competent selection of poetry, written by Poles at home and abroad,
mainly since 1956, translated into English. The anthology does not include the
works of Julian Tuwim, whose poetry the author considers to be untranslatable. The
work contains ninety poems by 21 authors, and the translations are mainly
by Miłosz who is himself a Nobel Prize winner. His selection illustrates both his
belief that Polish poetry has an intrinsic unity, unbroken by geographical dis-
tance, and his preference for positive, effective thinking as opposed to that form
of poetry, which indulges in negation and in a sterile anger.

729 **Polish authors of today and yesterday.**
Irena Morska. New York: Vanni, 1947. xvii+213p.
This volume provides translations of work by Gojawiczyńska, Orzeszkowa, Prus,
Rey, Reymont, Sienkiewicz and Żeromski.

730 **Ten contemporary Polish stories.**
Edmund Ordon, introduction by Olga
Scherer-Virski. Detroit, Michigan: Wayne State University
Press, 1958. xxix+252p.
Translations of both homeland and émigré writers including Choromański,
Dąbrowska, Gombrowicz, Hłasko, Kuncewiczowa, Bruno Schulz, Wierzyński and
Zawieyski.

731 **Five centuries of Polish poetry, 1450-1950.**
Jerzy Pietrkiewicz, Burns Singer. London: Secker &
Warburg, 1960; Philadelphia, Dufour, 1962. 154p. 2nd rev.
ed. Oxford: Oxford University Press, 1970. 138p. Reprinted,
Westport, Connecticut: Greenwood Press, 1979. xxx+138p.
(with new poems translated in collaboration with Jon
Stallworthy).

This beautifully produced volume reproduces very good examples of Polish poetry.
The translations were produced by a team including a known Polish poet and
professor of Polish at the University of London as well as an English poet.

732 **The modern Polish short story.**
Olga Scherer-Virski. The Hague: Mouton, 1955. x+266p.

The author covers the period from Romanticism to the Second World War and
discusses the Polish short story against the background of contemporary European
literature.

733 **Bitter harvest: the intellectual revolt behind the Iron Curtain.**
Edmund Stillman, introduction by François
Bondy. London: Thames & Hudson; New York: Praeger,
1959. xxxiii+313p.

Contains poems, short stories, and essays by East European (including Polish)
writers. They express dissent, and anger and frustration against the conditions
created by the Stalinist bureaucracy.

734 **Polish writing today.**
Celina Wieniewska. Baltimore, Maryland; Harmondsworth,
England: Penguin, 1967. 208p.

An anthology of eleven indigenous prose writers and poets.

The Arts

History and preservation of art

735 **The art of the Renaissance in Eastern Europe: Hungary, Bohemia, Poland.**
Jan Białostocki. Ithaca, New York: Cornell University Press, 1976. xxiv+312p. illus. bibliog.
A clear and expert presentation of the spread of Renaissance art to Central Eastern Europe, by a distinguished professor at the University of Warsaw. The author deals in detail with Tuscan and Northern Italian influence on the Mid-European architecture of the castle, church and town.

736 **Conservation and protection of historical treasures in People's Poland.**
Konstanty Kalinowski. *Polish Western Affairs*, vol. 15, no.1 (1974), p. 46-62.
The Polish authorities are directly responsible for conservation in several central municipal districts (Cracow, Warsaw, Toruń, Gdańsk) and entire towns (Zamość, Sandomierz, Kazimierz, Chełmno), and oversee 14 castles and palaces (Wawel, Malbork, Wilanów, Krzyżtopór, Łańcut etc.), 22 churches, many town halls, wooden synagogues, burgher houses, wind mills as well as Skansen outdoor rural museums (which gather together and protect scattered ancient rural objects). Conservation policies are also extended to: prehistoric and early historic settlements (Biskupin, Wiślica etc.); archaeological and historical sites; the natural environment; handicrafts; and archival and library materials. The 'Polish school of conservation' (known also for its achievements in many foreign countries) is characterized by some specific policy principles including: the removal of later additions in reconstructed objects; the reconstruction of entire districts in the style of one epoch to retain its harmony; and the incorporation of the reconstructed districts into the contemporary environment. The author is the professor of the history of modern art at the University of Poznań.

737 **Polish art.**
Stefan Kozakiewicz. In: *New Catholic Encyclopaedia.* New York: McGraw-Hill, 1967. vol. 11, p. 490-97.
A brief but clear profile of the general history of Polish art by this well-known late professor of Warsaw University.

738 **Renaissance in Poland.**
Stefan Kozakiewicz, Helena Kozakiewicz. Warsaw: Arkady, 1977. 332p. illus. bibliog.
A profusely illustrated monograph and album on the Renaissance and Mannerism periods in Poland. The author covers all branches of art and indicates the characteristic Polish variants of each style. This work is part of a series which will eventually cover each period of Polish artistic history and the following volumes are now being compiled: *Romanesque art in Poland* by Zygmunt Swiechowski; *The Gothic in Poland* by Tadeusz Dobrzeniecki; *The Baroque in Poland* by Mariusz Karpowicz; and *Neo-Classicism in Poland* by Stanisław Lorentz and Andrzej Rottermund.

739 **The art of Poland.**
Irena Piotrowska (Głębocka). New York: Philosophical Library, 1947. iv+238p. illus. bibliog.
A useful introductory work with chapters on architecture, painting, sculpture, graphic arts, decorative arts, folk art, and conservation.

740 **Protection of historical monuments in Poland.**
Jan Zachwatowicz, translated by Christine Cenkalska. Warsaw: Polonia, 1965. 147p. illus.
This brief book, written by a prominent historian of Polish architecture, describes the organizational framework of the conservation and reconstruction of buildings of artistic and historical value in Poland, and lists the most important historical town centres, castles, manors, churches, etc.

Biuletyn Historii Sztuki. (History of Art Bulletin.)
See item no. 870.

Cracow, city of museums: the most beautiful works of art from seven museums.
See item no. 895.

Guide to museums and collections in Poland.
See item no. 900.

The National Museum in Cracow: the Czartoryski collection; a historical outline and selected objects, Album.
See item no. 901.

Visual arts

Architecture

741 Atlas of Warsaw's architecture.
Juliusz Chrościcki, Andrzej Rottermund. Warsaw: Arkady, 1978. 248p. illus. maps.
This book is divided into three parts which provide: a history of Warsaw's architecture and urban development; a street by street catalogue of historical and contemporary buildings; and a pictorial album.

742 The architecture of Poland: a historical survey.
Zbigniew Dmochowski. London: Polish Research Centre, 1956. xxvi+429p. illus.
A comprehensive history of Polish architecture, with emphasis on the period before the Second World War.

743 The architecture of Poland.
Brian Knox. New York: Praeger, 1971. 161p. illus. maps. bibliog.
A highly recommended and attractively published book on the architecture of Poland within its post-1945 borders. The work is profusely illustrated and has 216 excellent pictures of churches, castles, palaces, town plans, etc. The narrative is chronological by region and begins with the Middle Ages.

744 Guide to architecture in Poland.
Jerzy Zygmunt Łoziński, Adam Miłobędzki. Warsaw: Polonia, 1967. 286p. illus. maps.
Examines the historical development of architecture in Poland and provides a list of architectural monuments, organized by place. Professor Łoziński is in charge of an enormous project the aim of which is to produce a national inventory of all Polish art treasures.

745 The royal cathedral at Wawel.
Michał Rożek. Warsaw: Interpress, 1981. 400p. illus.
A history of the ancient cathedral of the Polish kings located near Wawel castle. In the cathedral there are preserved the most precious treasures of Poland's heritage and tradition collected during the millennial history of the country.

746 Polish architecture.
Jan Zachwatowicz, translated by Marek Latyński. Warsaw: Arkady, 1967. 526p. 346 plates.
A beautifully produced and well-translated history of Polish architecture divided into the eight classical periods of art history. The author participated in the preservation and reconstruction of many of the important monuments of Polish

architecture, including the old town in Warsaw, for which Poland became so famous.

Painting

747 **Bernardo Bellotto.**
Stefan Kozakiewicz. London: Elek; New York: Graphic, 1972. 2 vols. illus. bibliog.

A consideration of the life and work of this Italian painter (1720-80) who worked in Warsaw. His twenty-six views of Warsaw made possible the reconstruction of the old town and the royal tract of the Polish capital as they were in 18th-century.

748 **Polish painting from the Enlightenment to recent times.**
Edited by Tadeusz Dobrowolski. Wrocław, Poland: Ossolineum, 1982.

An album of colour and black and white illustrations.

749 **Buckingham Palace panoramas.**
Feliks Topolski. London: Quartet Books, 1977. 112p. illus. (distributed by Horizon Press).

Reproduces pictures of the British Royal coronation by this famous Polish artist. The book includes a biographical essay on Topolski by Peter Ford, and an essay on Topolski's art by Bernard Denvir.

750 **Contemporary Polish painting: trends, goals, works.**
Aleksander Wojciechowski. Warsaw: Interpress, 1977. 188p. illus.

An examination of the developments in Polish painting, 1944-74. The author describes the increase of creative activities and the effort to reconcile originality and the uniqueness of the individual artist with the social goal of disseminating art experiences as widely as possible. The work also considers art and the state, and art and technology and separate chapters deal with various trends including those labelled: historicist; neo-romantic; expressionist; constructivist; pop-art; grotesque; and neo-primitive. There are 128 illustrations.

751 **Contemporary Polish painting.**
Jerzy Zanoziński. Warsaw: Arkady, 1975. 141p. illus.

A biographical guide to contemporary painters which briefly recounts their individual characteristics. The author also provides a preliminary discussion of contemporary Polish painting and its various trends. Includes sixty-three coloured reproductions.

Sculpture

752 **Contemporary Polish sculpture.**
Hanna Kotkowska-Bareja. Warsaw: Interpress, 1974. 158p. illus.

A richly illustrated album containing an introductory essay followed by bio-bibliographical sketches of major contemporary Polish sculptors.

753 **Contemporary Polish sculpture.**
Andrzej Osęka, Wojciech Skrodzki. Warsaw: Arkady, 1978. 160p. illus.

After an introductory essay on the general style of Polish sculpture, the book describes various trends and concepts that predominate at present. The inspiration of Polish sculptors is derived from folk art as well as from individual visions. Includes biographical notes on fifty major sculptors.

Graphic arts

754 **Polish poster today.**
Szymon Bojko. Warsaw: Agencja Autorska, 1972. 168p. illus. bibliog.

Polish poster art is internationally respected and Poland is the home of both the International Poster Biennale and the world's first poster museum. This volume provides a history of Polish poster art and a catalogue of fifty two artists including Tadeusz Cieślewski, Henryk Tomaszewski, Waldemar Swierzy, Franciszek Starowieyski and Roman Cieślewicz. Each entry has a brief biography and reproduces samples of the artist's work. Another interesting book is *The Polish Poster* (Krajowa Agencja Wydawnicza, 1979. 216p. illus.) which is an album of political, theatrical, musical, film, exhibition, commercial, tourist, sport and circus posters exhibited at the Poster Biennales in Warsaw since 1966. In addition Stanisław Szczuka's (ed.) *Polish Poster* (Warsaw: Agpol, 1977) is also of value. This work is a folder of thirty colour plates depicting a selection of the best posters (political, travel, business, cinema, theatre, social relations, traditional and avant-garde) produced during the period 1965-75.

755 **Contemporary graphic art.**
Irena Jakimowicz. Warsaw: Arkady, 1975. 253p. illus.

A thorough survey of the history of the graphic arts in Poland since 1945 with references to the inter-war period. The author discusses the works of all the artists, who made a significant contribution to the development of graphic arts and provides bio-bibliographical information.

Decorative arts

756 Decorative arts in Poland.
Adam Bochnak, Kazimierz Buczkowski. Warsaw: Arkady,
1972. 30p. of text. 341 plates.
This book covers jewellery, metal work, armour, stained glass and furniture made
in Poland, or commissioned by Poles abroad, during the Romanesque, Gothic,
Renaissance, Baroque, Rococo, Neoclassical and Biedermeier periods.

757 The Flemish tapestries at Wawel Castle in Cracow.
Edited by Jerzy Szablowski. Antwerp, Belgium:
Mercatorfonds, 1972. 506p. illus. bibliog.
A particularly fine book which consists of a number of articles dealing with the
unique collection of 16th-century tapestries made to order in Flanders for King
Sigismund II Augustus Jagellonian of Poland. The tapestries were woven to fit
the exact dimensions of the walls of individual rooms in the castle. At the time of
their execution the Flemish art of tapestry weaving was at its height. The articles
are by Belgian and Polish scholars.

Performing arts

Music

**758 Music of the Polish Renaissance: a selection of works from
the 16th to the beginning of 17th centuries.**
Józef Chomiński, Zofia Lissa, translated by Claire
Dąbrowska. Kraków, Poland: Polskie Wydawnictwo
Muzyczne, 1955. 370p. illus.
A collective work by well-known Polish musicologists which also contains facsi-
miles of musical scores.

759 Treasured Polish songs with English translations.
Edited by Josepha K. Contoski. Minneapolis, Minnesota:
Polanie, 1953. 352p. illus.
A selection of anthems, military songs, highland songs, lullabies, Christmas carols,
hymns, ballads and humorous songs.

760 Music in Poland.
Ludwik Erhardt. Warsaw: Interpress, 1974. 192p. illus.
An outline history of Polish music from its origins to the present day, by a
well-known music critic who is editor-in-chief of *Ruch Muzyczny*. The author
considers Polish music in the context of its European background, and describes
currents in Polish music, recent musical publications, music schools, festivals and
competitions.

761 **The golden book of Polish songs: a collection of best known Polish songs.**
Adam Harasowski.   London: Księgarnia Polska Alma, 1955. 191p.

One hundred and thirty songs written for piano accompaniment together with twenty choral arrangements. The original version was in Polish with an English translation.

762 **Polish music.**
Edited by Stefan Jarociński.   Warsaw: Państwowe Wydawnictwo Naukowe, 1965. viii+327p. illus. map.

A miscellanea of articles on various periods of Polish musical history, Polish musical life, composers and folk music. The *Musical Quarterly* dedicated a special issue to a survey of contemporary European music (vol. 51, Jan. 1965) to which this author contributed 'Polish music after World War II' (p. 244-58).

763 **An outline of Polish music.**
Tadeusz Ochlewski, translated by M. Mierowska-Paszkiewicz.   Warsaw: Interpress, 1979. 198p. illus. bibliog.

A history of Polish music arranged according to period. The volume examines: modern Polish music; music study and teaching; orchestras; competitions; publications; and archives and museums. This book is one of the official profiles of various aspects of Polish life intended for the foreign reader.

764 **Merrily we sing: 105 Polish folksongs.**
Herriet M. Pawłowska, with an analysis of music by Grace L. Engel.   Detroit, Michigan: Wayne State University Press, 1961. xi+284p.

A selection of folk-songs sung in the United States by immigrants from various regions of Poland. The Polish text is accompanied by an English translation which attempts to preserve, whenever possible, the spirit and metric pattern of the original, although this is sometimes achieved at the expense of the rhyme.

765 **Chopin.**
Arthur Hedley.   London: Dent, 1963. 222p. illus.

A masterly and evocative account of Chopin's life and the development of his character which emphasizes Chopin's uniqueness.

766 **Frédéric Chopin: profile of the man and the musician.**
Edited by Alan Walker.   London: Barrie & Rockliff; New York: Taplinger, 1966. 350p. illus. bibliog.

An excellent all-around study of Chopin's life, character and music. A collective work with ten participants.

767 **The life and death of Chopin.**
Kazimierz Wierzyński, foreword by Arthur Rubinstein,
translated by Norbert Guterman. New York: Simon &
Schuster, 1949. xvi+444p. illus. bibliog. Reprinted, 1971.
One of the best books on Chopin, and certainly the best written by Wierzyński, a
writer and compatriot of Chopin. The emphasis is on Chopin's youth, family life,
patriotism and the cultural pattern of his life and the approach is that of a
writer's and not a musicologist. Wierzyński also shared with Chopin the nostalgic
feeling of an expatriate intellectual.

768 **Chopin: a new biography.**
Adam Zamoyski. New York: Doubleday; London: Collins,
1980. 374p. illus. bibliog.
A perceptive and witty biography which dispels the Romantic aura that surrounds
Poland's greatest composer and gives a clear exposition of his creative genius and
personal life. The author does not pretend to provide an in-depth analysis of
Chopin's works but stresses the composer's life-long connection with the Polish
cause. Includes a complete list of Chopin's works arranged by date.

769 **Lutosławski and his music.**
Steven Stucky. New York: Cambridge University Press,
1981. 252p. illus. bibliog.
An accurate and critical assessment of the musical contribution of this great
contemporary composer is accompanied by a biographical sketch.

770 **Moniuszko: father of Polish opera.**
Bogusław Maciej Maciejewski, foreword by Sir Lennox
Berkeley. London: Poets' and Painters' Press, 1979. 156p.
After Chopin, Moniuszko (1819?-72) is the second major representative of
Romanticism in Polish music. Although he composed songs, folk dances and
sacred music, it is for his operas that he is best remembered. His operas included
Halka (Annette), *Hrabina* (The countess), *Verbum noble* (Gentleman's word),
and *Straszny dwór* (The haunted manor) which is considered to be his master-
piece.

771 **Ignacy Jan Paderewski: a political biography.**
Marian Marek Drozdowski. Warsaw: Interpress, 1981.
288p.
Examines the life and career of this famous pianist, composer, Polish representative at the League of Nations and prime minister. His political ideas were akin to
those of the Christian Democrats.

772 **My young years.**
Arthur Rubinstein. London: Knopf, 1980. 512p.
The volume cited above together with a second volume entitled *My Many Years*
(London: Knopf, 1980. 640p.) form an autobiographical account of the life of this
great Polish pianist and patriot who is generally acclaimed as the successor to
Paderewski. When the United Nations was founded at San Francisco in 1945,
with only Poland conspicuously absent from the constitutional assembly, Rubin-

stein, who was asked to play an introductory prelude, chose to play Chopin's Revolutionary Etude.

773 **Leopold Stokowski: a profile.**
Abram Chasins. London: Dutton, 1979. Reprinted, New York: Da Capo. 1981. xvii+313p. illus.
Of mixed Polish-Irish parentage, Leopold Antoni Stanisław Stokowski (b.1887) was one of the most prestigious orchestral directors of all time. He was universally appreciated for his musical interpretations and commanded tremendous personal prestige. His transcriptions of Bach and his music for Walt Disney's *Fantasia* are especially famous.

774 **Karol Szymanowski: his life and music.**
Bogusław Maciej Maciejewski. London: Poets' and Painters' Press, 1967. 148p. illus. bibliog.
A pioneering biographical essay on this great Polish composer, who during the inter-war years attempted to 'modernize' Polish music. The Kościuszko Foundation sponsored the publication of a photographic album tracing the musical career of Szymanowski compiled by Teresa Chylińska (New York: Twayne, 1973. 228p. illus. bibliog.).

775 **The music of Szymanowski.**
Jim Samson. New York: Taplinger, 1981. 220p. bibliog.
A major study of this great Polish composer, who is now achieving wide recognition abroad. Szymanowski fostered a national school of musical composition which attempted to purge Polish music from foreign influence.

The tradition of Polish ideals: essays in history and literature.
See item no. 7.

Polish Music.
See item no. 856.

Theatre

776 **The Polish theatre.**
Edward Csató. Warsaw: Polonia, 1963. 172p. illus.
An introductory outline which needs to be supplemented by more recent publications covering the last twenty years, a period which has been rich in new developments and achievements.

777 **Twentieth century Polish theatre.**
Bohdan Drozdowski, translated by Catherine Itzin. London: Calder, 1980. 256p. illus.
This book was previously published as a special double issue no. 33-34 of the *International Theatre Review Gambit* in collaboration with the Warsaw monthly *Dialog*. The work contains essays and other contributions by prominent Polish theatre critics and writers like Konstanty Puzyna, Stanisław Witkiewicz, and by

theatre directors like Józef Szajna, Tadeusz Kantor, Andrzej Wajda and Jerzy Grotowski. Also includes a bibliography of Polish drama.

778 Contemporary Polish theatre.
Witold Filler, translated by Krystyna Keplicz. Warsaw: Interpress, 1977. 128p. illus. bibliog.

A popular guide to Polish theatre by a well-known critic. The author describes various types and aspects of theatre arts (avant-garde, cabaret, variety, television, student theatre) and provides a history of the Polish theatre and brief accounts of stage design, music, prominent artists and schools of dramatic arts.

779 The persistence of freedom: the sociological implications of Polish student theater.
Jeffrey C. Goldfarb. Westport, Connecticut: Westview Press, 1980. 156p. illus.

The cabaret and student theatre remain the strongholds of free expression for intellectuals in Poland. Be it 'Pod Baranami' in Cracow or 'Stodoła' in Warsaw, the rebel and freedom-loving spirit of Polish students has remained unconquered even in the darkest hours of repression.

780 Polish theatre directors.
August Grodzicki. Warsaw: Interpress, 1979. 188p. illus.

A collection of essays on leading contemporary stage directors (Jerzy Grotowski, Tadeusz Kantor, Józef Szajna, Andrzej Wajda and others) and their major achievements during the last thirty-five years. The author, a prominent theatre critic, offers a readable profile of the avant-garde theatre, whose standards are internationally recognized. This same Polish critic is also the author of a short history which covers: the Polish theatre and its main contemporary characteristics; stage designers; playwrights; puppet theatres; festivals; theatre schools and journals; and the opera, ballet, operetta, philharmonic and chamber music theatres. This book is entitled *Polish theatre today* (Authors' Agency, 1978. 64p. illus.). In addition Wydawnictwa Artystyczne i Filmowe of Warsaw published in 1963 an album of photos and designs entitled *Theatre in modern Poland* which included commentaries by Grodzicki.

781 Modjeska: her life and loves.
Antoni Gronowicz. New York: Yoseloff, 1956. 256p.

This book recounts the life and loves of this great Polish actress, who became famous in the United States and especially in California, in the last quarter of the 19th century. Modrzejewska (her real Polish name) was admired for the beauty of her recitation, her personal grace, her poetic attitude and the classic containment in her stage manner. The actress's autobiography *Memoirs and impressions* has also been published (Macmillan, 1910. ix+571p. illus.). According to some admirers, she was able to make her audience laugh or cry by modulating her voice while reciting the alphabet.

782 **The theatre in Poland.**
Roman Szydłowski. Warsaw: Interpress, 1972. 176p. illus.
bibliog.

An examination of the development of Polish post-war theatre (including television and experimental theatre) presented by a well-known critic. The book includes profiles of prominent directors, stage designers and playwrights.

783 **Theatre in Poland/Le théâtre en Pologne.**
Amsterdam: Elsevier, 1957. 56p. illus.

An introductory survey of the contemporary Polish theatre. This work was originally a special issue of the journal *Le Théâtre dans le Monde*.

Poland from inside: a symposium.
See item no. 5.

The Theatre in Poland.
See item no. 869.

Cinema

784 **Contemporary Polish cinematography.**
Władysław Banaszkiewicz (et al.). New York: W. S.
Heinman, 1963. 173p. illus.

The author considers pre-war Polish cinematography, feature and documentary films, prizes and awards, festivals, and the motion picture industry.

785 **Roman Polanski: a guide to references and resources.**
Gretchen Bisplinghoff. Boston, Massachusetts: Hall, 1979.
x + 116p. illus.

Discusses Polanski's motion pictures and their plots and themes. A bibliography is also included. Other publications on Polanski include Thomas Kiernan's *Roman Polanski: a biography* (New York: Grove Press, 1981), Barbara Leaning's *Polanski, his life and films* (New York: Simon & Schuster, 1982) and Ivan Butler's *The cinema of Roman Polanski* (New York: A. S. Barnes, 1970).

786 **Polish cinema.**
Jacek Fuksiewicz. Warsaw: Interpress, 1973. 166p. illus.

Deals with: the origins and the present organization of the motion picture industry; feature films; documentaries; television movies; and Polish participation in film festivals and the awards gained. The book also includes a who's who.

787 **Screen series, Eastern Europe: an illustrated guide.**
Nina Hibbin. London: Zwemmer; New Jersey: A. S.
Barnes, 1969. 230p. illus.

An attractive reference book which covers the film industry, film producers and movie stars in nine East European socialist countries, including Poland. This volume provides something akin to a who's who of the East European cinema.

788 **Contemporary Polish film.**
Stanisław Kuszewski.   Warsaw: Interpress, 1978. 138p.
illus.

An overview of the history of the Polish motion picture which concentrates on the last thirty years. Special emphasis is placed on the development of various schools and themes of art, statistics, festivals, prominent directors, and the setting of films within the national tradition and social context.

Polish Film.
See item no. 855.

Folklore, Folk-art and Customs

789 Old Polish legends.
Fay Sibyl Marie Anstruther, illustrated with wood engravings by Józef Sękalski. Glasgow: Polish Library, 1945. 66p.

In addition to the above work there have been several other editions of Polish folk tales, fairy tales, legends and sagas including: Elsie Byrde's *The Polish fairy book* (New York: Stokes, 1925. 226p. illus.); Aleksander Chodźko's *Fairy tales of Slav peasants and herdsmen* (London: Allen, 1906. xiii+353p. illus.); Antoni Józef Gliński's *Polish fairy tales* (London: Lane, 1920. xiii+96p. illus.); Virginia Hoveland's *Favorite fairy tales told in Poland* (Boston, Massachusetts: Little Brown, 1963. 90p. illus.); Lilian McCrea's *Polish folk tales and legends* (London: Pitman, 1959. vii+88p. illus.); Lucia Merecka Borski's (Szczepanowicz) *Polish folk tales* (New York: Sheed & Ward, 1947. 123p.); Suzanne Strowska's *The Polish folk tales* (London: Burns & Oates, 1929. vii+150p. illus.); Sigmund H. Uminski's *Tales of early Poland* (Chicago: Endurance, 1968); Stanisław Vincenz's *On the high uplands: sagas, songs, tales and legends of the Carpathians* (New York: Roy, 1955. 344p. illus. by Zdzisław Czermański); and Zoe Zajdler's *Polish fairy tales* (London: F. Muller, 1959. vii+190p.).

790 Song, dance and customs of peasant Poland.
Sula Benet, preface by Margaret Mead. London: Dobson; New York: Roy, 1952. 247p. plates. Reprinted, New York: AMS Press, 1979.

Provides an insight into the soul of the Polish peasant and his life. The author covers dress, melody, language and ethnography.

791 Z. D. Chodakowski and the discovery of folklife.
Peter Brock. *Polish Review*, vol. 21, no.1-2 (1976), p. 3-22.

Zorian Dołęga Chodakowski (real name: Adam Czarnocki) was a pioneer in the rediscovery of Slavic folk life, which he regarded as the mainspring of cultural regeneration. Several nationalistic and popular groups, rightists and leftists alike, adopted Chodakowski's enthusiasm for a common Slavic past and advocated his beliefs as if they were their own.

792 Folk art in Poland.

Irena Czarnecka. Warsaw: Polonia, 1957. 234p. illus.

A beautiful album on traditional Polish folk-art, and its recent revival in, for example, interior decoration, textile and ceramic patterns and costumes for dance ensembles.

793 Souvenir of Poland.

Teresa Kuczyńska. Warsaw: Interpress, 1978. illus.

An outline history of the associations for the encouragement of folk-art in Poland established since 1901 is followed by a pictorial guide to applied and decorative arts inspired by folk design. Various areas of souvenir art are discussed including: costumes; jewellery; earthenware; wooden objects; cloth; coloured paper clippings; and glass paintings.

794 Made in Poland: living traditions of the land.

Louise Llewellyn (Jarecka). New York: Knopf, 1949. 14+289+viip. bibliog.

Deals with Polish folk costumes, and their expression in arts and crafts, and folk festivals. The author's vivid style, and the delightful drawings make this book especially suitable for the young.

795 Polish dances.

Irena Ludwig. London: Orbis, 1963. 8p. of text. illus.

An album of coloured plates and scores which illustrate different Polish folk-dances.

796 Guide to folk art and folklore in Poland.

Marian Pokropek. Warsaw: Arkady, 1979. 450p. illus. maps.

The book mainly deals with wooden objects (including sculpture and objects in everyday use) but it also covers such areas as sacred art, coal, rock salt sculpture, earthenware, embroidery and kelem-style rugs. Includes detailed maps and 393 illustrations.

797 Treasured Polish Christmas customs and traditions.

Illustrated by Zofia Stryjeńska. Minneapolis, Minnesota: Polanie, 1974. xii+198p. illus.

Christmas traditions, into which many pagan Slavic customs have been absorbed are very rich and varied in Poland.

Folklore, Folk-art and Customs

798 **Journey to glory.**
Marjorie B. Young, photographs by Adam Bujak. New York: Harper & Row, 1976. 203p.

An album of photographs depicting Polish festivals. The author also explores the origin and meaning of festivals as a collective spiritual experience. Roman Catholic Uniate (Greek-Catholic) and Mariavite celebrations, as well as festivals of remote pagan extraction, are included. An interesting record of one aspect of Poland's folk heritage.

Polska Sztuka Ludowa. (Polish Folk-art.)
See item no. 883.

Cuisine

799 **Old Polish traditions in the kitchen and at the table.**
Maria Lemnis, Henryk Vitry. Warsaw: Interpress, 1981.
2nd ed. 304p. illus.
A Polish cookbook made more attractive by beautiful reproductions of ancient engravings, old Polish recipes, anecdotes, and examples of special types of Polish cuisine including hunters' courses and food for festive occasions. The authors also explore culinary habits at various social levels.

800 **Polish cookery.**
Maria Ochorowicz-Monatowa, translated by Jean
Karsavina. New York: Crown, 1959. 314p.
This book is a selection of recipes which have been adapted from a Polish cookbook which has been a bible for Polish housewives for the past two generations. Most dishes can be prepared from ingredients readily available in the West, but the book also includes recipes requiring such delicacies as black truffles, rare game or berries.

801 **Old Warsaw cook book: hundreds of Polish specialities.**
Rysia (*pseud.*). New York: Roy, 1958. 304p. illus.
bibliog.
The main part of this book describes Polish dishes with such characteristic ingredients as sour cream, mushrooms, rye bread and smoked fish. It also includes an abundance of hors d'oeuvres, soups, sauces, and pastries as well as recipes for international dishes which have influenced Polish cuisine, or are common in Poland.

802 **Treasured Polish recipes for Americans.**
Edited by Maria Sokołowska, Irena Jasińska. Minneapolis,
Minnesota: Polanie, 1951. 4th ed. 169p. illus.
A short Polish cookbook published by a Polish-American cultural association, which is an active popularizer of the Polish heritage.

803 **The art of Polish cooking.**
Alina Żerańska, illustrated by Janina Domańska. New
York: Doubleday, 1968. 366p. illus.

A book for family use containing recipes which are typically Polish from pickled
cucumbers to hunters' *bigos*, and from cheese *pierogi* to yeast *babka*.

Sport

804 Sport in Poland.
Zbigniew Chmielewski. Warsaw: Interpress, 1980. 130p.
illus.

A study of the development of sport during the last thirty-five years which also
provides a historical outline of the growth of sport since the 18th century. The
author refers to the international victories of Polish champions; the present structure and organization of sport; famous sportsmen; and also provides a list and
description of various sports federations.

805 Sport in Poland.
Stefan Sieniarski. Warsaw: Interpress, 1972. 180p. illus.

Discusses the history and organization of Polish sport, and its various branches.
Attention is paid to the achievements of the most prominent Polish sportsmen, the
prizes won by them in international competitions and the records that have been
established.

Poland: the country and its people.
See item no. 10.

Przegląd Sportowy. (Sports Review.)
See item no. 885.

Encyclopaedias and Directories

806 **[Poland: a special issue].**
Edited by Adam Bromke, John W. Trong. *Canadian Slavonic Papers*, vol. 15, no.1-2 (spring-summer 1973).
This special encyclopaedic issue contains a unique collection of often contrasting articles on Poland by Polish scholars resident in Poland and abroad. The subjects considered include: the downfall of Władysław Gomułka; the strikes and riots of December 1970; political change and economic policy under Edward Gierek; trade; industrial workers; agricultural change; the reform of rural administration; the role of intellectuals in Poland; the social sciences and the reform of the education system; Roman Catholicism and church-state relations; foreign policy in the 1970s; and Poland and European security. In addition selected documents are also provided.

807 **Area handbook for Poland.**
Eugene K. Keefe (et al.). Washington, DC: Government Printing Office, 1973. xii+335p. bibliog.
A handbook prepared by the Foreign Area Studies Department of the American University designed for the use of US military personnel. The emphasis is on political, socioeconomic and military institutions in Poland.

808 **Poland: nature, settlement, architecture.**
Jerzy Kostrowicki. Warsaw: Arkady, 1972. 584p. illus.
A pictorial handbook which provides information on Poland's: climate; geology; natural life and resources; history; folklore; regional characteristics; cities; architecture and town planning; and social and economic problems. This book is richly illustrated and many of the photographs are in colour.

809 **Polish research guide.**
Edited by Jerzy Kozłowski. Warsaw: Państwowe
Wydawnictwo Naukowe, 1974. 638p.

A guide to the institutions of learning in Poland which lists: all departments,
institutes, branches and committees of the Polish Academy of Sciences; universi-
ties; institutes of technology ('polytechnics'); colleges; archives; museums;
libraries; and learned societies. The work also reports on the activities of all the
above institutions. This is the most recent English language edition; the Polish
edition, entitled *Informator nauki polskiej* is published biennially by the Centrum
Informacji Naukowej, Technicznej i Ekonomicznej in Warsaw.

810 **Who's who in the socialist countries: a biographical
encyclopaedia of 10,000 leading personalities in 16
communist countries.**
Borys Lewytzkyj, Juliusz Stroynowski, translated by Stephen
Pringle, Ulla Dornberg. New York: K. G. Saur, 1978.
xi + 736p.

A pioneering reference work which attempts to supply information under the
following headings for each entry: date and place of birth; educational background; career; bibliography of major publications. The amount of data depends
to some extent on the importance of a given personality and to an even greater
degree on the availability of information.

811 **The Soviet Union and Eastern Europe: a handbook.**
Edited by George Schöpflin. London: Blond, 1970.
xii + 614p. maps.

An indispensable work for scholars and students of Eastern European affairs. This
guide provides a country-by-country survey by distinguished analysts who deal in
depth with such topics as: ideology; political structure; military affairs; national
minorities; economic policy; social structure; church-state relations; education;
law; and technological development. Statistical surveys are also supplied.

Bibliographies

812 **Eastern European education: a bibliography of English-language materials on Poland.**
Nellie M. Apanasiewicz, Seymour Rosen. Washington, DC: US Department of Education, 1960-66. 64p.+35p.
An annotated selective bibliography.

813 **La Polonia in Italia: saggio bibliografico 1799-1948.** (Poland in Italy: a bibliographical essay, 1799-1948.)
Maria Bersano Begey, Marina Bersano Begey. Turin, Italy: Rosenberg & Sellier, 1949. 295p.
A bibliography covering the broad field of Polish-Italian relations with particular emphasis on literature and history. The bibliography, which is unannotated, covers both books and articles published in Italy.

814 **East European and Soviet economic affairs: a bibliography, 1965-1973.**
Alexander Bieńkowski, Lewis A. Tambs. New York: Libraries Unlimited, 1975. 170p.
A bibliography containing 1,200 citations of books and articles dealing with East European economic affairs, including limited circulation reports and working papers. The bibliography is arranged by country and by topic within each country, and published as the first part of a series.

815 **Bibliography of American publications on East Central Europe, 1945-1957.**
Robert F. Byrnes. Bloomington, Indiana: Indiana University Press, 1958. 213p.
Lists monographs and articles on the humanities and social sciences published in English outside Eastern Europe. This bibliography was continued as an annual publication under the title: *American Bibliography of Russian (Slavic) and East European Studies* (1956-).

Bibliographies

816 **La conoscenza del mondo slavo in Italia: bilancio storico-bibliografico di un millennio.** (Knowledge of the Slavic world in Italy: a historical-bibliographical summary of a millennium.)
Arturo Cronia. Padua, Italy: Stediv for Istituto di Studi Adriatici di Venezia, 1958. 792p.

An encyclopaedic work containing extensive information collected during the course of thirty years of research. This bibliography covers competently and comprehensively Italy's relations with Slavic countries over a period of a thousand years. The entries are arranged by periods and bibliographical footnotes are included although there is no subject index.

817 **Poland, past and present: a select bibliography of works in English.**
Norman Davies. Newtonville, Massachusetts: Oriental Research Partners, 1977. xxi+185p. map.

A selective bibliography of books and articles on Polish history and civilization. Some items in languages other than English are included, when no English-language materials are available. There are no annotations, and the compiler has overemphasized history and politics and devoted very little space to literature, language, the arts, and the history of science. Includes over 1,800 entries which are categorized under 18 headings.

818 **Russia, the USSR and Eastern Europe: a bibliographical guide to English-language publications 1964-1974.**
Stephan M. Horak, edited by Rosemary Neiswender. New York: Libraries Unlimited, 1978. 488p.

This bibliography covers a decade of Soviet and East European studies in English-speaking countries and all major fields are represented. A critical review of the literature is provided. The work contains 1,600 entries.

819 **East Central Europe: a guide to basic publications.**
Edited by Paul Louis Horecky. Chicago: University of Chicago Press, 1969. 956p.

An excellent guide to selected reference works, major texts, classics of literature and bibliographies concerning East Central Europe, with concise but comprehensive annotations in English. The Polish chapter (p. 599-798) was compiled by Janina Hoskins (Wójcicka).

820 **Early and rare Polonica of the 15th-17th centuries in American libraries: a bibliographical survey.**
Janina Hoskins (Wójcicka). Boston, Massachusetts: G. K. Hall, 1973. xii+193p. illus. map. bibliog.

A painstaking compilation of over 1,200 old and rare titles in 250 major US libraries. This 'labour of love' reflects the wealth of the Polish cultural heritage in America. The work is supplemented by other material including Old Slavonic books in Cyrillic published in Cracow, Hebrew titles printed in Cracow and

Bibliographies

Lublin, Unitarian religious literature from Raków and Lutheran works from Królewiec (Königsberg).

821 Polish books in English 1945-1971.
Janina Hoskins (Wójcicka). Washington, DC: Library of Congress, 1974. 163p.

A fairly comprehensive record of over one thousand English language books relating to the humantities and the social sciences. The books have either been published or translated into English, in or outside Poland. As the Polish bibliographer of the Library of Congress, the author is particularly well-qualified and has enjoyed ready access to all the publications concerned.

822 Recent studies related to the history of the Jews in Poland from earliest times to the partitions period.
Gershon Hundert. *Polish Review*, vol. 18, no.4 (1973), p. 84-99.

An evaluative survey of Polish Jewish historiography followed by a bibliography of studies (published between 1960 and 1972) on the history of the Jews in Poland from the earliest times to the end of the 18th century. The work is divided into the following sections: general works; town studies; religion; intellectual and cultural history; and socioeconomic history and conditions. There are also specific sections on: rabbinical studies; Hebrew books and printing; Frankism; and Hasidism.

823 Slavic Europe: a selected bibliography in Western European languages comprising history, languages and literature.
Robert Joseph Kerner. Cambridge, Massachusetts: 1918. 402p. Reprinted, New York: Russell & Russell, 1969. xxiv+402p.

An early but still valid and useful bibliography. The Polish chapter (items 2,005-2,555) covers: Polish history; geography and travel; archaeology; anthropology; socioeconomic, political, and military history; auxiliary sciences of history; ethnic problems; regions; and language, philology and literature. A separate chapter deals with the Masurians (items 2,714-2,720) and with the Cassubians (items 2,685-2,697).

824 Polish economy of the years 1918-1939 in Polish post-war publications.
Zbigniew Landau. *Acta Poloniae Historica*, vol. 5 (1962), p. 141-63.

Studies the inter-war Polish economy as reflected in books published in Poland. The compiler is a professor of economic history at the Higher School of Planning and Statistics in Warsaw.

825 **A bibliography of Slavic dictionaries; Volume 1: Polish.**
Richard Casimir Lewański. Bologna, Italy: Editrice
Compositori, distributed by the Kraus-Thomson
Organization, 1973. viii + 197p.
A comprehensive listing of general and specialized dictionaries (monolingual,
bilingual, polyglot). The bibliography has 1,762 entries, and an author and sub-
ject index is included.

826 **The literatures of the world in English translations: a
bibliography; Volume 2: the Slavic literatures.**
Richard Casimir Lewański. New York: Ungar & New
York Public Library, 1967.
Contains a section on Polish poetry, prose and drama which lists translations of
Polish writers published in books, anthologies and periodicals (p. 72-145).

827 **La Pologne en France: essai d'une bibliographie raisonnée.**
(Poland in France: an attempt at an annotated
bibliography.)
Jan Lorentowicz, Aleksander Maciej Chmurski. Paris:
Institut d'Études Slaves, 1935-41. 3 vols.
A bibliography of French publications pertinent to Poland published in franco-
phone and other countries. The authors cover the political as well as the cultural
aspects of Franco-Polish relations. Volume one deals with literature, theatre and
art; volume two with general works, language, travel and history; and volume
three with geography, sciences and law. Supplements are also provided.

828 **Czechoslovak-Polish relations, 1918-1939: a selected and
annotated bibliography.**
Chester Michael Nowak. Stanford, California: Hoover
Institution, 1976. xxii + 220p.
A selective bibliography covering the inter-war period which puts particular stress
on the social sciences.

829 **Polish society: studies in methodology; bibliography of
sociological works.**
Wrocław, Poland: Ossolineum, 1977. 202p.
A bibliography of sociological works written by Polish authors in languages other
than Polish between 1945 and 1973.

Bibliographies

830 **The international relations of Eastern Europe: a guide to information sources.**
Edited by Robin Alison Remington. New York: Gale, 1978. 273p. (International Relations Information Guide Series, vol. 8).
This repertory lists books and periodicals from eight Eastern European countries including Poland. The guide includes 1,300 titles on foreign relations, accompanied in most cases by a brief annotation.

831 **Legal sources and bibliography of Poland.**
Edited by Peter Siekanowicz, Vladimir Gsovski. New York: Praeger, 1964. 311p.
A selective bibliography of reference works, monographs and articles on Polish law and the legal system. Works in various languages are included.

832 **A selected bibliography of Slavic linguistics.**
Edward Stankiewicz, Dean S. Worth. The Hague: Mouton, 1966-70. 2 vols.
A selective and analytical bibliography which includes a thorough index of authors. The Polish section is subdivided as follows: general; phonology; morphology; syntax; standard Polish and its history; orthography; orthoepy; lexicology; lexicography; onomastics; regional dialects; social dialects; child talk; stylistics; poetics; versification; relation to other Slavic and non-Slavic languages; and texts. Volume one covers Slavic prehistory, Balto-Slavic, Common Slavic, comparative Slavic, Old Church Slavonic and Southern Slavic; and volume two Western Slavic and Eastern Slavic.

833 **The studies in nationality and nationalism in Poland between the two wars (1918-1939): a bibliographical survey.**
Konstanty Symmons-Symonolewicz. New York: Polish Institute of Arts and Sciences, 1944. 73p.
A brief bibliographical survey of one of the crucial problems of inter-war Poland: a multi-ethnic state where demands for autonomy on one hand and for assimilation on the other created great tensions.

834 **Polonica Canadiana: a bibliographical list of the Canadian Polish imprints for the years 1848-1957.**
Wiktor Turek. Toronto: Polish Research Institute in Canada, 1958. 138p.
A supplement published in 1978 (414p.) covers the period 1958-70.

835 **Polish-American serial publications 1842-1966: an annotated bibliography.**
Jan Wępsieć. Chicago: 1968. 191p.
Serials (newspapers, journals, bulletins) published formally and informally in the United States in any language are included. The following information is sup-

plied: title, date and place of publication, frequency, changes in the title, editor's and publisher's name and library holdings.

836 Bibliography of books in Polish or related to Poland published outside Poland since September 1, 1939.
Edited by Janina Zabielska. London: The Polish Library, 1953- . In progress.

This is the most complete bibliography of Polish publications published outside Poland since the outbreak of the Second World War. The work is produced using the resources of the largest Polish library abroad. The format is unfortunately rather inconvenient and individual volumes are slow to appear. So far three volumes have been published: volume one: 1939-1951 appeared in 1953; volume two: 1952-57 was published in 1959; volume three: 1958-1963 was made available in 1966; and volume 4: 1964-1969 is still in preparation. These volumes are in effect a cumulation of *Books in Polish or related to Poland* which is published by the Polish Library in London on a quarterly basis.

837 Polish-American history and culture: a classified bibliography.
Joseph W. Żurawski. Chicago: Polish Museum of America, 1975. 218p.

A valuable aid to research on US 'Polonia'. There are 1,700 entries, almost exclusively in English, classified by broad subjects. Another related work which is of interest is the annotated and classified guide by Joseph M. Gowaskie entitled *The Polish community in America* (1978. Burt Franklin Ethnic Bibliographic Guides Series).

Newspapers and Journals

English language

838 Acta Poloniae Historica. (Polish Historical Records.)
Wrocław, Poland: Ossolineum, 1958- . annual.
This is the most important Polish historical journal. The contributions are mainly in English, French and German and concentrate on Polish history, although there are also articles on the territories of Central-Eastern Europe which had cultural, economic and political ties with Poland. The journal is sponsored by the Institute of History of the Polish Academy of Sciences.

839 American Slavic and East European Review.
Philadelphia: 1941- . quarterly.
Articles on Polish life, traditions, history and culture can be found in the review along with papers on other nations in this region.

840 Antemurale. (The Bullwark.)
Rome: Institutum Historicum Polonicum, 1954. annual.
This publication contains contributions by Polish émigré scholars and pays particular attention to Polish Church history, Poland-Vatican relations, and Polish historical sources in Western European archives and libraries. As the title indicates, the journal presents Poland as a bullwark of Christianity and of Western civilization in opposition to the maxim 'ex Oriente lux'. The articles are in Italian, Latin and English.

841 Archeologia Polona. (Polish Archaeology.)
Wrocław: Ossolineum, 1958- . annual.
A scholarly English-language journal with occasional articles in other major languages. The periodical deals with Polish archaeological research in general and

with the civilizations that preceded that of the Poles in the Vistula-Odra River basins including those of the: Scyths, Goths, Wends, Lusatians and Sarmatians. The work is sponsored by the Institute of Civilization of the Polish Academy of Sciences.

842 **British Broadcasting Corporation, Monitoring Service: Part 2-Eastern Europe.**
Reading, England: British Broadcasting Corporation, 1948- . daily.

The Monitoring Service covers local, national and international news as interpreted by the broadcasting networks of East European countries including Poland. Includes daily translations and interpretations of news from Poland. No retrospective index.

843 **Catholic life in Poland.**
Warsaw: Pax. monthly.

This periodical, published in several foreign languages, is not sponsored by the hierarchy of the Polish Roman Catholic Church, but by 'Pax' - a Catholic organization enjoying exceptional governmental privileges. Thanks to this special position 'Pax' is able to publish books and journals which would otherwise probably not be available to the Polish reader.

844 **Daily News.**
Warsaw: Polska Agencja Prasowa. daily.

An information bulletin issued by the official Polish press agency PAP.

845 **Geographia Polonica.** (Polish Geography.)
Warsaw: 1964- . irregular. maps. charts.

Publishes articles on all aspects of geography, environmental and spatial studies with stress on Poland and research by Poles. The papers are mainly in English, but some are in French. The journal is sponsored by the Institute of Geography and Spatial Economy of the Polish Academy of Sciences.

846 **Journal of Central European Affairs.**
University of Colorado, 1943- . quarterly.

A periodical mainly concerned with historical, political and socioeconomic matters pertinent to Central Eastern Europe. Includes articles, comments, notes and book reviews.

847 **Law in Eastern Europe.**
Leiden, Netherlands: 1958- .

A series of monographs and translations from East European sources on jurisprudence and legislation. This publication is sponsored by the Documentation Office for East European Law, Leiden University.

Newspapers and Journals. English language

848 **New Polish Publications: a monthly review of Polish books.**
Warsaw: Agpol Press, 1953- . illus.
A well-edited and pleasantly presented periodical containing: announcements of new publications; the editorial plans of Polish publishing houses; reviews of major new books; lists of books about to appear; essays on prominent writers and scholars; calendars of forthcoming cultural events; and articles dealing with the Polish literary world.

849 **Oeconomica Polona.** (Polish Economics.)
Warsaw: Polskie Towarzystwo Ekonomiczne, 1974- .
quarterly.
A scholarly journal sponsored jointly by the Polish Economic Society and the Committee on Economic Sciences of the Polish Academy of Sciences.

850 **Panorama Polska: Nasza Ojczyzna.** (The Polish panorama: our fatherland.)
Warsaw: 'Polonia' Association, monthly.
An illustrated magazine addressed primarily to Poles living abroad which contains articles on all aspects of Polish life and on Poles in foreign countries. An English-language section of twelve pages is contained in each issue. Special features include: Polish lessons for English-speaking persons; humour; and double-page colour reproductions of Polish paintings.

851 **Poland.**
Warsaw: Interpress, 1954- . illus. quarterly.
Probably the best review published in Central Europe. It has a modern layout, interesting and stimulating articles, splendid illustrations, and a diverse contents including: articles; discussions; reports; interviews; and translations of short stories by Polish writers.

852 **Polish-American Studies.**
New York: Polish-American Historical Association, 1944- .
semi-annual.
This publication is dedicated to the history of the Polish-American community. A cumulative index for the period 1944-1973 is available.

853 **Polish-American Studies.**
Warsaw: Uniwersytet Warszawski, 1976- . irregular.
A journal of American studies.

854 **Polish Economic Survey.**
Warsaw: 1961- . fortnightly.
An economic review containing statistical information with particular reference to foreign trade.

855 **Polish Film.**
Warsaw: 1949- . illus. fortnightly.
Provides information about the current developments in the Polish motion picture industry. A bilingual publication (English/French).

856 **Polish Music.**
Warsaw: Authors' Agency, 1966- . illus. quarterly.
A journal containing articles and a calendar of events.

857 **Polish Perspectives.**
Warsaw: Polish Institute of International Affairs, 1958- . monthly.
A journal dealing with various aspects of Polish contemporary life (political, cultural and scientific) which contains a book review section and a calendar of events. The periodical places stress on foreign relations and the role of Poland in the world community.

858 **The Polish Review.**
New York: The Polish Institute of Arts and Sciences in America, 1956- . quarterly.
A scholarly journal concerning Poland's past and present with contributions by American scholars of Polish descent, Slavists, friends of Poland, and Polish scholars residing in the United States. This is the principal publication of the most important learned society with Polish interests in America. The Review contains: a bibliography of materials written in English on Poland; items by Polish authors published in English; a calendar of events in Poland; and book reviews.

859 **Polish Round Table.**
Wrocław: Ossolineum, 1967- . irregular.
An interdisciplinary yearbook of the Polish Association of Political Science. Certain issues deal with special topics such as Polish contributions to the congresses of the International Political Science Association, current trends in local government, and political culture. The work also includes reviews, the proceedings of the Association, a calendar of scholarly events, and a bibliography of Polish works on political science. Ten volumes had appeared by 1980.

860 **Polish Sociological Bulletin.**
Wrocław: Ossolineum, 1961- . semi-annual.
This is the journal of the Polish Sociological Association and contributions deal with: Polish centres of sociology; current research; new publications; the contents of sociological journals; and the changing structure of Polish society. Notes, book reviews and obituaries are also included.

861 **Polish Western Affairs.**
Poznań, Poland: Instytut Zachodni, 1960- . semi-annual.
This periodical is mainly in English but has occasional papers in French and German. Each issue contains articles, details of coming events, reviews and a bibliography. The topics dealt with include: Poland's relations with Germany;

Newspapers and Journals. English language

Poland's Western frontier; access to the sea; the Western territories; and military affairs.

862 **Polish Yearbook of International Law.**
Wrocław, Poland: Ossolineum, 1970- . annual.
Publishes the conclusions of theoretical studies on Polish international law and the opinions of Polish lawyers on current international problems. The Yearbook also considers the legal problems associated with Polish foreign trade. The work is sponsored by the Institute of Law and Government of the Polish Academy of Sciences and is published in English and French.

863 **Radio Free Europe: Polish Press Survey.**
Munich, Germany: Radio Free Europe Research Department. irregular.
Provides translations and abstracts of texts, reports, evaluations, and comments based on Polish daily and periodical publications. In addition *Situation reports* are published in a separate series.

864 **Review of Polish Heritage.**
Falls Church, Virginia: 1949- . illus. quarterly.
This is the official organ of the American Council of Polish Cultural Clubs. It is a periodical propagating Polish culture in the United States and is a bulletin rather than a journal.

865 **The Review of the Polish Academy of Sciences.**
Warsaw: 1956- . quarterly.
A quarterly journal containing: articles; a who's who in Polish learning; a calendar of events in Polish learning and higher education; details of anniversaries; information about international contacts involving Polish scientific institutions and Polish scholars; reports of meetings and seminars; and descriptions of the activities of research centres.

866 **Slavonic and East European Review.**
London: 1922- . quarterly.
A scholarly journal published by the School of Slavonic and East European Studies of the University of London. It includes contributions on several subjects including literature, history and ethnography and covers the Slavic countries including Poland.

867 **Studia Historiae Oeconomicae.** (Studies in Economic History.)
Poznań, Poland: Uniwersytet Poznański, 1966- . annual.
This journal covers general economic history but pays particular attention to Polish economic history. The articles are in either English, French or German.

216

868 **Studies on International Relations.**
Warsaw: Polski Instytut Stosunków Międzynarodowych,
1973- . semi-annual.

This periodical covers international affairs in general but presents the Polish view on international issues and examines Poland's participation in world affairs, and the study of international relations in Poland. Fourteen volumes had appeared by 1981.

869 **The Theatre in Poland.**
Warsaw: Institut International du Théâtre, 1958- . illus.
monthly.

A beautifully illustrated magazine, sponsored by the Polish Centre of the International Theatre Institute and the Polish Authors' Agency. It features: new performances in Poland; the Polish theatre abroad; new productions; books on the theatre; press reviews; news about directors and actors; and forthcoming events. The articles are in English and French.

Polish language

870 **Biuletyn Historii Sztuki.** (History of Art Bulletin.)
Warsaw: Instytut Historii Sztuki PAN, 1949- . quarterly.

A journal published by the Institute of the History of Arts of the Polish Academy of Sciences which deals with all aspects of the figurative and performing arts and which pays particular attention to Polish art.

871 **Dziennik Polski.** (The Polish Daily.)
London: 1940- . daily.

This is the newspaper of the Polish community in the British Isles founded during the Second World War. The Saturday edition entitled *Tydzień Polski* (The Polish Week) was first published in 1946 and incorporated the *Dziennik Żołnierza* (Soldier's Daily) which had been published during the Second World War period.

872 **Dziennik Związkowy.** (Alliance Daily.)
Chicago: 1881- . biweekly.

A newspaper sponsored by the Polish National Alliance in the United States for the Polish community in America. Now appears twice a week.

873 **Ekonomista.** (The Economist.)
Warsaw: Polskie Towarzystwo Ekonomiczne, 1900- .
fortnightly.

A scholarly journal which covers economics, statistics, economic history and sociology.

Newspapers and Journals. Polish language

874 **Kwartalnik Historyczny.** (Historical Quarterly.)
Warsaw: 1887- . quarterly.
The most prominent Polish language historical journal. It is sponsored by the Institute of History of the Polish Academy of Sciences and publishes English, French, German and Russian summaries of articles.

875 **Kultura.** (Culture.)
Paris: Instytut Literacki, 1946- . bibliog. weekly.
A Polish émigré journal published since the end of the Second World War. It strives to maintain close contact with the homeland, but is highly critical of the present administration in Poland. This periodical claims to represent Polish progressive thought in exile and the views of the Polish émigré (and sometimes the homeland) intelligentsia. The journal is not limited to literature and embraces the entire range of Polish civilization with special emphasis on contemporary events and the dissident movement in Poland.

876 **Narodowiec.** (The Nationalist.)
Lens, France: 1909- . daily.
A newspaper which principally serves the old Polish émigrés in Northeastern France.

877 **Nowe Książki: Przegląd Literacki i Naukowy.** (New Books: Literary and Scholarly Review.)
Warsaw: 1951- . biweekly.
Includes articles on recent Polish literary criticism, prose and poetry, culture and scholarship as well as reviews of recent publications. A literary and publishers' chronicle.

878 **Nowy Dziennik.** (The New Daily.)
New York: 1970- . daily.
A successor to *Nowy Świat* (The New World) which was established in 1922. It is the most popular Polish newspaper on the Eastern Coast of the United States and is less influenced by American English style and vocabulary than other Polish-American newspapers. The paper is read by both old and more recent immigrants alike.

879 **Ostatnie Wiadomości.** (Most Recent News.)
Mannheim-Schonau, GFR: 1945- . triweekly.
Established originally for the Polish military guard units (Kompanie Wartownicze) in occupied Germany, it now serves the entire Polish community (refugees and immigrants) in West Germany.

880 **Pamiętnik Literacki: Czasopismo kwartalne poświęcone historii i krytyce literatury polskiej.** (Literary Diary: a quarterly journal devoted to the history and criticism of Polish literature.)
Warsaw: 1902- . quarterly.
Contains articles, notes, translations, surveys, reviews and correspondence. The journal is sponsored by the Institute of Literary Studies of the Polish Academy of Sciences.

881 **Płomyk.** (The Tiny Flame.)
Warsaw: 1945- . biweekly.
A magazine meant for teenagers which was established in the inter-war period. It is educational and entertaining and attempts to stimulate the interest of young readers as well as suggesting pursuits which they can follow in their leisure time.

882 **Polityka.** (Politics.)
Warsaw: 1957- . weekly.
The principal Polish weekly publication dealing with contemporary Polish and international politics. It expresses the views of the state but on occasions is allowed a degree of autonomy when it is able to advance 'constructive' criticism. After 1980 its editor-in-chief, Mieczysław Rakowski, became Poland's vice-prime minister and a leading political figure.

883 **Polska Sztuka Ludowa.** (Polish Folk-art.)
Warsaw: 1948- . quarterly.
In Poland, folk-art occupies an important place in the expression of national character and feelings. Both the state and the church encourage the continuity of folk costumes, sacred folk-art and folk design in arts and crafts. English and Russian summaries of articles are provided.

884 **Przegląd Humanistyczny.** (Humanities Review.)
Warsaw: 1957- . monthly.
This scholarly review founded by the late professor Jan Zygmunt Jakubowski, an acknowledged authority in literary criticism and history, extends its coverage to the broad field of the human sciences. Includes articles, reviews, diaries, information about conventions, and a table of contents in English.

885 **Przegląd Sportowy.** (Sports Review.)
Warsaw: 1945- . weekly.
This is the main Polish periodical devoted to all kinds of sport. The Review continues the traditions of a similar weekly publication which existed in the inter-war period.

886 **Przekrój.** (The Cross-Section.)
Warsaw: 1945- . illus. weekly.
The most popular Polish illustrated weekly comparable to *Time* or *Newsweek*. The paper, printing and illustrations are of a poor quality.

Newspapers and Journals. Polish language

887 **Rocznik Slawistyczny.** (Slavic Studies Yearbook.)
Wrocław, Poland: Ossolineum, irregular.
A journal devoted to the Slavic language, and Slavic philology and linguistic history. Contains bibliographies. Prior to 1981 forty-one volumes had appeared.

888 **Szpilki.** (The Pins.)
Warsaw: 1935- . illus. weekly.
A satyrical periodical.

889 **Trybuna Ludu.** (People's Tribune.)
Warsaw: 1944- . daily.
An organ of the communist Polish United Workers' Party which presents the official views of party and governmental leaders.

890 **Twórczość: Miesięcznik Literacko-Krytyczny.** (The Creativeness: a monthly journal of Literary Criticism.)
Warsaw: 1945- . monthly.
Poland's most prominent literary journal.

891 **Tygodnik Powszechny: Katolickie Pismo Społeczno-Kulturalne.** (Universal Weekly: the Catholic Social and Cultural Publication.)
Cracow, Poland: Znak, 1945- . weekly.
This periodical represents most faithfully the views of the Church hierarchy, Catholic intellectuals and the 'Znak' ('Sign') political group. Circulation is kept low because of limited supplies of newsprint paper. The journal also contains theatre and film reviews and bibliographies. The term 'Powszechny' refers indirectly to its Greek etymology i.e., 'Catholic', while the term 'Znak' is associated with the sign of the cross pre-announcing the victory of Constantine the Great at the battle of Milvian Bridge (312) at Rome.

892 **Żołnierz Wolności.** (The Soldier of Freedom.)
Warsaw: 1945- . daily.
The official organ of the Polish armed forces which expresses the views of the military high command.

893 **Życie Literackie.** (Literary Life.)
Cracow: 1951- . illus. weekly.
Literary review of the Cracow cultural milieu which covers literary and general cultural themes and includes book reviews.

894 **Życie Warszawy.** (The Life of Warsaw.)
Warsaw: 1944- . daily.
A popular daily information paper. A German-language edition is also published occasionally during the tourist season.

Libraries, Archives and Museums

895 **Cracow, city of museums: the most beautiful works of art from seven museums.**
Jerzy Banach (et al.), translated by Neil Jones. Warsaw: Arkady, 1976. 182p. illus.
A lavishly illustrated volume which depicts a selection of the most beautiful works of art from the Wawel collection, the Cathedral Treasury, the National Museum, the Czartoryski collection, the Museum of the Jagellonian University, the Jagellonian Library, the Archaeological Museum, and the Historical Museum of the City of Cracow. The selections were made and described by the directors of the respective museums.

896 **Slavic and East European resources in Canadian academic and research libraries.**
Bohdan Budurowycz. Ottawa, Canada: National Library of Canada, 1976. xv+595p. tables.
Evaluates the Slavic holdings in academic and other research libraries in Canada. The Western part of Canada apart, Polish resources come second only to Russian material in Canadian research libraries.

897 **East Central and South East Europe: a handbook of library and archival resources in North America.**
Edited by Paul Louis Horecky. Santa Barbara, California: ABC-Clio, 1976. 466p.
A descriptive guide to major Eastern European holdings and collections in the United States and Canada. The guide includes exclusively Polish libraries, as well as general and specialized libraries strong in Polonica (e.g. Harvard University, the Hoover Institution, the Library of Congress, and the New York Public Library).

Libraries, Archives and Museums

898 **Eastern Europe and Russia/Soviet Union: a handbook of West European archival and library resources.**
Richard Casimir Lewański. New York: K. G. Saur, 1980. xv+320p. bibliog.

A guide to archival and library holdings of Slavic and East European interest (including those concerning Poland) outside the Slavic-East European area of Europe. Each entry contains comprehensive bibliographies and lists especially important and rare items. The work is arranged schematically and provides union catalogues of Slavic and East European materials in individual European countries.

899 **Guide to Polish libraries and archives.**
Richard Casimir Lewański. New York: East European Monographs, distributed by Columbia University Press, 1974. x+209p.

A comprehensive guide to almost 100 major Polish libraries and archives. The volume was sponsored by the American Council of Learned Societies. In addition to providing information normally supplied in library guides, the author sets out complete listings of publications by and about individual institutions, as well as providing information about prominent and unique holdings.

900 **Guide to museums and collections in Poland.**
Stanisław Lorentz. Warsaw: Interpress, 1973. 348p. illus. plans. map.

Discusses the history and describes the collections of 348 Polish museums and art galleries. The collections cover various fields including: art; archaeology; military; technology; and natural history. The author is a distinguished art historian and a former director of the National Museum in Warsaw. Provides complete information about each museum. This is a useful guide for visitors and researchers.

901 **The National Museum in Cracow: the Czartoryski collection; a historical outline and selected objects, Album.**
Marek Rostworowski (et al.). Warsaw: Arkady, 1980. 196p. illus.

Discusses the history of this collection which is housed in the oldest Polish museum. The collection was originally established by the Czartoryski family at their residence at Puławy in 1801, and was removed to Cracow in 1876, when it was combined with the Czartoryski collections from Sieniawa manor and from the Hotel Lambert in Paris. This collection represents one of the most precious treasure chests of Polish civilization and includes paintings, engravings, illuminated manuscripts, militaria, arts and crafts.

Early and rare Polonica of the 15th-17th centuries in American libraries: a bibliographical survey.
See item no. 820.

Bibliography of books in Polish or related to Poland published outside Poland since September 1, 1939.
See item no. 836.

Index

The index is a single alphabetical sequence of authors (personal and corporate), titles of publications and subjects. Index entries refer both to the main items and to other works mentioned in the notes to each item. Title entries are in italics. Numeration refers to the items as numbered.

224

230

236

238

243

245

247

opera 770
Paderewski, Ignacy Jan 771
Rubinstein, Arthur 772
songs 759, 761
Stokowski, Leopold 773
Szymanowski, Karol 774—775
Music in Poland 760
Music of the Polish Renaissance: a selection of works from the 16th to the beginning of 17th centuries 758
Music of Szymanowski 775
Mussakovska, O. 249
My Many Years 772
My name is million: an illustrated history of the Poles in America 285
My young years 772

N

Nagel guide to Poland 52
Nagórski, Z. 460, 465
Nagórski, Z. Jr. 581
Naimark, N. M. 132
Napierski, Kostka 597
Napoleonic Wars 116
  Polish campaign 117
Napoleon's campaign in Poland, 1806-1807 117
Narkiewicz, O. A. 426
Narodowiec 876
Narodowy atlas Polski 47
Naruszewicz, Adam 706
Nashe Slovo 249
National Democratic Party 411
National Education Commission 648
National identity 7
National income and outlay in Czechoslovakia, Poland, and Yugoslavia 549
National Museum 895
  Czartoryski collection 901
National Museum in Cracow: the Czartoryski collection; a historical outline and selected objects, Album 901
National Radical Camp 374
National Socialist German Workers' Party
  in Danzig 221

Nationalism 97, 118—119, 121—123, 125—126, 244, 339, 396, 398, 411, 453
  bibliography 833
  Slovak 489
  Upper Silesia 37
Nationalism in Eastern Europe 244
Nationalities 27, 136, 240, 439, 629
  Cassubians 246—247, 263
  Germans 263—264
  Karaites 265
  Masurians 263
  problems 31, 33, 38, 143, 145, 241—244
  Scots 266
  Ukrainians 248—249
Nationalization 541
  church land 344
Naval history 82
Navies
  Polish ships in Second World War 198
Navy, Merchant 568, 613
Nazi rule in Poland, 1939-1945 154
Nazis 147, 149, 154—155, 157, 167, 170, 221, 469, 617
Neiswender, R. 818
Netherlands 362
Nettl, J. P. 427
New Catholic Encyclopaedia 352, 737
New economic systems of Eastern Europe 546
New Polish poetry 725
New Polish Publications: a monthly review of Polish books 848
New regime: the structure of power in Eastern Europe 443
Newman, B. 197
Newman, S. K. 514
News
  periodicals 842, 863
Newspapers 844, 871—872, 878, 882, 889, 892, 894
  émigrés 879
Niagara Falls 273
Nicolaus Copernicus and his epoch 649
Niegolewski, A. 603
Niemcewicz, Jan Ursyn 281
Nitra, Diocese 334
Nobility 7, 81, 129, 132, 382
  18th-century European 367
Normandy
  invasion during Second World War 192

251

252

255

263

265

Map of Poland

This map shows the more important towns and other features.

BALTIC SEA
CASSUBIA
Hel
Gdynia
GDAŃSK
Elbląg
WARMIA MASURIA
LITHUANIA
Suwałki
POMERANIA
Olsztyn
KURPIE
Narew
Szczecin
Bydgoszcz
CUYAVIA
Toruń
Noteć
BIAŁYSTOK
Bug
PODLACHIA
BELORUSSIA
Berlin
GREATER POLAND
Włocławek
Płock
POZNAŃ
Warta
WARSAW
MAZOVIA
USSR
Odra
Kalisz
Łódź
Pilica
Wieprz
EAST GERMANY
LUBUSZ
Radom
LUBLIN
Chełm
WROCŁAW
LOWER SILESIA
Częstochowa
(Jasna Góra)
Kielce
Opole
UPPER SILESIA
Vistula
LESSER POLAND
San
THE UKRAINE
KATOWICE
CRACOW
PODHALE
Przemyśl
Lwów
CARPATHIANS
CZECHOSLOVAKIA

Cities with over 300,000 population
Regional capitals
Land over 450 m
Economic planning regions
UPPER SILESIA etc. Historical regions

BALTIC SEA
Wilno
Niemen
Berlin
Vistula
Bug
Warsaw
Odra
San
Lwów
Polish boundaries
1938
1945

0   50   100   150 km